WORLD WAR ME

WINNING THE WAR WITHIN

World War Me
Published by Casting Seeds Publishing

Scripture quotations unless otherwise indicated are from the ESV ® Bible (The Holy Bible, English Standard Version), Copyright © 2001 by Crossway. Used by permission. All rights reserved.

Copyright © 2014 by Joshua Eze
Cover design by Ruben Rodriguez | rubenrodriguezinc.com
Edited by Joann Francis

Published in the United States by Casting Seeds Publishing an extension and aid to UNPLUGGED.

***

Thank You
Thank you Catherine Smith and Kelly Andrews for your words of encouragement during the final stages of publishing this book. Your words helped a lot!

<u>Websites and Social Media sites:</u>
Website: IAMUNPLUGGED.COM | CastingSeedsPublishing.org
Facebook: /MyCoachJosh /IAMUNPLUGGED
Twitter: @MYCOACHJOSH @UNPLUGGEDCLT | IG: @UNPLUGGEDCLT

I dedicate this book to You. Keep the faith

***

The War is Won.

Table of Contents

3 Parts | Page 5

The Whole Armor | Page 11

Put On | Page 25

Choices |Page 33

Captive | Page 36

Conformed | Page 51

Preparation | Page 54

Fastened | Page 66

The Guarded Heart | Page 73

Shoes for the Journey | Page 95

Faith vs. Fear | Page 115

The Greatest Weapon | Page 120

The Power of Prayer | Page 127

The Finale |Page 135

List of Scriptures | Page 139

Chapter 1: 3 Parts

Before we embark on a journey of understanding the demonic, let us first understand who we are as human beings. When God spoke, "Let us create man in our image and in our likeness," he spoke within himself. God, who is three parts, chose to create us in three parts. We are a spirit. We have a soul, and we live in a physical body. We are three part beings like God (God the father, God the Son and God the Holy Spirit). Within God's three parts is the whole redemptive plan for mankind: God the Creator, Jesus the Savior and the Holy Spirit the regenerator. All of His parts are one; God working from eternity through time.

Our Three Parts

- Our Bodies give us world consciousness
- Our soul gives us self-consciousness
- Our spirit gives us God consciousness

Our body gives us a consciousness of this world. Our bodies let us know when we are cold and when we are hot. Our senses give us the ability to see, hear, smell, taste and feel what is in this present world.

Our soul gives us the consciousness of self. Our soul lets us know how we feel, causing us to be aware of our self. The soul harbors our thoughts, memories, ideas, perceptions, knowledge, emotions and our will.

Our spirit gives us a consciousness of God and who He is. Our spirit connects with the heart of God, whether through love, direction or correction.

These three parts are vital to our everyday survival. If one lacks attention, the others are affected. If I am overly consumed with the world and myself, my spirit is affected and will lack Godly inspiration and direction. If I am overly consumed with my spirit but neglect my body and my soul, I will be wise in God but ineffective in reaching people. I will be malnourished and will be unable to relate to people, since I cannot relate to myself. Each and every part is vital and must be balanced. If one area is lacking, the other areas will become vulnerable to an attack from Satan and the demonic.

Satan's ultimate agenda is to deprive the spirit man, to knock out our intelligence and sensitivity towards God so that we will lack direction, self-control and correction. He wants us dumb to God but keen to the world, causing our systems to become clogged and blocking the flow of God into our lives. When we do not pray, fast or read our Bibles, we become as dead men and dead woman walking. Our sin nature takes over, and we become unbalanced in our minds and disoriented in our will. We cannot win this war called life without God!

Satan deprives the spirit of its necessities or its ability to guide so that the individual will become addicted through their senses to facilitate the voids within their soul. Without the Holy Spirit active, we may have good morals and may not do much "wrong", but we are still dead; this leaves us open to be used and abused by Satan and his demonic influence. Balance is key; our whole being must be led by the spirit. If any other part is leading instead of the spirit, the whole being is heading towards a disastrous end. This disastrous end will be either early death or eternal damnation in hell.

IF:

If our Body leads, it will cause us to become overly consumed with the pleasures of this world. We will desire a successful and luxurious life over a content and humbled one, causing our pride to be in this world and not in the kingdom of God. When we are caught up in this world, we will live our lives through our senses. Our body will run rampant with no guide.

If our Soul leads, we will become unbalanced and guided by a confused mind. We will be overly consumed with ourselves and will aim to fill our voids through the desires of our body. We will use people for our own gain; we will become leeches aiming to heal our own bleeding wounds. When a person is caught up too much in themselves, they lead their lives focused on their hurts, gravitating towards the world instead of God to heal them.

If the spirit leads, we will be focused not on this life but our eternal one. We will understand fully the meaning of life and embark to help others understand also. The carnal things of this world will become distasteful to us; we will desire God, and our hearts will beat for him. Our flesh will continuously be crucified, dead, no longer living. Our body will be a tool used to do the will of God and not the will of our personal desires. Our soul will be balanced. Our emotions will be balanced. We will have emotions, but our emotions won't have us. Our hearts will be pure towards God, others and ourselves. Our minds will be renewed and not conformed to the thinking of the world and we will be humbled and completely guided by God. This can happen but only through faith in Jesus and discipline.

Romans 8:5-13 describes the difference between those that are led by the spirit and those that are led by the flesh. The Bible says:

5 For those who live according to the flesh set their minds on the things of the flesh, but those who live according to the Spirit set their minds on the things of the Spirit. **6** For to set the mind on the flesh is death, but to set the mind on the Spirit is life and peace. **7** For the mind that is set on the flesh is hostile to God, for it does not submit to God's law; indeed, it cannot. **8** Those who are in the flesh cannot please God.

9 You, however, are not in the flesh but in the Spirit, if in fact the Spirit of God dwells in you. Anyone who does not have the Spirit of Christ does not belong to him. **10** But if Christ is in you, although the body is dead because of sin, the Spirit is life because of righteousness. **11** If the Spirit of him who raised Jesus from the dead dwells in you, he who raised Christ Jesus from the dead will also give life to your mortal bodies through his Spirit who dwells in you.

Heirs with Christ

12 So then, brothers, we are debtors, not to the flesh, to live according to the flesh. **13** For if you live according to the flesh you will die, but if by the Spirit you put to death the deeds of the body, you will live.

Let's take a deeper look:

Romans 8:5
The Bible says for those who live according to the flesh (solely on their world consciousness) set their minds (self-conscious) on the things of the flesh or the world, but those who live according to the spirit (solely on God) set their minds (self-conscious) on the things of the spirit (God).

Those who live according to their flesh, having their lives consumed with this world, will automatically have their emotions, heart and minds set also on the things of the present life. This causes them to be "prideful" of this life.

But those who live according to the spirit (solely on God) will automatically set their emotions, hearts and minds strictly on the leading of the spirit of God. This causes them to be focused on the things of God and ignore the influences and temptations of this world.

Rom. 8:6 for to set the mind on the flesh is death, but to set the mind on the Spirit is life and peace.

The Bible in Romans 8:6 shows us the contrast between setting our minds on the things of the flesh and on the things of the spirit. Our soulish realm is our core. It sits in the middle of our spirit and our body. Whichever one is the strongest will dictate our emotions and will. Whichever part of us is being deprived has less of an influence against the one that is being catered too or aided the most.

To set our mind on the flesh is death.

Spiritual death is the conceptual stage of natural death which leads to eternal damnation in hell, the ultimate death. When we set our minds on the flesh, we are constantly bound by our selfish and worldly desires. This way of thinking is that of the unbeliever who pursues happiness and contentment in this world only and has no true concern about their eternity. Life begins once your spirit is illuminated or lit by Jesus. If Jesus has not altered your life in any way, your life or spirit remains dark and leaves your body and soul as prime real estate for the demonic. When we set our minds on the spirit, we yield all our members to the guidance of the Holy Spirit. We think like God, because our minds have been renewed by the Word. Our hearts are pure because we have humbled ourselves in the hands of God for him to purge them. When we set our minds on the things of the spirit, our emotions are balanced and our lives are balanced, giving us a peace that surpasses all understanding. Our hope is not in this world but in God, and our lives are not altered or affected by what happens here, we can fix our eyes on eternity and on an assurance that Jesus will never leave us nor forsake us. But if our lives are fixed on the world, then our eternity is damned.

7 For the mind that is set on the flesh is hostile to God, for it does not submit to God's law; indeed, it cannot.

The mind that is set on the flesh is hostile towards God. The Bible says that those that love God will keep his commandments. Satan's deceptive ways have had many of us breaking God's commandments because we have allowed him to consume our lives with so much (work, church, careers, hobbies, habits etc.). Our busyness has deprived our spirit and we have lost sight in keeping His commandments (not through rituals but through a loving relationship with Him). This makes us enemies of God because we have chosen to ignore God and gratify our sin nature.

Verse 8 shows that those who are in the flesh cannot please God. In other words, it is impossible to please God because the body is contaminated with evil. When we are in the flesh or consumed with our selfish desires, Satan uses us as his advocates to damage the lives of others.

Verse 9
You (those that are in Christ) are not in the flesh but in the spirit, if the spirit of God dwells in you. The scripture continues to say that anyone who does not have the spirit of Christ does not belong to him. In other words, the distinction is made between those that are and those who are not of God. The results of their lives are either after God or after the world. The content of their heart is either pure and purged or contaminated and defiled.

Verse 13 is the key scripture that clearly states the options we have either to live after the flesh and die or to personally mortify the deeds of the flesh and live.

The scripture says that if you live after the flesh you will die but those through the Spirit who mortify the deeds of the body will live. Those that die to themselves will live, but those that choose to live (for this present life) will die.

We are in a war within ourselves and a war against spiritual wickedness in high places. Each and every one of us is in the middle of this war, some bound by their desires and others free. Some are fighting for God and some working for Satan. Until we first understand our lives (our whole being), we will lose sight or remain ignorant to Satan's strategies. This book aims to open your eyes to the demonic and to reveal to you the deceptions that are plaguing many of our lives. The jewel of this book is the revelation God has given me from Galatians that talks about the full armor. We cannot win this war without armor, and we cannot win if we do not know how to effectively use it. I pray this book helps you and helps you grow even more in your relationship with God.

***

He's Coming
Will You
Be Ready?

This book is interactive. There is a page on UNPLUGGED's website (IAMUNPLUGGED.COM) called WWM3 and on that page is a list of videos that will amplify a lot of what I share in this book. Throughout this book you will see a play button with a bold sentence under it that will tell you the name of the video to watch on the site. With that being said take a seat, sit back, relax and prepare your heart and mind for war. Whether you like it or not, you are in a war.

[Watch World War M3 Part One online now] IAMUNPLUGGED.COM | WWM3

Warning
The content in this book is extremely valuable. Satan and those associated with him will do their best to keep you from obeying God and reading this book. He aims to completely destroy your life, and he does this by limiting your knowledge of God and of his strategies. Before you can expect to win this war, you have to first know your enemy. Take time to know your enemy because he has definitely taken the time to know you.

Chapter 2: The Whole Armor

Armor, by definition, is "protection for a soldier".

We all are soldiers whether we are fighting for God or for Satan.

We as humans are trapped in a war that has been going on since the beginning of time and that is the war between good and evil. Satan and God are not equal. God created Satan, and a creation will never succeed its creator. The creator knows everything about his creation, and the creation only has a limited understanding of its creator. What we do know is that evil wants control over good, in order to reduce its power and influence. Evil wants to demoralize and completely obliterate the essence of good, making what was once good evil. Each and every one of us was born with morals. We all were instilled with a conscious of God and a set of boundaries within the lines of morals and common sense. We instinctively know what is right and wrong, and our conscious bears witness to it. At one point, we all were naive and innocent, waiting to be nurtured and instructed in the proper ways of life and of God. But what happened? What caused us to be (as a society) so evil, immoral, anti- Jesus and anti-life? Many would say our environment. Others would say peer pressure or the influence of people. Many would say exposure to bad things at a young age.

All these are true but not the right answer. The answer to why we are so contaminated is simply put; we have let down our armor. Without armor, there is no protection from outside intrusion. Without armor, we are vulnerable. Without armor, we are lost and easily influenced by evil. My question to you: "do you have your armor on?" Everything in life conveys to us the importance of armor; look at our skin. Our skin is the armor for our body. It protects against not all but many intruders that try to get into the body. Even our skin needs armor depending on activities, war, weather, etc. What about tree bark, banana peels, siding, bricks, and walls? All these things protect (to a degree) what is important on the inside. Without outer protection, whatever that is on the inside will not be protected or encouraged to mature and grow normally. If exposed, whatever is on the inside would become vulnerable to decay or destruction. Armor is important not only in our natural life but also our spiritual one. The lack of spiritual armor is worse than the loss of natural protection because the lack of spiritual guards will cause us to pull down our natural ones. For instance, if we are vulnerable in our emotions and our armor is down, it will cause us to let down our physical guards which may lead to overeating and addictions that can cause cancer, STD's and emotional distress. All of these things will contribute, (if not dealt with) to an early death. If we allow our spiritual guards to fall, it will automatically pull down our natural ones. We have to understand how serious life is. Demons are real. Satan is real. Their agenda operates out of deception and confusion, both working interlocked to tear down our defense systems and leave us vulnerable to invasion and destruction.

A lot of things in our natural world aim to tear down. Everything from the poisons in our food to the pollution in the air aims to tear down our God given healing system, the immune system. Scientists have found that if you want to kill people off, tear down their immune systems. If you tear that down, there will be nothing to fight off diseases and cancers. Tearing down the immune system is an easy way the evil elites can slowly kill us off. Lucifer the one behind the evils of our world knows the importance of tearing down systems both naturally and spiritually. If he can tear down your intelligence of God, take you away from praying, fasting and renewing your mind with God's Word, he will have instant access to your soul through your body. Think back through your life. Remember the times when you were living recklessly, sinning or even the times when you slipped? During those times, were you praying and reading the Word like you should, or were you kind of drifting from God?

Our soul (mind and will) become vulnerable when our spirit man is dead or being detained. Lucifer knows that when a person has a consistent relationship with God, consistently fasting, praying, and meditating on scripture, that person is less likely to fall and be destroyed. But the ones who do not do these things or maintain these things are vulnerable prey. This is why the Bible says that he roams around seeking whom he may devour. Seeking means that he weeds out, searches through seeing who is vulnerable. The key word in my statement earlier is consistency. The only ones that are less likely to fall or be utterly destroyed are those that are consistent and determined, motivated with a fixed and marked goal. HE CAN NOT DESTROY THESE; he may tempt, attack and test but if they remain consistent, they will not be utterly cast down.

Vulnerability comes with pulled down guards or armor.

No armor = vulnerability.

Partial Armor = vulnerability

Almost all armor = vulnerability

All armor = no vulnerability

The main question that needs to be addressed is: "what is vulnerable when our armor is down?" I doubt a body guard entertains anything until they first addressed their protection strategies, their security systems and their armor. After these things have been addressed or dealt with, then they look to entertain other things. Ironically, in our lives we entertain everything but our armor. Every person that has anything of any type of value always makes sure that thing is protected, whether it be their cars, houses, spouse or children. What bothers me and has motivated me to write this book is that we protect things more than we protect ourselves. How valuable do you see you? Do you believe you are?

***

Now I know we have great security systems, 401 k plans, hiding spots for our valuables, but we have not even come close to guarding our lives. We allow lust to ruin our marriages, pride to ruin our careers, hate to keep us away from forgiving, anger to push us to kill and murder, insecurities that causes us to rape, steal, lie, cheat and hate ourselves. We have protected everything we see as valuable but have neglected what God sees as valuable, which is a person's life and soul. My question to you is, is your armor on? Are you vulnerable? Are you being defeated in your life? People run around churches, sing praises about how Satan is defeated but never realize how Satan keeps them defeated. If he is so defeated, then why are we so defeated in our lives?

Take some time right now to write down the areas in your life that are vulnerable and I want you to utilize the scriptures in the back of this book to help you find out what God says about those areas.

***

Remember when I talked about our three parts (body, soul and spirit) and our consciousness (world, self and God)? These areas need armor. Our Body needs armor that will keep it alive and addiction free. Our soul needs armor to keep its emotions balanced, mind renewed and heart purged from the things of this world. Our Spirit needs armor that will keep it vibrant, alive and strong and give it the ability to lead and guide our bodies and to balance, renew and purge our soul. It needs the proper checks and balances that will keep it dominant and not detained.

Our body needs armor to guard our senses:

- Sight
- Touch
- Taste
- Smell
- Hear.

Armor is needed for these areas to protect against:

The lust of the flesh
The lust of the eye
The Pride of life.

For the remainder of the chapter I will be covering how to protect each of our five senses. Let's start with sight.

Impaired Vision

When something is impaired, it is absent or lessened, either temporarily or permanently. When our vision is impaired (spiritually) it is absent, completely gone, or lessoned, deteriorating until it is absent. Whatever has our eyes has our will, emotions and energy.

The Bible says in Matthew 6:22- 24

22 "The eye is the lamp of the body. So, if your eye is healthy, your whole body will be full of light, 23 but if your eye is bad, your whole body will be full of darkness. If then the light in you is darkness, how great is the darkness!

24 "No one can serve two masters, for either he will hate the one and love the other, or he will be devoted to the one and despise the other. You cannot serve God and money.

The Light of the body is the eye:

The eye is the window of the soul. Through one look or glance the intentions or motives of a person's heart can be revealed. The eye within its abilities is an area in which deception is prevalent. A look of love and concern can camouflage the motives and the intentions of lust. One look of care and concern can be a cover up to backbiting and jealousy. The eye is very deceptive. The Bible says that it is the light of the body, meaning that it is the glass in which either light or darkness shines through. Through the eyes one with discernment can see the soul of a person (their intents and motives.)

If your eye is bad, your whole body will be full of darkness

The eye only reveals the content of a person's soul. The eye only reveals what lies in the heart or in the mind, nothing more nothing less. Whatever is solely dominant in a person's heart will flow through the eye of an individual with the hope and intent of gratifying their greater lust, which may be the pride of this life, the accolades, and the fame. Satan knows the heart yearns to be praised. He knows that people yearn to be appreciated, draped with fine linens, and deemed great in the eyes of the masses. He knows that our hearts search for acceptance and love and he facilitates this appetite with the luxuries of this world that can only satisfy the flesh but cannot save the soul. Therefore, those that bite on this trap and have their eyes fixed on their desires; develop their resumes to achieve greatness instead of humbling themselves in order to be great.

If then the light in you is darkness, how great is the darkness!

Darkness in its original form is never appealing. If we could see down the road many of us are on, we would definitely make a U-turn. Satan is a deceiver and strives to creatively enhance his abilities to deceive, so he presents half-truths in our lives and before our eyes that is strategically contaminated with lies. He knows that if what we see seems like truth, we will bite on it.
Our society mostly governed by Satan but eternally governed by the hand of God, is fixed on what they see, never to strive to see beyond what they are shown. Most people don't test the spirits to see if what is being presented is either a counterfeit or genuine. We believe what we see because we have built such a connection with it. This is the art of deception, presenting lies wrapped in truth that appeal to our senses causing us to be hooked and prey for deception. We believe news anchors because of their nice suits and ties. We believe people because of their warm smiles and gentle hugs. We believe because we have grown to love deception, for it makes us comfortable. Never believe everything you see, but always seek to find the truth behind everything you see. If it is true, it will be true from the beginning. Truth never has lies. If there is any lie, the intent behind what is being said or presented was never true but a lie from the beginning in order to facilitate an agenda from the desk of Lucifer himself.

24 No man can serve two masters: for either he will hate the one, and love the other; or else he will hold to the one, and despise the other. Ye cannot serve God and mammon.

The Bible continues to read that no man can serve two masters: for either he will hate the one and love the other or else he will hold to one and despise the other...

THERE IS NO GREY AND NO IN BETWEEN! You will either love one or hate the other, not love one and kind of sort of like the other. The next portion of the scripture brings it down to the end result of everything. It says you cannot serve God or mammon (money).

God strategically places the root of everyone's concern in their need to be provided for. Pro (providing) for one's vision. Either they will trust in God for physical (body), emotional (soul) and spiritual (spirit) provision or for money, which purchases the needs of them all causing addictions.

Satan has built a system that has made people impatient. We have fast internet and fast food. Nothing wrong with that, but it can flow over into our spiritual life with a God that does not operate off of impatience, but maturity. God moves when maturity is presented. He is not moved by whining or complaining. With such impatience we heap for ourselves provisions. We work hard. We work long hours, all to obtain a certain way of life. Satan promises all of us that certain way of life with no intents of following through. He is a liar and the father of lies. Even if you do obtain success through your means of provision, you are still bankrupt spiritually and emotionally. I guarantee there is not one successful person that is truly happy without Jesus because there is still a void left, leaving a missing piece of a broken heart and a tormented mind. People who seek provisions for themselves are earthly rich but eternally poor. Money is only paper and does not have the components to restore a depressed soul. There is not enough money in the world that can permanently heal a broken heart; temporarily yes, but permanently no. Anything outside of Jesus is a false hope that has no foundation. Only Jesus Christ is sturdy and stern enough to hold any weight of sin and will eternally crush its hold on your life. We have been brainwashed into believing a lie from Satan. From culture to culture, everyone's eyes are fixed on money as their means of providing for their carnal visions, but they forget that money's source originates from a tree that the ultimate provider created. Why trust a byproduct of something when you can trust the One that made it. All money is not wrong, but money has an ability to pull the worst out of people. Money itself is good, but the motives behind it and the love of it leads to evil.

Blurred Lines

I am sure you have heard of the statement, "perception is the new reality," and this statement is true in a lot of people's minds. The reality of most people's lives lies within how they perceive things, and this is the basis of their life's principles. Satan's goal is to distort or pervert our perception of how we hear and see things through our senses. He desires, through his system and through those associated with it, to influence us to have a view of life that is contrary to God's view. Perception is not what you see, but how you see. He wants to alter the way you see the opposite sex, money and life in general.

All of us are currently blinded by something. No matter how mature we are, all of us are currently under some level of deception. What we are not adequately informed about or ignorant to can or has been used against us to deceive us. This is why it is important for us to seek wisdom in everything and in all our ways acknowledge God so that our paths will always be directed. God wants to renew how you see things. He wants you to perceive things through the lens of love, joy, longsuffering and goodness. He wants you to see humanity, sin, poverty, social injustice and sex through his eyes.

Satan designed his system to have you to connect what you see with your heart. He wants you to develop an internal connection with what is outside of you, causing you to idolize it. He knows that if he can get people to formulate opinions about the opposite sex or to other races contrary to what they are to be viewed, those opinions will be their guide instead of God's opinion. This is why there is racism, classism, sexism or any other isms because society has engineered us to see things either far greater or far less, causing us to either be drawn to or driven from certain things. It is always important for us to pursue the correct way of seeing things.

The reason why we cannot see what is ahead of us clearly is because we have not seen what has been done for us clearly. The real reason why many people have not truly been impacted by the gospel is because they have not quite understood the significance of it. I am sure the people who saw the crucifixion and our savior rise from the dead, who walked with him 40 days after his death in the upper room, took their relationship with Jesus seriously and appreciated it more. But we are so far removed that what Jesus really did has not really gripped us. Knowing what He did for us will help us understand what we need to do for him; if that has not been made clear, then surely seeing Him will not make it clear.

How to develop a Clear Vision

Developing a clear vision is three fold. One is self-evaluation. Two is to seek His vision. Three is to apply what He shows you. Let us look at self-evaluation. One top thing that is avoided in our daily walk is self-evaluation. We should always desire to examine our motives. Before we do anything, it is our responsibility to take the time to look at our hearts and see if we are truly doing things with the right motives. When it comes to sight, it is imperative that we examine what we have an unhealthy eye for. Below are some questions that I would like you to think about. Use the space below to answer the questions.

1. Yes or No | Do I have 20/20 vision when it comes to:
   a. The opposite sex _____
   b. Money _____
   c. Success _____
   d. God _____
2. What are those things I just cannot keep my eyes off of, and why do I allow myself to be so enamored by them?

[Watch Blurred Lines online now] IAMUNPLUGGED.COM | WWM3

The Subtle Touch:

There are different types of touch that we can receive. We can receive an aggressive touch, a perverted touch, a touch of love or a touch of embrace. Each of these touches triggers or stimulates a mood or a feeling lodged within the soul. From this trigger or stimulant, whatever is lodged within the soul of a person will strive to manifest. For example, a sexual touch can stimulate a feeling or a mood that will strive to manifest sex. An aggressive touch can stimulate a feeling or a mood that will strive to manifest some type of self-defense. Every touch will in some way (without self-control) strive to produce a product of an internal mood or feeling. Touch can be dangerous because a touch of so-called love can be one of lust. A touch of embrace can be one that leads to a betrayal similar to Jesus and Judas. Touch can be very deceptive because what is in the heart can be camouflaged behind an innocent touch. Lies are behind most touches. Deceit and malice are behind many touches. We can be easily deceived through an innocent touch that could lead us down a path of sin and destruction.

Many women after being physically abused have been embraced by their abuser, causing them to be confused and often falling back into those abusive hands. Love is the strongest force we have, and the feeling of love can sometimes dominate any other feelings that we have. The only way the abused woman can escape is through the renewing of her mind. The same thing goes with sex outside of marriage. Satan loves to build or heighten emotions. He knows that the faster he builds emotions, the quicker the couple will want to progress in their relationship. Knowing this he knows that if the feelings escalade too soon, the couple will strive to entertain or be a part of something that is too difficult for them to handle. He builds their feelings off of infatuation not love. Infatuation produces multiple touch, feelings and moods that usher in the complicated products of sex. Soul ties, damaged homes, abortions, single moms/dads, and sexually transmitted disease can be products of sex outside of marriage. Satan knows that the final outcome to this path brings death, a death that kills the soul. The mind is confused with thoughts of so-called loved. Now the heart is latched on to those thoughts causing it to produce deceptive emotions. Your will has now been handed freely to Satan, regardless of if you call yourself a Christian. Satan does not care what you call yourself or what religion you profess. He will find a way to deceive you and entangle you with touch that inevitably brings defeat and failure. This path leads to depression and emotional imbalance. Professing Christianity does not exclude one from Satan's wiles.

T R U E
L O V E
W A I T S

Satan's ultimate goal, when it comes to touch, is to devalue what is valuable. He desires to cause you to view the things of most importance as if they are not important at all. He wants to devalue purity and purpose in your life. He wants all of us sexually, morally, mentally and emotionally impure, in order to block heaven. He knows that if he can get you to have impure thoughts and to embrace an impure life, those impurities will close heaven to you. It is not falling in sin that God hates most but dwelling in it that he abhors. If Satan can devalue how we view the purity of mind and heart, then we will associate and attach ourselves to more and more impure things. This will cause us to live far below how God originally intended for us to live. The second main thing Satan wants us to devalue is our purpose. The one question he does not want you to seek the answer to is "why am I here? Why do I exist?" He knows the power of a person fueled by purpose. He knows the relentlessness that embodies a person driven by purpose. That person will stop at nothing to fulfill his or her purpose. He knows that if he can get a person caught up on the shallow things of life, they will roam through life never having the chance to feel what it is like to live with a purpose.

When it comes to touch, Satan's aim is to get things within your external and internal personal space. He will use the laws of attraction to attract things into your personal space that will be used to control you. What are you attracted to? The thing that catches your eye, you will most likely bring into your personal space. Your heart is deceptive and will do whatever it takes to convince your mind of why it needs that thing. That thing will then awaken something in you through touch that will cause you to become addicted. Satan knows that anything awakened inside a person who is unprepared or unequipped to manage the emotions associated with what is awakened will hurt the individual. That thing that once was considered beauty to the eyes is now a disgrace. This is why I tell people, "Never say never." All of us at one time have said that famous phrase. We then end up doing the very thing we swore we would not because Satan knows that if we do not examine and hold ourselves accountable, our convictions will corrode.

Guard your sense of touch. Put up those armors. Never embrace a touch until you first discern the spirit behind the touch. Most touches can camouflage a deceptive internal motive that wishes nothing but to obtain for self.

[Watch the Subtle Touch online now] IAMUNPLUGGED.COM | WWM3

Hearing to Understand:

There is a difference between hearing to listen and hearing to understand. If you hear just to listen, you will believe only what is told to you. If you hear to understand you will seek to fully understand what you have heard, you will research and process with common sense and God's Word. The two main gates that Satan comes through are our hearing and our ability to see. Hearing is a channel that can be used for lies, gossip and bad news. Some of those things are deceptive and lodge in our brains producing thoughts that trigger negative moods, emotions and actions. For example, a negative word spoken about you can trigger a negative mood of anger which can then trigger an action of negative retaliation. Through the sense of hearing, we can be easily tossed to and fro if our lives are not founded on God and His Word. Our ears are constantly hearing and receiving. What we hear affects our thoughts and Satan uses that arena. Do you not think that demons are assigned to you or possibly in you to lure people into your life that will speak damaging things to you? This earthly world is highly influenced by the spiritual world. Our ear gate can be used to affect our minds with information that will either hurt or help us. When we hear only to listen, we are being too lazy to find out if what is being said is truth. Satan loves those who are hearers only because the Bible says they are deceiving themselves. Satan is very strategic. Why would he waste time doing the deceiving when he can cause the populous to deceive themselves? While people are busy deceiving themselves, Satan can put his attention on other areas of destruction before his time is up. The Bible says that Satan roams around seeking who can be devoured.

The Acquired Taste

Sin is a multi-billion dollar industry, and this satanic system will never relinquish on making sure you become addicted to what they are selling. It preys on your sin nature and causes you to identify with anything other than God. One of the senses used by this system is taste. Taste is a powerful sense. It is the smallest portion of our digestive system but the most compelling. A lot of people are enslaved by their taste buds and their cravings. Hunger and thirst are very powerful motivators. There are two types of hunger and thirst. One is natural and the other spiritual. The satanic kingdom is after your hunger. It wants to manipulate your hunger and cause it to desire things that are negative and physically and emotionally addictive. The formula is simple and is listed below:

- How this works
  1. Assess
     - Demons assess you to see when to intrude and what areas in your life are the weakest.
  2. Acquaint
     - Once they observe those areas, they begin to acquaint or introduce you to things that will begin to build your appetite.
  3. Appetite
     - Once they have assessed you and acquainted you with a supplement, they will begin to build your current appetite to an unbearable state.
  4. Addiction
     - Once your appetite is unbearable, you will then become addicted to a certain way of life or to a substance that will then lead you to your annihilation.
  5. Annihilate
     - The whole purpose of introducing you to a supplement and to build your appetite is to completely destroy and weaken you.

Satan's mission statement is to steal, kill and to destroy. He does this through infiltration and manipulation with the intent to make sure you are completely imbalanced. The state of your spiritual hunger will determine what you indulge in naturally. If you are malnourished spiritually, you will overly indulge physically. The symptoms of spiritual malnourishment are listed below:

- Symptoms of Malnourishment
  1. Emptiness || Lack of Fulfillment
  2. Confusion || Lack Of Clarity
  3. Addictions || Uncontrolled Desires
  4. Depletion of Fruits || (Lack of: love, joy, peace, forbearance, kindness, goodness, faithfulness, gentleness and self-control)

When the spirit is malnourished and is not being satisfied, it will cause our souls to feel empty and our minds to be confused. We will become enslaved to addictions. The qualities that we are to have that will ensure a stable life will become depleted. Instead of acting in love, we act in hate or lust.

The Bible says that no one seeks for God by default. We are drawn by our desire for something else to fulfill us. God is like vegetables or the one thing you use to not like but over time developed an acquired taste for.

Taste and smell are rarely used for mass deception, but there still is a deception that comes through these senses to destroy our health. Satan has engineered a strategic plan that will destroy the body through these senses. He knows that through our ability to smell we can be lured to taste and eat things that will damage our bodies. Our nose starts the deception by triggering the mind to eat what smells good. From there we become hooked to the mechanically engineered poisons present in our foods that were created to damage our immune systems, which damage our lives. It is what you do not know that will kill you, not what you do know.

[Watch the Acquired Taste online now] IAMUNPLUGGED.COM | WWM3

Chapter 3: Put On

11 Put on the whole armor of God that you may be able to stand against the schemes of the devil.

In verse 11, God has strategically placed the foundational formula for our success as soldiers in this war. We all, whether we know it or not, are soldiers, fighting for God or helping the devil. If you call yourself a Christian, this scripture and the ones that follow should be important to you. From this point on, I will break down Ephesians 6:11 and implement the components needed for revelation and understanding. The first thing that is said is, "Put on the (whole) armor of God." God operates out of wholes not partials. He desires that patience perform her perfect work that we will be whole lacking nothing. He desires for everything in our life to be genuine and whole. He is requiring that we have a heart that is "striving" for perfection. The keyword in the first statement is "whole." The passage does not say to put on some or most of the armor; it says all the armor. In this verse, we are told to "put on" the armor. The Bible, prayer, fasting and spiritual development is available. Truth, His righteousness, salvation and faith are all available armor. A soldier that does not put on his armor is already on the road of defeat. How would it look for a soldier to go into battle without his gear or armor? How would it look for a fireman to go into a burning building without his whole armor? How would it look for you and me to walk this Christian walk without our armor? Look around you. Can you see a lot of "defeated Christians"? Why do you think they are defeated in their health, finances, family, and career? It is because they are not putting on the whole armor. We have to understand that you cannot fight a spiritual war with natural resources. You have to fight a spiritual war with spiritual guards, and if they are down, your natural guards will be down as well. This parallel effect will cause cycles of defeat. The problem does not lie in God's lap but in ours. The reason why we need all of the armor is so we do not become vulnerable for attacks in either realm.

The next thing he says is "So that you may be able to stand." This is the reason why we need the whole armor so that we may be able to stand. Standing is a sign of strength and focus. It is a sign of a person having standards and not easily swayed. Satan prefers for you to be bent out of shape, whining, crying, complaining and doubtful, with no intentions of standing firm on truth. He prefers for you to stand on lies rather than to stand on or for truth. This is why deception is at an all-time high because the gospel is at an all-time high in its ability to reach billions. The moment technology increased, so did deception. Satan uses fluttery, cotton candy doctrines to have the babes and even the very elect confused. The armor of God will keep us standing and firmly holding our position against the grain because what we are standing on is firm and not loose like quicksand.

First, God warns us to "put on" our whole armor. Secondly, He tells us why we need it (so that we can stand). Now He tells us for what purpose. The purpose is so that we can stand against the schemes of the devil.

1st we need armor (all of it)

2nd so we can stand

3rd against the devil

So if we do not have our armor and we rarely ever stand, then that will leave us vulnerable to the schemes of Satan.

Satan is great at what he does. Look around and you will see that he has been busy. Some of us can even look at our own lives and see the success Satan and his demons has and is having. I know what you are thinking. No Josh! Satan is defeated, not us! Ok let us take a look.

Here are a few questions that will show whether you are or have been defeated by Satan.

Are you addicted to anything? (Drugs, porn, sex, masturbation)
How are your finances?
How is your family?
Do you spend a lot of time with your spouse and kids or are you too busy?
How busy are you? (B.U.S.Y. - Being Under Satan's Yoke?)
How often do you pray selflessly? Or do you pray selfishly?
How often do you read your Bible?
Can you quote ten scriptures quicker and faster than ten of the latest songs?
What is the first thing you do when you wake up?
Do you really trust God?
Are you often full of fear?
Can you quote three scriptures that have to do with overcoming fear?

What are the fundamental blocks of true salvation?
How assured are you about your salvation?

I can probably go on for days with questions, but you get the point. We are defeated in our lives because we have left ourselves vulnerable and drawn away by our own lust and enticed to sin. Satan is not dumb. He is clever and his demons know exactly how to strategically destroy your life, here and eternally. The Bible says that narrow is the way and narrow is the gate that leads to life and few will find it. But broad is the way that leads to destruction and many will be on it. I wonder why few and not many will be on the narrow?

The Narrow vs. the Broad (note from my blog)

Now I know many of us have heard the saying "repent and believe," but many of us may not understand it or may have a limited understanding of it.

"Repent and believe" is the fundamental foundation of the Christian life. It is the conceptual stage of eternal life.

You cannot walk through the gate without repentance, and you cannot walk the journey without believing.

The Bible says in Matthew 7: 13-14

13 "Enter by the narrow gate. For the gate is wide and the way is easy that leads to destruction, and those who enter by it are many. 14 For the gate is narrow and the way is hard that leads to life, and those who find it are few.

Verse 13 says to enter by the narrow gate. This is warning us that if we want to enter into life, we have to enter the narrow gate.

He then warns us about another gate that is wide, which is the gate we all entered in through us being born into sin.

Now this gate is wide due to its welcoming of sin and every fruitful deed born from it. Now as you continue to read, you will see that there is a way after the wide gate.

There is a way, the Bible says, that seems right to a man, but the end therefore is death. This way is the path that many are on, and possibly you.

This way is carnal, lustful and prideful. This way houses people who lie, steal, and cheat and those who harbor lust and pride in their hearts. This way includes coveters, manipulators and deceivers. This way, the Bible say's leads to destruction (eternal damnation in hell). It continues to read that many are on this path. Now Jesus has prophesied that many will be on this road. Why? This is because of man's unwillingness to do what the next verse says.

The Bible says that straight is the gate (repentance) and narrow is the way (believing) that leads to life and few will be on it.

Narrow gate: Repentance.

Many of us are unaware of the definition of repentance. Repentance means to come to your rightful place, to leave sin and grow into His righteousness. God says that the gate is narrow because not too many can walk through it. Your sins and bad habits have to be left outside of the narrow gate before you embark on the narrow way.

True repentance is the complete abandonment of self and sin. It is the complete abandonment of your plans and dreams to line your will under God's will.

Repentance is not I'm sorry it's I'm done.

At the gate we have to leave all the baggage at the door. As we walk through the gate, the gate will purge our hearts and renew our minds, causing us to walk through and leaving all behind. It is like a caterpillar and a butterfly. In order for the butterfly to fly it has to squeeze through the cocoon that once had it bound. The caterpillar, now butterfly, cannot trust (or believe) his wings until it first presses through the narrow opening. For the narrow opening gives the butterfly enough strength to trust the air under its wings. The same is for us. We cannot embark or walk with God until He first purges us through the narrow gate.

This is the season of brokenness where he breaks everything that is not like him in your life. This is where he molds your heart to want what he wants and to do what he requires, no longer desiring selfish things. This is where your mind is renewed and you no longer think like the world or think selfishly, but you have the mind of Christ.

"You cannot be whole until you are first broken."

Once you have been purged, God exalts you and you now have to believe him as your provider. The Bible says that there are two masters, God and money. Both are the means of provision.

Let us look at the people entering the wide gate on the broad path. What are they chasing? What is their means to provision? What do they serve? Is it money?

Satan knows the human heart. He knows what will drive us and have us chasing money instead of God.

In order to be saved you must repent and believe. Repent and forsake all of your sins, career goals, dreams and ambitions, and seek the face of God. Make him your master. Walk through that narrow gate, and allow him to purge you. While you believe and walk this life, trust him only to provide for you.

There is a reason why HE says few. Many of our hearts do not want to let go of the throne of our lives and hand it to God. We do not want to be purged. We do not want to give up our lucrative businesses or jobs. We do not want to let go of the porn, sex, drugs or fame. We do not want to let go because we love the options and the diversity of choices on the broad road. We love the freedom that we have on that path, not knowing that road leads to hell. Today do a u- turn. Repent and believe.

***

Transition: Satan's strategies: We wrestle not with flesh and blood.

What are we wrestling against?

The fight that we have in life is not really against people but against Satan and his demonic forces. There are people that say not everything is demonic, but a lot is. People are being influenced by the unseen. Who does lust belong to? Ask yourself; what is the influence behind pride, envy, jealousy, hate, rape and addictions? What about the increase of black magic and new age Satanism? Why are these things increasing nationally and globally? Satan knows that the more people open themselves up to the demonic, the more vessels will be available to destroy the lives of others. He hates you and he hates me. He hates anything that reminds him of God. Satan will try to distract, deceive and derail the masses from the Loving arms of God and lead them to eternal damnation in hell! So why not have people hate, envy and be jealous? Why not have people rape and kill each other? This behavior will only keep them thinking that there misfortune was everybody else's fault. This deception keeps the attention off of the true culprit of destruction, Satan. How much longer will we be deceived by Satanists in preacher's robes and bishop's garments? How long will we adhere to false doctrine, never to be trained in how to see clearly? This is why this book was written so that you can see and can hear. Satan does not want you to read about him. He wants you to keep believing that he does not exist so that you will continue to quarrel and fight amongst each other. We are a human race, created in the image and likeness of God. Satan and the fallen ones have declared war on us. They want us all dead and eternally damned to hell. Are you going to continue to fight against people or will you fight against those behind the person?

His strategy is simple. He wants to:

Deprive the Spirit (our God conscious)

Numb the Body (our World Conscious)

Possess or control the soul. (Self-conscious: mind, emotions, heart and will)

Satan knows the human soul is delicate and sensitive, if not guided by the Spirit of God. He knows the soul houses a person's emotions, mind, and will. He knows that this core of the human body will determine the body's success or failure, its ups and downs, and its destiny. He knows that if the mind is not renewed, then it will lead the body down a road the Bible says seems right to a man but the end there of is death. He knows that if the heart is defiled, then it will take the body deeper into sin and deeper into depression. He knows that if he controls the mind and the heart, then he will be behind the will (wheel) of the person's life, leading them down a dark road.

The 4 C's: Canvas, Choice, Captive & Conformed:

In everything there is a strategy, a plan. Even if you do not know you have a plan, there is one. Everyone has a strategy and a plan; even Satan. In this section, I will show you the formula that Satan uses to destroy the countless lives that are not fully armored.

The 4 C's:

1. Canvas
2. Choice
3. Captive
4. Conformed

In order for us to be successful in this life, we have to know our enemy. An army makes sure that before it attacks, it has some solid intelligence about its enemy. The lack of intelligence or knowledge about one's enemy will lead to a quick defeat.

It is not what you know that will kill you, but what you do not know.

Deception always enters, not through the locked doors, but the open window. The Bible says that God's people perish due to a lack of knowledge. Let us look deeper into this.

Satan loves to paint a picture on the canvas of our minds, a picture that constantly shows our dreams of success and our inner desires. He loves to drop thoughts of suicide, depression as well as thoughts full of hopes and dreams. He loves to clog our minds with everything but the Word of God. He will leave some of the Word in your mind but use the Bible verse out of context, to keep you bound by a system he has placed within our Christian circles. He loves the mind, because it houses everything;

It houses our;
Thoughts
Memories
Emotions
Ideas
Perceptions
Knowledge

This is why he desires our mind, because it houses so many components that interlock, potentially affecting the others. If he can torment your thoughts, those thoughts will affect your mood or emotions. If he can have your emotions imbalanced, then those emotions could trigger bad memories and bad thoughts. If he can contaminate any one of these areas, he knows the domino effect would be damaging.

There is a reason that it is said that the MIND is a terrible thing to waste. What is ironic about this is that we waste our minds, often entertaining negative things. We entertain F.E.A.R. (false evidence appearing real), false hopes and dreams. We entertain any and everything but rarely entertain God. Why? This is because of what we have allowed to be painted on the canvas of our minds. If we allow Satan a brush and an opportunity, he will paint a masterpiece.

In my previous book, UNPLUGGED, I go into more detail about the mind. Feel free to check that section out or go to my website to order your copy.

The first thing that Satan attacks is the mind. The mind can be reached through two passageways that causes us to be world conscious, and that is through our abilities to see and hear. Through those senses, Satan can manipulate the mind to receive satanic influences that will open doorways for demons to enter and alter the mind. What we perceive dictates how we see things; it dictates what we remember or choose to save in our memory banks. Perception can dictate how we see people and our motives behind what we desire to achieve. Hearing does the same. Our minds are vast and deep. If Satan controls 90% of your mind, then he will lead us to do and think on things that were created for our destruction.

His objective is to paint a false view of life. He is a salesman, and he comes to the mind to persuade you to buy his deception. He tries to persuade you to have sex and selfish desires. He knows that inside of each and every one of us is some type of genuine nature that has been altered and some type of kindness. He wants those morals corroded, and he starts with the deep thoughts of the mind.

[Watch Deep In Thought and Memory Lane online now] IAMUNPLUGGED.COM

Many of the mistakes in our lives were once conceived in our minds, and once conceived in our mind, they were nurtured in our heart. This gave birth to actions, whether through our lips or hands. Satan knows that if he can have us entertaining deceptive thoughts and memories, it will lead us to the next step.

Chapter 4: Choices

Our Choices today produce the results of tomorrow.

Satan loves immediate choices, choices that provoke us to make an immediate decision or an instant reaction. He knows that if a person has been bogged down by their thoughts long enough, they will believe that their thoughts are a reality. If they think their thoughts are a reality, then they will make actions in reality from the false reality that is painted in their minds. So if a person believes they are worthless, they will make a choice or decision in reality, which will be something such as suicide or selling themselves short. The more you think on things, the more you enter into those things thinking they are true and real. When you entertain negative thoughts, you will produce negative actions, whether it is wasting time, doing drugs, having sex, being consumed with addictions or neglecting home with work. Negative thoughts will always produce negative actions, if not used as fuel for motivation. The results of your life today are due to the choices of yesterday. You are tired now because of your lack of sleep last night or well rested from your 8 hours of sleep last night. You are in debt today because of bad spending yesterday or you have a high credit score due to the good stewardship of your credit yesterday. Either way, today is formulated by the choices of yesterday.

Now think back, way back, before you made those negative or positive choices. What was your thought life like? Was it positive or negative? Be honest! Once you become honest with yourself, then God will begin to make some changes. The longer you choose to remain you will never gain!

Whatever we entertain in our minds will eventually boil over and become a reality in our lives. Satan and his demons aim to cause you and me to make quick choices without thinking. They love for us to make decisions off of impulse and not reasoning. Think to yourself. Before you had sex, took drugs, cheated on your spouse or ran up the credit card, did you really think about what you were about to do? Did you really think about it? Satan does not deceive us by moments but through a process. In other words, his deception is a process; it takes time. It does not just pop up; its wears you down until you are in the valley of decision. Deception is subtle. Just like with a painter, a master piece is not painted in an hour. The artist takes time with each brush stroke. He takes his time to insure that his painting comes out perfect. Satan does the same thing with the masterpiece of deception. He takes his time to observe the canvas and see where he should start, where we are vulnerable. He chooses what brush, temptation, he should start with, leaving you and me with a choice to make. He paints a picture so appealing and eye catching that we are manipulated and overly consumed by it. We become numb, give in and make a choice, not by the Word of God, but by the painting on the canvas of our minds. We have to understand that life is delicate and must be handled with extreme care. The more negative choices we make, the more negative the outcome. The moment we decide to change is the moment we begin to rebound and grow. But the longer we keep making bad choices, the more we will remain bound. Who is to blame? Many times we blame God for our negative choices. Who made the bad choices, you or God? This is your life, not mommas, daddies or your closest friend. If you continue to have your guard down, Satan will eat you alive, choice by choice.

Choices and Emotions

Satan wants every choice to be taken from heightened emotions and never from solid reasoning.

(Excerpt from my blog about heightened emotions 2009)

Every day we make countless decisions off our emotions. Decisions based upon an "indicator" of a present mood. When we make decisions off our emotions, we have no foundation, nothing to stand on but how we feel at the present moment. Satan loves for us to make decisions off our emotions. For when we do; the chances of us making a good decision become very slim. He knows that if we make decisions solely off our emotions, we will become vulnerable and susceptible to being deceived, injured, embarrassed or even loose our life.

We are to make decisions off of reason, not off of impulse or heightened emotions. When we think and use the organ that is between our ears and really reason everything, the chances of us failing and being deceived will be quite slim. In our society, we have been trained and brainwashed to make decisions off of how we feel. We abort babies because of how we feel. We murder people based on how we feel. We cheat on each other based on how we feel. We lie, manipulate and deceive based on how we feel. We do all these things based upon an indicator. Imagine if every person thought before they made a decision. Do you really think our world would be like it is today?

The plan of Satan is to place each and every one of us in a situation that leads us into making a rash decision. Once we are in a place of decision, he will place things within that environment that will heighten our emotions. Once the emotions are heightened, those emotions will leave us in a position where the brain is not currently being used. When the brain is not currently being used to think and reason, then a decision will be made off of impulse and emotion, leaving you and me in a compromising and vulnerable state. It happens every day! Think about it? When two people are alone, some same sex or opposite, sexual emotions are heightened. Once those emotions are heightened, the chances of those two people using reason or wisdom becomes quite slim. Then what happens? Usually a sexual sin occurs. Once the sin has taken place, it produces a consequence for the two people involved. Once the consequence occurs, what happens? Another set of heightened emotions occur, which lead the two to produce a negative answer for the consequence. This answer could be an abortion. Satan only provides for the consequences of sin, and most sins occur through heightened emotions. If we think and use reason before we make a decision, the chances of us being deceived will be slim.

The Bible is our foundation. Within it lies everything for you and me to remain balanced. Without a foundation, how can we stand? Without a foundation, how can our emotions become balanced? When we meditate on God's Word and it becomes a part of us, we have something to come against the deceitfulness of Satan and our rampant sinful nature. Every day that we choose not to lean and meditate on God's Word, we will continue to be deceived by Satan and enslaved by our emotions.

Today and for the rest of your life, think and use that brain God gave you. It is up there for a reason.

***

Satan knows that if he can have you make decisions based off of your emotions, the chances of those decisions being balanced are slim. He wants to trigger, through our thoughts, heightened emotions that will cause us to make immediate decisions. If he can paint a picture on our minds and lure us to make immediate choices, then he will have us captive.

Chapter 5: Captive

CAPTIVE- **prisoner:** a person or animal that is forcibly confined or restrained, especially somebody held prisoner

Many times our choices will lead us to become prisoners without bars, limited and restricted in our minds. We can become bound by addictions and bound by thoughts. Many of our bad choices will lead us down a dark road where we become confined and limited. Satan wants us to believe that he does not exist or that he is not one to take seriously so that while we are ignorant of his strategies, he will slowly lure us in to invisible cages keeping us limited, subtly confined and restrained. Our thoughts are the guards that keep us restrained and confined, limiting us from ever achieving freedom and greatness. The word captive means a prisoner, a person or animal that is forcibly confined or restrained. Satan has no power over the believer but he can deceive and manipulate him or her to imprison themselves. Look back in the beginning with Adam and Eve. Did Satan make Eve eat the fruit? Did he force it down her throat? No. He slowly deceived her into taking and eating the fruit herself. Deception is an art. Through the mind, one can become so fixed on themselves that they begin to defend themselves and have self-pity. Once the person is in a state of focusing on them self, he then begins to harbor those internal emotions that outweigh all logic. Those emotions cause the individual to start building on a thin foundation, a foundation of emotions. Once the emotions have reached the boiling point, the individual now makes a choice. Now Satan has control over the individual's will. If the person continues to act, they will slowly become addicted to the choice they have made. For example, fornication (sex outside of marriage) does not begin with the actual act of sex; it always begins with a thought.

For men:

Satan always attacks us through our natural born senses and longings. With a man, he will attack us when we immediately hit puberty. Satan knows that if a young man is not taught on what to do in this transition, he will become instantly vulnerable. The demonic mostly attacks everyone during transitions. During puberty, if the young man is not taught on what to do or how to balance his emotions, he will be opened and vulnerable to sexual perversions. Satan knows that men are visual creatures, and through sight they are turned on sexually. During this time in a young man's life, Satan will immediately aim to implement the stages of lust. Once lust sets in, the first stage begins with thoughts that entertain that lust. The young man enters manhood by jacking off, masturbating and things of that nature. Once he has entertained these things privately, he will now publically seek the progression of his inward desires. He was once innocent, now he has become addicted to the feeling of self-gratification which leads him to explore the possibilities of sex outside of marriage. What men have to understand about Satan is that his lust has no boundaries. Everything you said you would not do in this area, have you not done? In some cases you have done things you swore you would never do, such as having sex with men. Satan wants perversion, and it only comes through addictions.

For woman:

He knows that women are emotional, which is not necessarily a bad thing, but can be dangerous. He knows that if he tilts one emotion too far left or right, it will cause an imbalance. A woman's mind is where her security lies. What she thinks determines her value and level of balance. She can look in a mirror that morning and feel secure, but one negative look can instantly throw off her security. Satan wants to plant in her mind a sense of worthlessness or zeal to be accepted. He enters in due to the level of attention she receives at home. Satan thrives on young ladies who did not have fathers in the home because he knows that a father is key in the home. He knows that if there is no natural father, the child will have a hard time understanding how God is as a father. This distortion is the key thing that has destroyed and perverted society. How can we know

God as a father if we do not know our own fathers? This now opens the door for demonic intrusion that will lead the young lady into a mindset of striving to be accepted. With this mentality, she will become prey to the man that is brainwashed mentally through his lust, which now leads her into a vulnerable spot of sexual immorality.

God Loves you and desires for you to be Free!

Addiction

Addiction means devotion; or great interest in a particular thing, to which a lot of time is devoted. Whatever has your thoughts will ultimately have your devotion or free will. Whatever occupies most of your time will occupy most of your choices, which will either have you walk in freedom or bound in slavery.

Devotion:

Devotion means great dedication and loyalty. Society has done a great job of initiating us into these secret societies where we become forced to join the fellowship of our inward lustful desires. Satan has built a system that focuses solely on deception, desiring to slowly usher you and me down a road of satanic devotion. He builds a system with pawns that we adore and follow so that subliminally we make a decision to pledge allegiance to Satan. We unknowingly are walking and following these pawns towards the pits of hell. The things we allow ourselves to entertain will slowly lead us either to heaven or hell. Everything is influenced by one of two things, good and evil. If this was not true, then why is there such a distinction between good and evil? We have to understand that we are soldiers in this war called life, and both sides aim to have us either free or captive. Your lifestyle determines who you are loyal to. Look at your lifestyle and ask yourself who you are loyal to.

Whoever has your devotion will have your drive. Whatever captivates your mind or intrigues you the most will ultimately, for a season or a time, have your dedication. For example, throughout our lives, something has had most of our time and energy. For some of us college, or in some cases parties, had most of our time and energy. Engagements and wedding planning had most of our time and energy. Whatever holds your time and energy has your devotion. Satan plants distractions as bait. These things aim to distract you so that what should have your time and energy slowly dies. This is why he has parents so busy that their children deteriorate. He has husbands so busy at their job that their home deteriorates; they may still have a house, but within that house there is no home. Satan may have us so focused on being in a relationship that we lose sight of our own personal development, leaving us partially capable of surviving a marriage. People do not break marriages; marriages break people. The standards of marriage break people because they were not ready for it. Satan wants the immature trying to handle mature things so that those things can crush them. Maturity always reigns over immaturity. This is why Satan wants your devotion so that he can eliminate all endeavors to mature. If we continue in the cycle of immaturity we will never obtain freedom from the vicious jaws of deception.

Great dedication is in the definition of devotion. You can look at your life and see the great dedication we have to our addictions. A lot of our addictions and desires get more attention than God. Satan, through our senses, builds a strong connection with the addiction. He brainwashes us to believe that the addiction fills our voids. Addictions can only temporarily heal what God can permanently heal. Addictions can heal a wound only for a time, but Jesus can permanently heal and leave no scar. With Satan, we are deceived to build such a great dedication to find an ecstasy that will leave us permanently satisfied. But what we fail to realize is that to every climax, there is another side with a downward journey. Satan's system was built to have you chase something that is only a dream. He wants you strongly dedicated to chase this dream so that you will be burnt out. Society now has increased the fire of addiction by adding different woods, spices and flavors so that you remain addicted, even with knowledge of God's commandments. Deception leads to damnation. Truth leads to life. Wherever there is deception, there lies the process of death. Wherever there is truth, there lies the process of life. On one of these roads lies what we ought to devote ourselves too. If we continue to leave our guards down and remain deceived, we will think we are on the right road but only be deceived.

Before there is great dedication, there is great interest. This goes with the bait of the canvas. Satan draws us through interest. Without great interest, there is no great dedication. Satan and his demons do not come in with a pitch fork and horns and say, "Follow me to hell." He will strategically and subtly wash away your morals, removing God slowly from your heart. He will bring people in your life to open the doors of your mind and heart to his deception and hook you on a cycle of self-defeat.

There is nothing worse than self-deception. The greatest deception is self-deception.

Satan wants us to be conformed to this world so much that we adhere to his deception and deceive ourselves. It is one thing to be deceived by Satan's system, but it is another to deceive ourselves. Deception by definition is the **practice of misleading somebody:** the practices of deliberately making somebody believe things that are not true. It says that it is the practice of being constantly mislead, the practice of deliberately making someone believe that a lie is the truth. Self-deception involves continuously believing a lie, even if there is evidence of truth. Ignorance, confusion and deception are the three corded rope that Satan aims to wrap around the necks of every individual. He knows that we are vulnerable through the areas we lack knowledge, and with that vulnerability, he aims to gain entrance. He loves to use ignorance to blind us from the truth, so he places within our natural environment pawns that will fund countless dollars into schemes and tactics to keep you ignorant of truth in all areas. He knows that there is a 99.9% chance that humans mimic their environment. And if there are things that promote ignorance or the diluting of truth, then the human within the environment will mimic the negativity within it. Ignorance and confusion go hand in hand/ Confusion is a state or a season in which someone is confused, tossed in between two ideals. Below is a note I wrote on October 12th 2009 on confusion.

"Satan is the author of confusion."

(My random thoughts)

A confused army never wins a war

A confused team never wins a game

And a confused person never wins in life.

Confusion is the enemy of confirmation. It aims to completely overshadow God's confirmation. God confirms and Satan confuses. Anything that God confirms, whether in our lives or through His Word, Satan will immediately try and overshadow.

Many of us are confused in our minds, through our emotions and by influences. Many of us are stagnant, unmovable. Confusion hates clarity, because clarity brings comfort and stability. When we are clear on what we are to do, we are assured and propelled to complete and accomplish what we have clarity about. Satan knows that when a human becomes disciplined and focused, hardly anything can alter their course. But the moment they begin to lack some disciplines and slightly lose focus, the door opens for complacency and confusion to destroy their lives.

The moment we lose sight of what God has confirmed, we will open the door for Satan to implement suggestions, opinions, ideas and lies from others that will question the validity of what God has spoken into our hearts.

The Bible says, "Let God be true and every man a liar."

God, from His eternal position, knows and sees all. He, through His sovereignty and providence, knows each and every one of our endings from our beginnings. If the suggestions and opinions from others are limited and do not line up with what God has already confirmed, why trust them? We need to immediately address the spirit behind anything that goes through our ears. The Bible says to try the spirit by the Spirit. Every opinion and suggestion has the opportunity to either help or to hinder, if it is not helping, then it is hindering. If it is not hindering, then it is helping.

Satan will use anyone with any kind of influence on our lives to try and confuse us, in order to alter the plans of God for our life. Too many voices in one head can be detrimental to your life. When we listen and entertain thoughts and opinions, they can overshadow or even cause doubt to manifest. This can cause us to become stagnant in our faith.

Everything that God speaks into our lives requires faith. Without faith it is impossible to please him. It becomes impossible because faith requires trust, and when we lack faith, we lack trust.

Trust God with your whole heart. We cannot say we fully trust God when we only trust him in some areas of our lives. A person who trusts God is one who completely trusts him with their health, finances, present circumstances and promising future. If you lack trust, you will become easily confused. Trusting in everything else but God will fail you, but when you trust God, no matter how tough it is, your foundation will never fail.

Satan loves to use hurts and disappointments to cause us to not trust God. Satan knows that if we cannot trust those who we can see, it will be even harder for us to trust someone whom we cannot see. Hurts and disappointments from people will cause us to doubt God, whom we cannot see, because we have been disappointed by people who we see every day.

Satan does not want you and your purpose to meet. Eternally, God knows your purpose. His objective is to help you and your purpose to meet. When you meet your purpose, it will cause damage to Satan's kingdom. The only way we can meet our destiny is to solely trust God and cling to him, having our ears solely tuned to his radio station.

Satan never sleeps, nor will his demons stop planning. Every day they will aim to destroy your life, to alter it from having a rendezvous with destiny. They want you to remain confused, ignoring God's confirmations. They want you to doubt and disbelieve what God has shared in your heart. They want you emotionally bound so that you will ignore and have excuses about why you should not marry the one that God told you to. They will have you go to colleges and universities because of your preferences instead of God's preference. They will have you mingled and entangled with sins, ignoring the truth of the Bible that has the power to save your souls. They will do any and everything to keep you off track and confused about what God has already spoken to you.

[Watch the Sixth Sense online now] IAMUNPLUGGED.COM | WWM3

God does not have to speak in order to communicate. Often times we get so caught up on hearing from God that we veer off the path He is leading us on. A stop sign does not speak but it communicates. God is diverse in his ability to communicate with us. He can speak through circumstances, experiences, people and things that happen in our lives. When God speaks, it will never contradict His Word, and it will never leave us confused. Peace, unlike our emotions, is unconditional. Do not let your emotions have you sidetracked or veering off of the course God has for you. A clear sign that something is from God is that Satan will test it. Satan does not want you happy or successful. If you have peace about a relationship you are in, and, out of nowhere, start to feel confused, find out if the devil is attacking that relationship. Why is he attacking the relationship? That person may be God's best for you. Satan may also attack decisions about moving or what college to attend. If your peace is being constantly bombarded by Satan, know that you are on the right path. Do not turn your heart away from God due to emotions or other's suggestions.

Trust God
Numbers 23:19

"God is not a man, that He should lie,
Nor a son of man, that He should repent.

Has He said, and will He not do?
Or has He spoken, and will He not make it good?

Today analyze your life. Seek what God wants for you and stick with it, because at any moment. Confusion will knock at your door. Take some time now to write down what you know God has confirmed in your life as well as the areas you feel confusion. With the areas that you feel confusion look in the back of this book for scriptures that you can meditate on that will help you gain clarity about those particular areas.

Satan works through ignorance and confusion to produce the aura of deception. He needs his prey to be:

1. Ignorant
2. Confused

If people ignore truth, they will easily believe a lie. If Satan places behind truth something that is more appealing to the flesh, then a person that is ignorant will always remain confused on it. Satan loves to place in front of us options, options that appeal more to our flesh instead of our spirit man. If the spirit is depraved, we will naturally gravitate to our flesh, which will leave us open for deception and the potential of eternal damnation in hell. So when God says there is **one way**, Satan presents alternate paths that look like or seem to be the right way. Ignorance and confusion are needed in order for deception to cloud the mind.

Now once Satan has the will, he aims to have us captive by our choices, bound within cycles.

Cycles - **repeated sequence of events:** a sequence of events that is repeated again and again, especially a causal sequence. When a person is entertaining deception, ignoring truth and remaining confused, Satan has the opportunity to implement within our lives cycles. Anything repeated over and over again will produce growth or hindrances, depending on what conceived the cycle. Satan knows that through human vulnerability and through their unguarded weak areas, he can implement strategically cycles that will leave individuals within sequences of deception. Satan does not want to work hard on deceiving everyone on a personal scale. He is not omnipresent as God is. He knows that the best way to destroy millions, while doing less work, is by scientifically initiating addictive cycles that will damage lives. He wants us bound by these cycles:

Drugs
Depression
Success
Fear
Lust
Self Defense

What we have to realize is the influence that Satan has on this world through his selective elite. He has scientifically produced diseases, schemes, propaganda and governments to destroy the image of God. This is why he has instituted abortion and homosexuality to kill the image of God within the individual and within the context of the family. He has destroyed through strategically luring us within addictive cycles that will, through our lust and desires, lead us into hell. He knows that the longer someone stays bound, the harder it is for them to be free, if they choose to never pursue humility. Satan hates humility. This is why he elevates our emotions of pride. Pride can propel us deeper and deeper into sin and farther away from the arms of a loving God.

The Bible says in John 3:36

36 He who believes in the Son has everlasting life; and he who does not believe the Son shall not see life, but the wrath of God abides on him."

When we are in Christ, we are new creatures. The old creature is dead and gone. When we believe in Jesus, we understand that he is now Lord over our lives. Once we have fully understood the gospel from a logical standpoint, we can embark in it. It is with understanding one is able to grow. When we have Jesus in our lives, we are immediately being prepared for eternal life, being imperfect people being sanctified into perfection. The Bible says that he (those that are saved) that believes in the son (not just confessing but with trusting in Jesus to change the heart) will have eternal life. Immediately following it says that those that do not believe or trust or fully understand or endeavor to allow the Holy Spirit to change their hearts, the wrath of God abides (rests or dwells) on them. Wow! Satan loves to hide this scripture. This scripture is within the same chapter that Satan has used to deceive millions, John 3:16. Yes, God is love, and he gave through love. But it did not change his wrath resting on those that remained in darkness. Satan loves for ignorance to initiate cycles that will leave us under the wrath of God. He loves for us to be under cycles comfortable and complacent, not willing to have the discipline to seek hard after truth. God hates the slothful and the lazy, those that want to remain dead and not pursue life. The reason why God hates those is because we have the audacity to reject truth, to remain buried in our lust and sin. How long will you remain deceived? Are you winning this war?

Cycles were aimed to have us on automatic, constantly bound with no intent of being free. Would you not call a person crazy or stupid if they were in prison for twenty years, had the opportunity to be free but did not take it? That is crazy right? What is ironic about this is that many of us are like the prisoner that has been bound, some for five years, twenty years or their whole life. When Jesus comes to set us free, we should not reject him and remain bound by our desires. When are we going to trust Him? This life is serious. Millions upon millions are being thrown into hell due to them deliberately choosing to remain under God's wrath. I can image Satan counting the numerous amounts of lives he has strategically deceived. Look at the path you are on. Are you on the boulevard of deception or back on the road of truth?

Let us take a look at some of the common cycles that I listed earlier:

Drugs
Depression
Success- The pursuit of happiness
Fear
Lust
Self Defense

Drugs:

Satan has scientifically engineered countless drugs that aim to numb the senses, in order to possess the soul. Like I said before, he aims to deprive the spirit and numb the body, in order to possess the soul. He loves the power of drugs, for it provides a temporal sense of ecstasy that disrupts a person's environment. Drugs alter the mind, leaving it open to the environment to heighten emotions that will lead the individual to make decisions from emotions instead of reasoning. He wants you hooked on drugs so that you will remain depressed and disoriented, unable to reason. What does a drug really do for your body? Does it heal your wounds permanently? Everything that Satan offers aims to only temporarily heal what God can permanently heal. Satan knows that if he takes care of them temporarily, they will be hooked on a cycle. Every time they are depressed or sad, they will not reach out to God but to drugs that deteriorates the body. Do you not know that God is going to hold us accountable on how we use the body he has leased to us? Drugs are in no way helping the nourishment of the body. Drugs kill the body. Drugs destroy your immune system and kidneys, along with your life. Many people may think that since no one cares about them, drugs can fill that void. My question to you is, "How will you feel after the drugs take your life, and you stand before God?" "What will he have to say about your choices?" Drugs were made with the intent to destroy your life. Everything that God created (naturally) aims to help the body, right? What do you think Satan is going to do with what God has created naturally? He will distort and pervert it, in order to destroy the body. Drugs are really not worth the time, money, loss of family and loss of your life. D.A.R.E. to say no to drugs.

Depression:

Depression is a state of unhappiness and hopelessness. Depression is one of the main goals of Satan. He targets us, not when we are balanced or strong inwardly, but when we are emotionally unhappy and full of hopelessness. When we are in a state (or season) of unhappiness or hopelessness, we either find things to make us happy or we pursue hopeless things in our quest for hope. Joy is a fruit from God. He wants us full of joy because joy transcends all other components of happiness. Satan hates joy because joy is not based on conditions; it is an unconditional attribute from God. Happiness is based upon conditions. Certain conditions such as people, titles, property and things can dictate that happiness. With joy, God is our ultimate trust. If we have God but still do not have things, we are still full of joy. God transcends all things. Satan places things within our environments that will take our eyes off of the One that transcends.

He gives you

A. a false hope
B. he attaches with the false hope conditional happiness
C. he adds an automatic clock that has a set time which will dictate how long the

happiness last
D. then he allows the happiness to subside causing you and many to fall into a state of depression

When we are depressed we become vulnerable. Now Satan can implement countless things that will cause us to be bound in cycles. False hope leads to depression, and depression can lead to everything outside of Jesus Christ.

Success:

It is so amazing how we have been influenced to chase things that are conditional. We have been programmed by the media to be in the pursuit of happiness, a pursuit after something that has no foundation. Happiness is conditional because in order to have happiness, certain elements have to be in place. This means that before I am happy, I must have certain things. The only thing we need is God and He will bring us true happiness and joy. What Satan wants to take is our creativity, gifts and talents and diverts them from being used to impact lives for God. He wants us to raise our stock while our families stock decreases.

What are the things/ people you feel you need to feel happy and how do you think these things can be used against you?

_____
_____
_____
_____
_____
_____
_____

Some may say cars, houses, opportunities or fame. Notice that God is nowhere on that list. Satan wants us to pursue everything but God. He will even counterfeit some of your plans and have you believe that you are doing something For God. You cannot have success naturally until you are successful spiritually. God can care less about what you obtain in this natural life if you are still bankrupt on the inside. Satan wants to place within your environment things that will entice you to use your gifts for him and not God. For example, a person is gifted in singing. He or she has been singing for years and is very talented. Everyone knows that this person was destined to sing. What do you believe are his or her choices? Choice one: he or she could master that gift and use it for the church or in the world for God. Choice two: he or she could be tempted to exchange a deal with Satan to have their gifts be used by him and in return receive "happiness". Anything Satan offers is a counterfeit of what God has already ordained. Success does not mean you are blessed. Cars, houses or money do not determine that you are blessed. Jesus in your heart is what defines being blessed. Why pursue something that was created when you can pursue the one who created and can grant you access to all things?

Fear:

Fear paralyzes. The cycle of fear is probably the most lethal within Satan's arsenal because it builds phobias that will hinder anyone from growth and from God. God desires faith because faith is trust. He says that without faith or trust in Him, it is impossible to please Him. Satan knows this and implements the opposite, fear. It is not wrong to feel fear, but it is a sin to be subject to it. Many of today's issues were birthed in fear. Fear paralyzes. We cannot endeavor to walk in faith while we continue to stand in fear. Satan knows that he has to place within our environments things that will disappoint us and deteriorate our trust in God. No trust in God equals no faith. We have been programmed to only believe what these natural eyes can see. We have been taught to trust ourselves and to never trust a God we cannot see. God works within time, and with time comes maturity. Satan works from impulse, and with impulse there is immaturity. Faith needs development, but the one lethal injection that can kill faith is fear. Look at your life today. Are you bound by fear? Is fear hindering something you have a peace about? The Bible says that He gives us a peace that passes all understanding, able to keep our minds and hearts through Christ Jesus. This means that peace passes all of what we know or do not know, and with that peace we have to walk by faith so that we may please God and do His exploits. I would rather do something in faith, than to do nothing in fear. When you do something, you get an outcome. When you do nothing, you reap no outcome.

Lust:

Lust is a strong desire or longing for something. Lust is a cycle that we all have to fight. For it was injected in us through the fall of man. Lust is a nature that strongly longs to exceed normal bounds in order to fulfill its strongest desires. Love has boundaries; lust does not. Satan wants our lives to be contaminated by lust. He wants us to act from 99.9999999% of lust and maybe .9999999999% from love. He knows that we have desires, and he wants those elevated by what we see with our eyes. From our eyes and the development of our lustful desire, we will become prideful in this life. Sound familiar?

Lust of the Flesh
Lust of the Eye
Pride of Life.

Satan wants the lust inside to be dominant and in control of your will, emotions and mind. The demonic wants to lure you into environments that will incubate certain emotions and pull lust out of you. The tree, in Genesis, represents the world that we daily live in. Satan and his demons are still coming into our lives with subtle question meant to lure us into Satan's system. Are you biting the fruit from his system?

Self defense

It is one thing to defend something of value, but it is another to defend something that you are not knowledgeable of. Satan loves for us to be attached to things and people or religion that we will defend, even if there is evidence there to solidify that what you are naively defending is false. He knows that when people's hearts latch on too strong, they will naturally defend a lie over accepting truth with evidence. This happens to people all of the time. People are presented with truth and still choose not to accept it. How many of us defend what God hates? How many of us listen to things that openly profess against Christianity, family, marriage and anything that is holy to God? How many of us have a statement to justify why these things are okay? There is a strategic system in place. Satan will present you with countless lies until you latch on to them and make them a part of your life. He will daily place his pawns in front of you through television and song so that you will latch on. He numbs the body by depriving the spirit, and once the spirit is deprived and the body is numb, he can control and pervert the soul. Once he has presented before you lies and perversion, he will entice you to entertain what is being presented. Once you entertain what is being presented, it leaves you open to the demonic scheme that was formulated within what is being presented. This is when he lures you to love or attach your soul to people, songs and things so that you will defend them, even if someone shows you the truth. This cycle is damaging because many people today are blind and being led by the blind, and they will both fall into the ditch. Do not defend lies. Follow truth.

The purpose for Satan having us in cycles is for us to live life on automatic, automatically addicted to porn, drugs, people and success. He wants us to be continuously bound by these things. He wants us to be like a mouse on a wheel that runs but gets nowhere, with our eyes fixed on a target but never reaching it. He wants us bound by jobs that will never fulfill our call and lust that we never learn how to truly love. He wants us bound by happiness that we never experience joy. He wants us impatient that we never allow patience to have its perfect work in us. What has you bound in a cycle? Write those things below. Be honest with yourself and write everything that you know that you are bound by or are cycled in and utilize the scriptures in the back of this book to help you understand how to overcome the cycles.

_____

_____

_____

_____

_____

_____

_____

_____

_____

_____

_____

_____

_____

_____

_____

_____

_____

_____

_____

_____.

Chapter 6: Conformed

Conformed means: to follow standards, to follow a standard or standards that have been fixed, regulated or required.

God has high standards; Satan has low standards. The higher your standards, the harder it is for things to overthrow you. The lower your standards, the easier it is for things, people, offenses, temptations, demons and everything else to overthrow you. Satan has standards that are fixed within his system, standards that have certain regulations and requirements. All of his standards were fixed to make sure that you and I break God's laws, drift away from Him, love the world more than God and enjoy this temporal life instead of striving for Eternity. Being conformed is the display of the conceptual stage of the canvas. He lures you into an environment that will incubate certain thoughts that will give Satan an opportunity to paint a picture on the canvas of your mind. Once you have entertained those thoughts, then he corners you in to making a choice off of emotions instead of reason. After the choice has been made, he hopes that you become addicted to the results of the choices you have made (drugs, sex, lying, greed, etc.), which cause you to be captive and bound to those results. After all this has happened successfully, you will become funneled into his fixed standards, regulations and requirements.

At this point, people are fully deceived into believing that there is no hope of change. For they love themselves more than God and people. They enjoy their sins. They have sold or exchanged their souls for the pleasures of this world. Full deception causes the numb effect. The body is numb to truth. The body walks around with no life because the soul is dark and the spirit is dead. Satan wants us to be numb and made into zombies and robots that are easily manipulated to abide under his fixed standards, regulations and requirements. Whatever television advertises, society initiates, rappers and pop stars portray, his zombies will gravitate toward. This makes his system stronger and darker. What we have to understand is that Satan operates from our energy and efforts. The moment we become dumb and numb, he willingly uses our energy and efforts to make evil dominant over good. This causes more and more people to fall and drift away from God. Look at television. Look at society. Listen to your music. Is this right? Is this good or is this evil? Is it common sense or perversion? The moment you reason and think things out is the moment freedom takes place. Satan does not want you to think! He wants you lazy and conformed to his way of thinking and doing things so that millions upon millions will be tossed over the cliff of life into the jaws of hell! Look where you are now. Are you on that broad road? Are you entertaining things that God hates? Are you brainwashed? Satan wants you brainwashed. He wants to condition (formulate) you to behave abnormally. He wants to induce you to continuously believe a lie. Normal is what God intends. Abnormal is what Satan wants to initiate. Normal is a husband and a wife, not a man and man or woman and woman. Normal is a family not shacking up. Normal is marriage, not divorce. Satan wants to distort (alter **shape:** to bend, twist, stretch, or force something out of its usual or natural shape) meaning and make what has meaning worthless. He wants to condition us to believe that what is normal is abnormal and what is abnormal is normal. He does this by possessing or owning the media or influential streams of society to constantly beat images and words on our minds, conditioning us to accept this new way of thinking. This will destroy the image of God and initiate a distorted view. Our minds are sponges. Our emotions are delicate, and our hearts is the core of our lives. If he can constantly pull the strings of your emotions, you will constantly act off of emotions and not your brain. Even if you do use your brain, it will be too late because it will be distorted.

This has been a brief overview of Lucifer's strategies for mankind. If you feel that you are trapped within one of these areas and may be battling in your mind, or faced with choices, dealing with addictions or maybe you feel you have reached the final stage of conforming to the world, then keep reading. I have answers from God's Word that are practical and can help you break away from the world and grow in God. It is not going to be easy. Contrary to popular belief, Christianity is not easy. In this life, you will have trials, test and opportunities to face persecution. You will experience satanic and demonic attacks. You know why? It is because you have truth, and the truth you have can set you and others free.

There is good news. When God created the earth, he knew that within the course of his creation there would be a fall. Before man was created, God spoke the words, "Let's make man in our image and in our likeness." Within that statement, he spoke subliminally the redemptive plan of mankind. He spoke within himself three beings: God the creator, Jesus the savior and the Holy Sprit the instructor. He spoke from Eternity though time his redemptive plan. When Adam and Eve fell, we all were injected with sin and lust. Once we received this injection, we were damned and destined for hell, until God stepped from eternity into time to redeem man back to Himself. He lived on earth as Jesus for 33 years. He healed the sick, raised the dead, changed hearts and also suffered persecution. The greatest event known to man is the moment at the cross where God, who was without sin, died for the sinner. He gave everyone an opportunity to choose life. When He died, the price for our sins was paid, but only for those that believe. Today, the Holy Spirit searches to and fro, plowing and breaking the hearts of men to accept Jesus as Lord. Those that believe and trust in Jesus are saved, but those who do not believe or obey him are still under His wrath. Do you believe? Is Jesus Lord over your life? Does he control how you think and live? Do you obey his commandments? He says that if you love Him, you will keep His commandments. If He is not Lord of your life, then you are still under His wrath. Today is the day of salvation. Today, get understanding and beware of Satan's devices.

***

Once we understand our enemy, we can prepare ourselves. Before a person is ready for war, he must go through boot camp. He must first go through training. God wants us to understand our enemy so that we may be prepared for anything our enemy throws at us. If we do not understand, we are ignorant. If we are ignorant, we are confused; with confusion and ignorance comes deception. What lies on the other side of this book is truth, truth that will open your eyes to be prepared and qualified for this war that we all face.

Welcome to World War Me, in other words, boot camp.

Chapter 7: Preparation

Preparation - **preparing something or somebody:** the work or planning involved in making something or somebody ready or in putting something together in advance.

Before an army goes to war, it must prepare. If generals and soldiers are not prepared, they will suffer casualties. Preparation is a word that many people do not adhere to, but is essential to life. If you do not prepare, you will fail. If you do not prepare or practice before a game or race, the chance of you winning is slim. If you do not prepare for a test, the chance of you passing is slim. If you do not prepare in this life, it will cost you in eternity. If you plan to be a soldier, you must be prepared, but preparation comes with a cost. It will cost you time and effort, but it will be well worth it. I would rather be prepared today than suffer loss tomorrow.

Foundation - **support for idea:** the basis of something such as a theory or an idea.

Anything without a foundation is destined to fall. Anything that has a solid foundation will never fall. A foundation is essential to everything. If a building does not have a foundation, it will fall. If a tree does not have roots, it will fall. If we do not have a foundation, we will definitely fall as well. Preparation should precede the pursuit of aspirations, just like reasoning and thinking should precede actions. Everyone needs preparation before they embark on destiny. Life is full of hurts, pains, disappointments, let downs, temptations, trials and tests. If you have not experienced these, keep living. Life is full of a lot of things other than promises and prosperity. If life is full of these things, how should I prepare for them?

Everything in life reveals God's plan of preparation. The ground is prepared before a seed is planted. A nest is prepared before an egg is laid. A bride is prepared before the wedding ceremony. A lot of things are prepared before something else can be done. What bothers me is that we prepare ourselves for pleasures but are never prepared for what else life has to offer. We prepare ourselves for everything but for eternity. You cannot build the structure of a house without first laying the foundation. Our life represents the structure. Our life represents the frame, the brick, the stone and siding. The question is, what is the foundation?

Parable (House on a rock)

The Narrow Way

13 "Enter by the narrow gate; for wide is the gate and broad is the way that leads to destruction, and there are many who go in by it. 14 Because narrow is the gate and difficult is the way which leads to life, and there are few who find it.

You Will Know Them by Their Fruits

15 "Beware of false prophets, who come to you in sheep's clothing, but inwardly they are ravenous wolves. 16 You will know them by their fruits. Do men gather grapes from thorn bushes or figs from thistles? 17 Even so, every good tree bears good fruit, but a bad tree bears bad fruit. 18 A good tree cannot bear bad fruit, nor can a bad tree bear good fruit. 19 Every tree that does not bear good fruit is cut down and thrown into the fire. 20 Therefore by their fruits you will know them.

I Never Knew You

21 "Not everyone who says to Me, 'Lord, Lord,' shall enter the kingdom of heaven, but he who does the will of My Father in heaven. 22 Many will say to Me in that day, 'Lord, Lord, have we not prophesied in Your name, cast out demons in Your name, and done many wonders in Your name?' 23 And then I will declare to them, 'I never knew you; depart from Me, you who practice lawlessness!'

Let's take a look 1st in Matthew 7:24-27

Matthew 7:24-27

24 "Therefore whoever hears these sayings of Mine, and does them, I will liken him to a wise man who built his house on the rock: 25 and the rain descended, the floods came, and the winds blew and beat on that house; and it did not fall, for it was founded on the rock.

26 "But everyone who hears these sayings of mine, and does not do them, will be like a foolish man who built his house on the sand: 27 and the rain descended, the floods came, and the winds blew and beat on that house; and it

fell. And great was its fall."

Matthew 7:13-23 represents what it takes or the requirements that will show what a person is building their life on. Let us take a deeper look.

Jesus begins to tell his disciples that whoever hears his sayings will be liken to a wise man who built his house on the rock. The rains descended; the floods came and the winds blew and beat on that house. And it did not fall, for it was founded on a rock. He continues to say that everyone who hears these sayings of His and does not do them will be like a foolish man who built his house on sand. And the rains and the floods came and the winds blew and beat on that house. The house fell, and great was the fall of it.

Let us break this down.

The house represents our lives. The two types of people listed are those who hear and do and those that hear and do not do (wise/foolish). These two types of people represent the house. The rains and the floods and the wind represent false persuasions, temptations and deceptions that come from Satan. They beat on our lives every day, through influential streams such as media, family, friends, and society. These elements, which beat on the house, all come to test the structures foundation. Jesus said that those that were wise built their houses on the rock, while the others built their houses on sand. Those that were built on the rock fell not. Those that built their houses on sand fell.

The foundations

Key word in this passage is the word "the". It said "the" rock, not "a" rock. Those that lay their foundation in Jesus Christ first are wise. He is "The" Rock not "a" rock. The Rock means that He is the Only Rock that we can build our lives on. A rock would present a view that He is a rock amongst many that we can build our lives on. Any builder will tell you that before you build a house, you must first lay a strong foundation. For the elements will not aim to test the structure but the structures foundation. If the house foundation is weak, then the house will fall. If the foundation is strong, the house will not fall; it may suffer damage but not a total loss. The sand represents anything else outside of Jesus. Jesus is the only way to eternal life. Anything else is a false persuasion. Why is sand bad? Any builder will tell you that if you build your house on sand, it is in vain. Sand is not strong enough to hold anything. Sand looks solid, but when rain gets in, it will cause the structure to slide. Satan wants you to build your lives on sand or things that seem strong. He is strategic. He will give you time to build your house, knowing that he will test it in the future. His tests and temptations will easily destroy the foundation because he packaged this in his plan from the beginning. He wants you to build your lives on your dreams, goals, aspirations and hopes. Jesus says that only what you do for Him will last. All of us at some point were building our house on sand. We were building it on sand because we had no knowledge or understanding of Jesus The Rock. We were building our lives on what we knew, which was grounded on selfishness, pride and lust. When Jesus comes into our lives, we immediately destroy our old house. We get the demolition team (the Holy Spirit) to completely tear that old house down to the ground so that we may build a new one on Jesus Christ, The Rock. Death is our ultimate test. When death comes it will show the difference between the wise and the foolish. It will show who built their lives on either sand or on The Rock. It will show who endured the false persuasions and the temptations that continuously beat upon their lives. When death comes to your life, will your house be left standing or will it crumble?

There are two types of people in this world, saved and unsaved. Many people think they are saved but do not truly know. Many people believe that they are saved because they said a prayer a few years ago or they were baptized. Many people believe that Jesus is just "a" rock that they can build on and there are other ways to heaven. These are just a few of the mass deceptions from Satan. Salvation is much more than just a prayer; it is a process. It begins the moment you became spiritually alive and ends when you are physically dead. The process begins in the heart, under the plowing hands of the Holy Spirit. Before there is salvation, the heart (the mind, emotions and will) must be broken. The heart represents the center core of human life. Our natural heart is the center core of our lives. If it stops, we die, making our natural heart the ultimate indicator in one's earthly fate. Our spiritual heart is also similar. In God's eyes, our spiritual heart (mind, emotions and will) determines our eternal fate. God is not going to judge you by the results of your actions but by the content of your heart. Let us take a look at the scriptures that preceded Matthew 7:24-27.

Matthew 7:13-14

The Narrow Way

13 *"Enter by the narrow gate; for wide is the gate and broad is the way that leads to destruction, and there are many who go in by it. 14 Because [a] narrow is the gate and difficult is the way which leads to life, and there are few who find it.*

Like I said earlier, humanity is separated not by races or ethnicity but by the saved and unsaved, found and lost, regenerate and unregenerate. These are the ultimate distinctions of mankind from the ultimate source, God. In verse 13-14, Jesus warns of two gates and two roads or ways, one gate narrow, the other gate wide. One way is difficult and the other easy. Jesus' first statement tells us to enter through the narrow gate. He then states the alternative to His gate which is the one that is wide (Satan's vast alternatives). He continues to say that this gate is wide and accepting and that it leads to destruction. There will be many who go in by it; the reason why many will go that way is explained in verse 14. The way of the narrow gate is difficult and leads to life. God warns that only few will find it. Wow! Deep stuff huh? Jesus tells us here that those who desire to enter the narrow way will have to leave somethings behind. Eternal life immediately calls for self-denial. Only the real and genuine can enter this way. And as you go through this narrow gate, it will purge and knock off everything that Jesus does not want. For those entering in the narrow gate, there will be a season of God purging our hearts.

The wide gate is wide because of its vast acceptance of everything but the ONLY way. Take a sincere look at the world today. The world accepts everything but Jesus? The things of God which are best for us are ridiculed and viewed as obsolete, while everything else is viewed as acceptable. Satan knows that man's flesh, if it exceeds a certain level, will gravitate towards the things of the world. This road is what many people are on, because this road satisfies our selfish desires, lusts and appetites. This road caters to our wants and not our needs. It lends a tender touch to our hurts, giving us false hopes to chase addictions that temporarily heal our wounds. The wide gate has leaders who were handpicked by Satan. Some of these leaders are singers, rappers, actors, politicians, pastors, bishops and influential leaders sent to catch the eyes of the weak and lead them down the dark and deceptive road to hell. Millions will be lead over the cliff into the abyss of eternal damnation. Are you on this road? The verse below explains who are all on this road;

2 Timothy 3

1This know also, that in the last days perilous times shall come.

2For men shall be lovers of their own selves, covetous, boasters, proud, blasphemers, disobedient to parents, unthankful, unholy,

3Without natural affection, trucebreakers, false accusers, incontinent, fierce, despisers of those that are good,

4Traitors, heady, high-minded, lovers of pleasures more than lovers of God;

5Having a form of godliness, but denying the power thereof: from such turn away.

The process of Salvation is difficult. Jesus tells us the reason why many will be on that broad road is because the narrow way will be difficult. The wise are those who count the cost and are true disciples. They do what Matthew 16:24-26 says.

24Then said Jesus unto his disciples, If any man will come after me, let him deny himself, and take up his cross, and follow me. 25For whosoever will save his life shall lose it: and whosoever will lose his life for my sake shall find it. 26For what is a man profited, if he shall gain the whole world, and lose his own soul? Or what shall a man give in exchange for his soul?

He says that those that desire to come after him will deny themselves (deny all of their old ways and dreams), take up their cross (their call from God and His will for them) and follow Him (strive for perfection and holiness). He continues and says that those that save their life (continue to build their house on sin and keep their plans) will lose it in eternity. And whoever will lose his life (leave it outside of eternal life's gate) will truly find life, a life that leads to eternal life with God. In verse 26 he says, "What profit's a man to gain the whole world but loose the only thing that lives on beyond the worlds restraints." Let me ask you a question. What profits you to have millions of dollars and a famous name but lose your soul in hell? Life is likening to a vapor, but eternity is like a continuous rushing wind; it is forever.

The verse finishes by saying, "What shall a man give in exchange for His soul?" This is something to ponder. What are you willing to give in exchange for your soul? Many people are exchanging their souls for fame, millions, opportunities, sex and pleasures. This war in life begins in us. Many of us are fools chasing false hopes and heading down a dark road. When are we going to be wise? The Bibles says that the fear of God is the beginning of all wisdom, and wisdom leads to life. Are you wise today or are you foolish?

Ripe or rotten fruits

You Will Know Them by Their Fruits

15 "Beware of false prophets, who come to you in sheep's clothing, but inwardly they are ravenous wolves. 16 You will know them by their fruits. Do men gather grapes from thorn bushes or figs from thistles? 17 Even so, every good tree bears good fruit, but a bad tree bears bad fruit. 18 A good tree cannot bear bad fruit, nor can a bad tree bear good fruit. 19 Every tree that does not bear good fruit is cut down and thrown into the fire. 20 Therefore by their fruits you will know them.

A wise person and a foolish person are not just only recognized by which road they are on but also by their fruits. You will also know them by who they follow. Many of us are blind and lazy. We would rather be fed than feed ourselves. Satan has built a system that aims to serve humanity quickly. This method will even carry over into the modern day church. Jesus says to beware of false prophets (teachers, pastors, bishops, prophetess, televangelist, evangelist or anyone with a "word from God") who come to you in sheep's clothing (a follower of God) but inwardly (in their hearts and motives) they are ravenous wolves (followers of Satan's). He says in verse 16 that you will know them by their fruits (actions). Before you entertain what you hear, look with your eyes. Just because people say they are of God does not mean that they are. The greatest tactic of deception Satan can use is to pose as his enemy. Satan will try to mimic Christ; he will try to act, talk and speak like Jesus. This form of deception has destroyed millions, making them lazy and unwilling to seek truth. Babies need assistance, not adults. Satan has developed a strategy to have people come under a false gospel instead of the true Gospel. The true Gospel combines God's love with God's wrath and tells of man's depravity. The gospel shows that we are in need of a Savior.

Many of today's alter calls only speak of one aspect of the Gospel. They mostly focus on His love for us and that if we say a prayer, then we are saved. Memo: nowhere in the Bible does it say that you are saved off of a prayer. It says to repent and believe. It says to deny yourself, take up your cross and follow him. It says to crucify your flesh daily. It says that if you do not obey or believe, God's wrath remains on you. Millions upon millions of people have followed wolves down the broad road thinking that they are saved. What if I was trying to sell you a product but the product I was trying to sell you was a counterfeit. If you bought that product and believed that it was real, does that make it real? No it does not. Satan has produced a system that herds millions in to believing the counterfeit. Most of what is going on is emotionalism. Emotionalism is when people use other's emotions to gain something for themselves. They keep you ignorant of the truth so that you will buy their lies. They will show you hungry people in Africa to have you send your money to them. They will give you false hopes because they know if they have your hope, they will have your money. They will distort and take scripture out of context to make you continue in their game. They will mix their lies in with truth. Think of it like this; if I gave you a glass of water and slipped some poison in it, could you tell? Out of ignorance and lack of discernment, you will drink it and it will kill you. This is what is going on now. They present something that is true but add just enough poison to do the damage. They encourage you to drink their water, causing you to slowly rot as they aggressively grow rich. The longer you remain ignorant, the longer you will remain their prey. We cannot always believe what we hear. We should first observe with our eyes before we entertain what we hear.

Fruit is what Jesus was trying to warn us about. He wants us to watch for their fruit. He wants us to look at how they treat people and observe their lifestyles and character. Sheep are sheep. Wolves are wolves. Sheep follow the shepherd. Wolves aim to scatter the sheep. Jesus says that if you are not sowing with Him, then you aim to scatter. Many are following false teachers and do not know it. Let us get back to the analogy of me selling you a product. I have come to you to sell you a product that is counterfeit. I advertise that it is real but you knew beforehand the difference between what is fake and what is real. Your knowledge beforehand saved you money and time because you knew the counterfeit from the real. Before you deem something to be real, first see if it is a counterfeit. What if I told you that many of today's mainstream ministers are not true? What if I told you that most of what you hear on TV is a lie? Would you believe me? Satan has worked hard to make sure you will not believe truth. You know why? It is because the truth will set you free.

I Never Knew You

21 "Not everyone who says to Me, 'Lord, Lord,' shall enter the kingdom of heaven, but he who does the will of My Father in heaven. 22 Many will say to Me in that day, 'Lord, Lord, have we not prophesied in Your name, cast out demons in Your name, and done many wonders in Your name?' 23 And then I will declare to them, 'I never knew you; depart from Me, you who practice lawlessness!'

The final few phrases where Jesus draws the distinctive line between the saved and the unsaved are found in verses 21-23. He says that not everyone that calls Him Lord (whenever the Bible repeats a word the writer is trying to strongly emphasize the word) will enter the Kingdom of heaven. He goes on to say that he who does the will of father will enter heaven. Many in that day (key word is many) will say to Him, "LORD have we not _____ in your name? And I will declare to them 'I never knew you.' Depart from me you who practice lawlessness (iniquity)."

Many in that day that never made Him Lord will call Him Lord. Back in the day, a slave was owned by his Lord. The Lord owned every aspect of that person. We have been programmed to think of Jesus as a friend, a homeboy, a pal, a comrade or even a Savior but never Lord. Those that are wise and those with eternal life make Jesus Lord over their life, finances, decisions, dreams, goals aspirations, gifts and talents. What are some things you are doing now that you think are okay in God's eyes but really are not? What are some things that you are doing now for God but are really doing them for yourself, for your name to be known? God does not care about the results of your actions, He cares about the content of your heart.

Not everyone that says they are a Christian is one. Just because they look the part, does not mean they are the part. In order to say you are a part of something, you must first seek to find out if you are doing what is required. How can you call yourself a Christian if you do not even know what being a Christian requires? Many people call themselves Christians but are doing things contrary to what the faith says. The danger of following wolves is that they will brainwash you and have you believe that God has changed. God has boldly said that he never changes and that he is the same yesterday, today and forever. Lawlessness or the iniquity in one's heart keeps them from being truly saved. Lawless means someone who is uncontrolled or unregulated (Someone without restraint or laws). When people deliberately do things outside of God's laws, they are lawless. Satan wants humanity to be lawless so that our laws derive from them and no one else or no one higher. The Ten Commandments are necessary for us. When we break one, we isolate ourselves from grace and embellish in His wrath. Deep inside each and every one of us is a moral law that came from the moral law giver, God. When we exceed those laws, due to our lust and pride, we remain under his wrath and away from grace. Satan has built a system that aims constantly, from every corner and every channel, to pull that lust and pride out of you. He wants that lust and pride to exceed a certain level so that you can be damned if you are an unbeliever or destroyed as a believer. Many people who say they are saved do not live under the laws or parameters of salvation. For example, if you were drowning in a pool, I rush in to save you, and then you jump back in, would you consider that foolish or wise? Would you blame me if I did not go back in there to save you again? Many people think that since they are under grace (so they believe) or that they have said a prayer that they can jump right back into sin. The Bible talks about people who started out with us but did not finish with us. The Bible says that those that endure shall be saved. Are you only in Christianity because of its benefits but are not willing to endure its requirements or persecution. A Job may have benefits but before you get those benefits, you have to meet certain "requirements" and "endure" the job. Many people want the benefits but are too lazy or not willing to meet the requirements or endure the task. Are you one of them?

The will of God is this that you love Him and keep his commandments. The will of God is for you to seek after, trust, forsake all (your dreams goals, aspirations, pursuits) and follow Him. Many of us are caught up on what is God's will for us tomorrow that we derail from what His will is for us today. If you do not do His will today but die today chasing His will for you tomorrow, where would you end up? If we seek him today and do what he requires of us, which is praying, seeking after him and examining our hearts working out our own salvation with fear and trembling, He will take care of what He has for us tomorrow. This could entail what city you will be in or who you will marry. But if you keep seeking after tomorrow, you will miss Him today. Today is the day of salvation, never tomorrow because tomorrow could be too late.

Before you can win this war, you have to first be prepared. This Christian life is not easy. Nowhere in scripture will you see or hear Jesus say "Hey Guys. This life as a Christian is easy." He says that there will be trials, tests, persecutions and warfare. If you are not willing to go through this life, then stop reading now because you are not fit for the Kingdom. The Bible says a man that puts his hand to the plow and looks back is not fit for the Kingdom of God. What does the world have to offer you anyway? The truth hurts, but let the truth heal you today.

Part 2

This section aims to reveal the practical ways to prepare for warfare mentally, emotionally and physically. Humanity has been at war with Satan and his demons since the fall of man. Before we aim to fight him and his system, we have to first prepare to win the war on the inside. A lot of you are hurting. Many are confused and lost. Within this section, we will discuss the main areas that need God's hands to heal.

Satan aims to get control of one or more of these things. If he gets a hold of your thoughts, he will heighten your emotions. If he can bring up bad memories, those too can heighten your emotions and produce bad thoughts. If he can get a hold of what you study, he can lure you to forfeit your will and use your knowledge for him. There are so many ways Satan can contaminate your mind.

The Bible says in Romans 12:1-2

1 I beseech you therefore, brethren, by the mercies of God, that you present your bodies a living sacrifice, holy, acceptable unto God, which is your reasonable service. 2And be not conformed to this world: but be ye transformed by the renewing of your mind, that ye may prove what is that good, and acceptable, and perfect, will of God.

Verse 2 is what I am going to focus on. It starts with the warning not to be conformed to the world and the conceptual stage of not being conformed to the world is to be transformed by the renewing of your mind.

Renew means: **to replace something that is worn**, broken, or no longer suitable for use. Many of our minds, within one of the 6 areas (Thoughts, Memories, Emotions, Ideas, Perception, Knowledge), have been worn, broken, or are almost non suitable for use. Satan has done a great job in entering in one of these areas. He uses open doors to contaminate and conform the mind to the ways of his system. His system aims to wear out the mind. If Satan can wear out the mind, he can heighten emotions and alter your will apart from God's will. Usually our minds dictate our days (positive thoughts positive day or negative thoughts negative day). God created our minds to be the motherboard of our lives in order to house all data that pertains to us, our loved ones and our experiences both good and bad. Our minds are like sponges. Whatever it entertains, it will soak up. Satan knows that the mind is a terrible thing to waste; this is why he has built a system that conforms the mind from being powerful and sharp to being weak and dull. A weak mind equals overall weakness. A strong mind equals overall strength. Consistency is key. That is why the key word is renewing. Renewing is a process, a process under the framework of consistency. Without consistency, there will be no lasting change.

The definition says that renew means to replace something that has been worn, broken or no longer suitable for use. Let us take a look at these words.

Worn: **showing effects of wear:** weakened or frayed by use.

Worn, by definition, means showing effects of wear, weakened or frayed by use. Our minds are always moving, from several thoughts throughout the day to intense dreams at night. Our minds keep moving. Satan loves to have our days dictated by our thoughts. He desires that our minds run with no breaks. He wants our minds running on constant worry and on auto anxiety. If our minds wear thin, so will our lives. If our minds never rest, then our emotions will never be balanced. If our emotions are never balanced, then our actions will be uncontrolled. Satan wants our minds worn down, showing effects of wear, weakened and frayed by over usage. When our minds are weak how will our emotions be balanced or our actions controlled. If our minds are weak, how can we be alert and focused and keen to details, both physical and spiritual? If our minds are weak, how can we discern spirits and attempt to win this war within and against Satan? Overly doing anything benefits no one. There must be balance, control and rest or the mind will wear out, weaken and fray.

God intends for everything to be whole, lacking nothing. In order for this to happen, everything must be in place. When things begin to be contaminated or tampered with, they will deteriorate and brake down. Broken means something is no longer whole: out of order. Is a laptop whole if it is missing a lot of buttons? Is a car whole if it is missing its tires? What about your phone. Is it whole if it is missing its battery? No. They are not whole, they are broken. Satan wants our minds to be so worn that it deteriorates and loses its intended wholeness. He wants our minds to be out of order. A person can be physically fit, but if anyone of those 6 areas is contaminated, destruction is impending. A broken mind equals a broken life. We will be no longer suitable for use.

Our mind is strong. It can hold so many things. The worst thing is for us to have our minds lose strength and become weak and dull. Satan has done a great job in brainwashing millions into his systems way of thinking. He has tempted millions to operate off of impulse and not from reason. He has lured people to make countless decisions off of one aspect of the mind, there emotions. He has contaminated our minds so that our minds are no longer suitable for use. We have heaped for ourselves politicians, preachers, actors and rappers to think for us. We have relied on them to dictate our thoughts, memories, emotions, ideas and perceptions. Why think for yourself when others can think for you?

Chapter 8: Fastened

We have come to the portion of the book where we will discuss our armor. I will be discussing what we need to put on in order to be successful in this Christian Journey and to prepare for the end times that we are in. We all are required by God to put on our full armor. God warns us to take up or put on our whole armor that we may be able to stand. We cannot stand firmly and win if we do not have on our armor; we will be vulnerable and open for attack. Life is serious, but many of us are living it loosely. We have to understand that it is what you do not know about your enemy that will kill you. There is not one soldier that will go into combat without his or her gear and gun. There is not one firefighter that will go into a burning building without his or her gear. God requires that no Christian enter his or her new life without their full armor. If we lack or leave behind part of the armor, it will affect our success in battle. It makes no sense to have a shield but no helmet, breastplate, bullet proof vest but no shoes. We have to have on the full armor in order to be effective in this war called L.I.F.E. When we lack one area, it will cost us in another.

Truth is essential
A belt may be a small piece of the armor but its purpose is extremely vital. Without a belt, everything is loose and out of place. Without a belt, everything is out of order. The same goes for truth. Without truth, everything in your life will be loose and out of place. Without truth, everything in your life will be out of order. Truth is solid and whole. In order to be secured, everything in our lives must have truth at its foundation. Your life is a house and, under it, a foundation must be laid. The main house and the garage are on the same foundation. In other words, you cannot have truth as your foundation in one area and a lie in the other. You are responsible to make sure that everything that pertains to you is founded on truth, if not, your life will be unbalanced. For example, you can be a Christian and your eternal foundation is laid but you have poor health. An unhealthy body will not last long enough to accomplish the spirit's purpose. Satan loves to implement lies within the parameters of truth. He will never attack those areas in your life where you have truth and an understanding of that truth. He will attack you where you entertain lies. His demons will attack you through your heath, finances and family. They will attack you where truth is not present. Truth is whole and it must cover every aspect of your life. We all know that we will make sure that we care for the things we love most. Satan has done a great job of unbalancing our being. He will have us so caught up on our soul realm that we neglect our bodies and our spirits. He wants us so caught up on what is on our minds, how we feel, and our own desires that we neglect

truth in the other areas of our lives. If a soldier does not have his belt, he will lose focus on the battle because his shirt is out of place or his pants are sagging. Satan wants different aspects of our lives to be loose that we remain loose without endeavoring to tighten things up. What are some areas in your life that are loose? What are those things that have you distracted and not focused? Look at your life and see what is keeping you from truth. Here are some questions you may need to ask yourself:

How is your health?
How are your finances?
How is your family structure?
How is your marriage?
How is your commitment to God?
How is your Character?
How is your Integrity?

All the things listed above are things we have the power to change. We must first get rid of those things that are hindering us and then implement truth that will save us. We have to learn how to stop looking at others and examine ourselves. Those seven questions above are vital for your life and truth must be laid as their foundation. Satan and his demons will come in those areas that are built on lies, infatuation, lust, and pride; they will come through these areas and deteriorate your strengths and have you dominated by your weaknesses. Without truth, everything will be loose. Is your belt fastened?

The belt holds everything in place. Without truth, everything will be out of place. You have to have truth in all areas. If one lacks truth, then many areas in their lives will be out of place.

Truth in your beliefs and in everything.
We must have truth in every area. If we lack truth in one area, it will affect the others. Truth begins in our beliefs. There are a lot of things that try to imitate truth. A lot of religions advertise that they are the way or that there are multiple ways. There can only be one truth, and that truth is the jumping board that everything springs from. If I say that I am rich, I must have evidence that attests that what I am saying lines up with what I have. If I say that I am healed, I must have evidence that what I am saying is true.

2009 was a tough year for me, in regards to truth. I was discouraged because of strong accusations that came against Christianity. In April of 2009, I almost left the faith due to the accusations that Jesus was compared to pagans and how the story of Jesus was a myth. The accusations were that the Bible was written by masons and the story of Jesus was a part of astrology. I heard so much that I almost strayed from truth. Thankfully the Holy Spirit told me to do deeper research. He took me through a journey that revealed in many ways that Jesus did live and die (proof from Historians). He took me through creation and how everything had to derive from one greater source. He showed me how the Bible is distinct in its ability to describe the human heart and our sinful nature (unparalleled to any other book). I searched out how the accusations were lies and false. The Holy Spirit showed me how accurate the Bible is on History, nature and human life. He showed me so much that I had to seek out truth for myself. Before you entertain what people say, seek truth out for yourself. Satan has handicapped us and his system has engineered laziness within our DNA so that we will entertain lies instead of seeking out truth. Many will fall away in the end times due to their lack of discipline.

This is so that when persecution comes, we will be caught in the valley of decision and many will choose to follow a lie rather than to stand for the truth. What a tragedy. Why follow a lie that is temporal when you can follow the truth that is eternal? The point of what I am saying is that you are responsible and the steward of your life. The pursuit of truth should be number one because it is the foundation. How can you build anything without first laying the foundation? When you die, you will be judged alone. No one will vouch for you. It is up to you to seek out your religion, denomination, affiliation and see if they are true. Truth can only be found by first recognizing the counterfeits. If you know the counterfeits and knock them down, the truth will remain standing. The Bible has stood the test of time as true. Jesus has stood the test of time as true. Remember this, truth is never popular. Why? Truth is not popular because there is money and power in lies. Look at your world today. Is the bible popular? What happens when you read it in American high schools? You are allowed to read the Quran and other books. What about Jesus? Why is his name so hated? Mohammed's name is not hated. Truth is never popular because the architect of the world's system knows the power in truth. What does the Bible say about the truth? It says that it will set you free. Satan cannot benefit from someone who is free, he can only benefit from people who are bound.

***

I dare you to do what I have done and research everything about Jesus and the Bible. Below are a couple of people that I listened to during that tough time in my life that really aided in my relationship with God. There were plenty of others but these two helped me the most. I hope they help you too:

Tim Keller
Ravi Zacharias

Truth is the foundation

Truth must be the foundation to everything. In order to have truth, you must have understanding. The deception comes when we sign in to things or entertain things with a limited or partial understanding. The aim is to do nothing without first understanding everything that pertains to it. A builder knows what he wants to build. He never lets his emotions or his impulsive nature propel him to build without taking the time to lay the foundation. A builder is patient because he wants what he builds to last and endure. Endurance does not come from the brilliance of the structure but from the strength of the foundation. You have to take the time to lay the foundation of your life. You have to take the time to count the cost of this thing called life. Satan has done a great job in making us impulsive and overly eager that we begin building the house without first laying the foundation. When we do this, Satan will engineer a storm with winds strong enough to destroy the house. He wants you so eager to have sex that you build your foundation off of infatuation and lust. He then engineers a storm with winds of STD's, babies out of wedlock and broken homes. Your house will be destroyed. God wants you to build things from love not Lust, joy not happiness, peace not chaos, kindness not hate, goodness not evil, faithfulness not laziness, gentleness not harshness and from self-control and not from a lack of it. When you build on the opposites you are building your life destined to fail.

Truth is vital and it must be laid first before we endeavor to build our lives. We have to count the cost of everything. Before you build on a relationship with someone first check their foundation and before you join into marriage build it on Truth. Before you consider a career count the cost and lay the foundation first and ask is this what God wants me to do? In everything before we build our lives on it we must first lay the foundation. What are you standing on today will it last or will it sink when tested?

Vulnerability

Imagine a warrior that did not put on his belt, his shirt was out of place and his pants were falling in the middle of battle? What would happen? The moment when everything begins to drift out of place is the moment when we begin to lose focus. When we lose focus on truth, we become vulnerable. Vulnerability is Satan's goal. We are only as strong as our weakest link. That link is whatever the weakest area in our lives is. Satan will never attack what is governed by truth. He cannot come through this area because there is understanding. With understanding, there are standards. The higher the standards, the less of a chance Satan has to attack. Satan attacks those areas that are built on lies. These areas are where we are ignorant and lack standards and understanding. When we lack understanding, we are ignorant. I cannot fool you into doing anything or buying a product if you fully understand that product. But I can fool you if you are limited in your understanding of the product. Where do you lack understanding? It is within that area that you will be vulnerable to attack. If you do not have truth, you will not have understanding.

We all become vulnerable when we do not have truth. If we lack truth in our health, we will become vulnerable for satanic attacks through our health. If we lack truth in our finances, we will become vulnerable to debt. Without truth, we are lost. If we lack truth when it comes to life, it will cost us in eternity.

What if things are not fastened?

This question speaks volumes. What will happen to you tomorrow if things are not fastened today with the belt of truth? Where will you spend Eternity tomorrow if your life is not fastened? Eternity is nothing to be taken lightly. This life is just a test to see where people will spend Eternity. It is a test to see who will pass or fail. If you do not have truth governing your life, will it speak up for you in eternity? Truth is everything, and without it, it will cost you everything. Think about all those that have died due to diseases, or those people who are in extreme debt. Think about those that are in prison or jail. I guarantee that every one of them that still have a sound mind will attest that they wish they would have acted differently. They wish they knew then what they know now. I guarantee that everyone that is in HELL right now would tell you that they wish they knew then what they know now! How are you living your life? Are you living it outside of truth?

The Bible says in Matthew 7:7-8

7 "**Ask**, and it will be given to you; seek, and you will find; knock, and it will be opened to you. 8 For everyone who asks receives, and the one who seeks finds, and to the one who knocks it will be opened.

We all know that no one who asks a question will leave immediately after asking if they have yet to receive an answer. Truth should be our number one priority because with truth comes understanding. With understanding our standards are lifted. If there is no truth, there is no understanding and we become vulnerable.

In the above scripture, Jesus tells the people to ASK. A. (ask) S. (seek) K. (knock). He tells them that if you want truth, you have to A.S.K. Him. You have to ask him your questions, because He has all the answers. You have to seek Him to find the path of truth, and you have to knock on His door of truth to get an answer. The only problem is that we are asking the wrong people, seeking the wrong things and knocking at the wrong doors. The subliminal message in this passage reveals that the people that ASK are persistent, consistent and dedicated individuals. People who ASK are patient not impatient. They are willing to wait, not eager to leave. They fully understand the value of what they are searching for, and they are willing to endure anything to obtain truth. Look around our world today. There are billions of people who are unwilling to ASK. They are not willing to ASK because they are not willing to submit and be humbled under the only One with the answers. Truth, as a category, does exist. If truth exists that means that there is only One truth. And if there is only one truth, then everyone should be following it. What is sad about this is that many are following lies and only few are following the truth. We have to endeavor to ASK because if we never do, then we will never obtain a true answer.

Truth hurts but truth Heals.

Truth is comprised of standards, and with those standards comes many discomforts. When truth is presented to a lie, immediately truth will cause discomfort. Let me make this plain. If I was to come to you and my breath is not its freshest, you would present me with the truth. The truth would be, "Josh your breath stinks; here is a mint." At that moment, I would feel uncomfortable because I realize I had been in everyone's face with my breath stinking. The moment that truth was presented, I became uncomfortable because the truth revealed my ignorance. With the truth presented, I can take the mint and heal my present condition, or I can remain in ignorance and remain with bad breath. This happens to a lot of us. When truth is presented, we often get offended and refuse to accept it. Satan has used offense to keep people in bondage to the truth. When we allow our worldview to be contaminated by lies, we will never ever gain freedom. We have to accept truth for what it is and endeavor to allow it to heal us. Yes, truth hurts but packaged within truth is a path that leads to health and well-being. Everything must begin with truth, and from truth, everything will grow. If truth hurts, trust and know that it will heal you, just like mints to bad breath. When you told me my breath stank and gave me a mint, believe that I will carry my mints to insure that my breath never stinks again. The same goes for life. When you embrace truth, it will help you to be prepared to never let your life stink again.

Chapter 9: The Guarded Heart

The breastplate is a piece of armor that covers the chest area. This armor is vital to anyone in war because it covers the most vital organ we have, our heart. If our heart ceases to work, we cease to live. The heart is considered the core of our being. Just like our natural heart is the center core of our natural life, our spiritual heart is the center core of our eternal life. Our spiritual hearts make up our soul realm. This is our mind and will. God is not going to judge us by the results of our actions but by the content of our hearts. Many people today are not guarding their hearts. They are leaving their hearts vulnerable to attack. Satan's ultimate aim is to continue to defile the human heart. He aims to make sure that a man or woman's heart continues to drift away from God. He aims for our hearts to remain dark, even if we profess that it is illuminated. With a blanket of deception, Satan covers our eyes and misleads us to follow a path away from God. If we do not know the condition of our hearts, how can we endeavor to stand with confidence on Judgment day?

The Bible clearly teaches on the condition of our heart. It has a wealth of information about how deceitful our hearts can be and how our hearts can be purged and clean unto righteousness and holiness. Life begins and ends with our heart, both naturally and spiritually. Our natural life spans from our first heart beat to our last, but our spiritual hearts span throughout eternity. The moment our natural heart stops, our spiritual heart will be judged. How is your spiritual heart looking? Satan endeavors to deceive so that we remain blind to the condition of our hearts. The Gospel of Jesus Christ targets the heart first because it is the core of our lives. The Gospel immediately targets our sins against God. It targets our selfishness and pride. It shows us that our hearts are at war with the things of God. The Gospel immediately addresses the heart. Since the fall of man, human beings hearts have grown wicked, panting more and more after wickedness and darkness. Their hearts beat impulsively after the things of this world while giving a deaf ear to the things of God. The moment sin entered our veins, we were destined for Hell. The Wrath of God was shadowing us. God's ultimate plan was to send a gift, a doorway, for those who genuinely love Him to walk through. The gift was through the life of Jesus Christ who, from His death and resurrection, sealed a covenant between true believers and God. From this pinnacle point in History, man now has to choose between darkness and light. The heart of man must choose to either pant after God or chase after the world. The sad thing is that many people really believe they are panting after God when, in reality, they are not.

The heart must first repent before it seeks forgiveness. The travesty is that many people do not know what true repentance is. The greatest deception Satan has ever done is to dilute the message of the gospel. This one move by Satan is probably the most genius move he has ever made. He knows that the Gospel has power. He knows that no partial gospel can save anyone. He knows that if he can drift people away from God and His Word, then people will lose sight of the message. The full gospel acknowledges first the condition of man's heart (repentance) while the partial Gospel only acknowledges the love of God (forgiveness). Before you can receive forgiveness, you must first be humble and repent. Salvation is much more than a prayer; it is a process. Before Jesus even stepped on the scene of time, His plan was already finalized in eternity. Before He created man, he foreknew man's disobedience. And with His foreknowledge and omniscience, He saw the solution of man's depraved heart. When he stepped from time into eternity, His earthly life wrote out the contract and His death and resurrection sealed and signed it. It is up to those who believe and trust in Him to sign their end of the deal. This is not about works but trust. The trust is to completely surrender to Jesus Christ. His natural life wrote out a contract (blueprint) that shows us how we ought to live. His perfect life embodied the message he was carrying, which was the gospel of the initiating of Gods kingdom. Jesus' first words herald "Repent and believe". He tells us that before we can say we believe, we must first repent. And before we repent, we must understand why we need to repent. The understanding portion of the Gospel has been left out of many preacher's and evangelist's presentations. They have also made repentance a gray area. Jesus made it very clear that the gospel is only accepted by those with an ear to hear. Now hearing here is not about the ability to hear but the ability to understand. Everyone or most people have the ability to hear, but only few have the ability to fully understand what they have heard.

Satan has packaged his partial gospel under the umbrella of impulsiveness and emotionalism, a system that imbalances a person's emotions and draws them into making an impulsive decision without reasoning. He deceives the masses to make a decision to sign a contract they have not fully read. They hear only about the Love of God who died for their sins or that he wants to forgive you or that everyone that is good is saved. What Satan leaves out is the condition of the human heart. He leaves out of his partial gospel the reason why we need Jesus. He leaves out the order of salvation, which begins with the brokenness of the heart by the Holy Spirit. He strongly advertises that a prayer or a baptism stamps their name in the Lamb's Book of Life. Salvation is much more than a prayer. It is a long but beautiful process. Satan's deception has caused more damage than good because millions believe they are saved when they do not know enough of the gospel to be saved. When the heart is not guarded, it lies open for attack and false doctrines. Those that have ears to hear will hear to understand, not hear just to say they have heard. Many have heard the gospel but only few have understood it. There are two types of listeners, both hear the same Word but have different outcomes. One heard the Word (gospel) and the other understood the Word (gospel). The one that heard it understood it only in his/her intellect but did not accept it in his/her heart. The Word was heard but never acted on. This person's outcome, if they do not change, will lead to hell. They heard the Word on Sunday but went back to the clubs on Saturday with no change. They heard the Word but remained lustful and prideful. They heard the Word but did not allow the Word to change their hearts. This is the results of millions. Now the one that heard and understood took the time to ponder the Word. The Word made him/her realize their present condition as a sinner. The Word made them humble and willing to open their heart for the work of the Holy Spirit. This person's outcome, if they continue, will be heaven because they have embraced the full message (gospel).

One Word
Two people
Two different outcomes

What outcome will you have?

Why is a full explanation of the gospel important? It is because the full gospel includes time for the individual to examine their present condition. When something is being fully explained to an individual, what is being fully explained will be fully understood. What will happen to the person who only gets a partial explanation? It is likened to a job. The efficiency of a business relies on the training of its employees. What is the difference between a business that thoroughly trains their employees and a business who carelessly trains their employees? The same is with life. Our life wraps around the hearing of the gospel. Everyone's life, whether a believer or not, wraps around the Gospel of Jesus Christ. They either obey and receive Eternal life or disobey and remain eternally damned. Either way, everyone's life is affected by the message of Jesus Christ, even those who have not heard.

No one is without excuse.

A heart that is left unguarded is one that will be left to rot. A heart that is fully guarded is one that will grow and flourish. The human heart is delicate and must take precedence. By it being the core of our lives, it must be examined daily. Truth holds everything together and is the beginning of everything. Without truth being presented, a person cannot live truthfully. When truth is presented, the heart now has to choose whether to adhere to truth or shun it. I am now going to explain the process of the human heart under the umbrella of the Gospel.

The formula of true repentance is found in 2 Chronicles 7:14. The Bible says:

If my people, which are called by my name, shall humble themselves, and pray, and seek my face, and turn from their wicked ways; then will I hear from heaven, and will forgive their sin, and will heal their land.

The four key words:

Humble
Pray
Seek
Turn

Humility:

Repentance begins with humility. It begins with the self-examination of our present condition that is at war against God. Once we have understood the message of Jesus Christ and have understood the content of our hearts, then we (those that are genuine) are forced to become humble. Humility is a part of the conceptual stage of salvation. It is the immediate response after a person fully understands. It is the state where men and women's hearts become open and receptive. A lot of people ask the question, "Why do bad things happen to good people" or "Why is there evil?" Evil exist for two reasons. The first reason is to reveal the attributes of God. The second reason is to open the hearts of people. Let us look at the first one. When evil happens, it reveals an attribute of God. If there were no rebellion, how could we know Him as savior? If there were no sicknesses or diseases, how would we know Him as a healer? If there were no evil, how would we know Him as God? Evil exists to prove the distinction between it and good. If there is evil, then there is good. If there is good, then there is a moral law that explains the difference between the two. If there is a moral law, then there has to be a person that gave the law. Evil is just the beginning of a long process that leads to the proof that there is a God. The second notion is that evil exists to open the hearts of people. God knows what will open the hearts of people that will influence them to change. He knows exactly what will get people on the right road. Sometimes, it takes the death of a loved one to open someone's heart. Sometimes, it takes earthquakes and hurricanes to open the hearts of people. Sometimes, it takes cancer to open the hearts of people. God would rather you suffer a little but make it to heaven than enjoy a lifetime of pleasure and end up in hell! The trauma or pain that we experience that causes us to be humble cannot compare to an eternity in hell! I would rather suffer a little here and remain saved than to enjoy the luxuries of this life but hit hell wide open. God knows what needs to happen, and if it takes a death in the, family so be it. If it takes cancer, so be it. If it takes an earthquake, so be it. Now is God the source of these catastrophes No! He just uses what's around us and the consequences of our sins to help humble us. Think about it. What would you rather choose? Suffer a little now or suffer for eternity.

God does what needs to be done to make sure we enter a state of humility. He knows that when a person is humble they are attentive and sensitive to direction. They are pliable they and useful because they are not about themselves. When a person is prideful, their ears are closed and their hearts are hard. Humility insures attention to reality. A person that is humble is led by commonsense and adheres to directions, but a person who is prideful makes up his or her realities. When the gospel is presented, it is followed by the toiling of the heart by the Holy Spirit. If we are not working with the Holy Spirit, our works are in vain and our labor yields no eternal reward. The Holy Spirit works on a person, leading to humility which leads to an open heart towards God.

Satan wants us to enter a state of Depression. God wants us to be humble while Satan wants us to be in a state of depression, both are the conceptual stages of either greatness or destruction. Satan knows how to use evil as a tool to cause us to be in a state where we are open to him. Depression is a counterfeit tactic opposite of humility. Humility leads to growth and maturity in God while depression aids the void that reaches out to be filled. Depression is a state where we are low, pressed down by our hurts and pains. Satan knows that the longer a person remains hurt, the more likely they will find themselves in the cycle I call "hurt and retaliation". This cycle begins with hurt, and that hurt then develops and leads to a retaliation. This cycle leads to hurt people hurting people and hurting people damaging society. Both humility and depression are conceptual stages to either greatness or destruction.

Prayer:

Anything new must be presented with proper communication. Without proper communication, the receiver and the sender grow apart. After we are humbled and walk in humility, we must communicate with God. Prayer is a tool that God has instituted as the main means of communication that leads to an expected end. Humility leads to prayer. Once we are in the process of repentance, we are first humbled and within the new life of humility, we grow in prayer. Prayer is key in life. Without prayer, we lose communication with God. Within that communication lays instructions, directions, and purpose. If we lose our communication with God, we lose instruction, directions and purpose. Prayer is the source to the heart while humility guards it. Prayer is God's direct line of communication that embodies wisdom to renew the mind, reshape the heart redirect the will. Humility is what insures that we remain focused on the true purpose of life and to make sure that we remain at a safe and balanced level. Humility produces balance and prayer fuels humility. Without prayer and a consistent relationship with God, pride corrodes our once humble state. Once our humility is corroded, next goes our morals and common sense. Satan hates it when you pray. He hates it when you are daily breaking bread with God. Satan knows that God knows everything and God will never leave His children ignorant of life and of Satan's plotted schemes. So if Satan severs the lines of communication, we lose intelligence. Imagine if a country's whole system of intelligence was suddenly down. Would that country be safe or vulnerable? What if you lose your signal on your cell phone in the middle of an important call? Would you be fully informed? The greatest thing an army can do is to sever the lines of communication and intelligence of their enemy. If their enemy is not being informed, then they are confused. Confusion is one of Satan's greatest resources. A confused army never won a war.

Humility leads to a consistent prayer life because your heart needs reshaping and your heart needs to be guarded. If you do not pray, your heart will not be guarded. Ask yourself, how often do you pray? How often do you start your day off in prayer? This is serious because one day all we are going to have is prayer. There is coming a day of great persecution and tribulation and all we're going to have is prayer. Prayer is too important not to use. Satan loves it when we rarely pray because that means that we rarely receive instructions. He loves it when we sometimes pray because that means we sometimes receive directions. A soldier lives and breathes on the instructions and directions from his or hers commander and chief. Any miscommunication can lead to defeat or the death of soldiers. When we do not pray, we cease to develop and grow.

Prayer is not just something we do, it is a necessity. It is the road that insures we reach an expected end.

Seek:

When we are seeking for something, we do not stop till we find it. The length it takes for us to seek depends on how important the product or person is that we are seeking. If we lost a penny, we would not take as long to search for it as if we lost one hundred dollars. A one hundred dollar bill has more value than a penny. The time we search depends on the immanent value of the person or item we are searching for.

The higher the value; the longer the search.

During this process, we are compelled to search or to seek after God due to his value. His worth to us is everything. His worth as a father and as Lord leads us to seek Him to obtain His attributes and to obtain His character. God implemented seeking because it is a part of the flow. First comes humility, the conception conceived by understanding. After the conception, there needs to be a system in place to nurture the seeds growth. That system is under the umbrella of prayer and communication. When we communicate, we want to be more and more like the One we are communicating with. Seeking God cannot be contained within a moment, it is a developing process. The more we remain PLUGGED into him, the more we die to ourselves and the more He lives in us. This has to be a process because we are constantly battling ourselves and our sinful nature. We have to remain focused because if we do not, our sinful nature will aim to be dominate. The work of Salvation cannot be contained within a moment but it flows within a process orchestrated by God. When we seek after Him, we lose sight of ourselves which leads to the death of our pride and our lust. We seek after Him, due to His value and our depravity. We only become somebody when we are in Him because it is only Him that receives the glory. The ground does not benefit in the harvest but the seed sower does. We do not receive anything because we are the ground. It is only God that receives because he is the sower. When our hearts are being fueled through prayer and guarded by humility, we gain by becoming good ground. We do not become good until we seek after the only one who is good, God.

Turn:

This is the core of repentance. Each and every process described above leads to the turning away of one's sins. Humility reveals the sinful condition of our hearts. Prayer reveals the need to trust in God so that we will not fall back into our previous condition. Seeking God is what will propel us to gain ground in Him and less in us. Prayer and seeking God help us to turn against sin. Our hearts have to be completely turned against sin. The influence of prayer and seeking God will motivate us to be purged not pleased, sanctified and not seduced. It will move us towards God. Without a guard on our hearts, how will we be protected from the influences that aim to cause our hearts to faint? If we do not guard our hearts, they will become callous, hard and an enemy of God. Sin leads to death. Repentance leads to life, and an understanding of the gospel leads to repentance. The Bible says that the goodness of God leads to repentance. You can also implement that the good news of God leads to repentance. Because of His goodness he sacrificed himself and opened the door unto salvation. He laid out a blueprint for us to follow. Do you really think God would do all this and expect us not to do anything? His life wrote the contract and His death and resurrection signed it. He is now waiting on you to sign your end. Are you willing to die so that you may live? Repent and believe.

Each and every one of us have morals that were established in our hearts. We all know what is right and what is wrong. We all know what is good and what is evil. Like I said before, evil proves there is good, and good and evil prove there is a law that determines such. The law proves that there is a law giver who is perfect because truth and justice have to derive from something that is true. If this person is true and just, he has to be omniscient (all knowing) because, in order for Him to judge correctly, he has to know everything. If the person is true and just, he would also have to be omnipotent (all powerful) because His power to judge lies within himself. He alone is perfect. If the person is true and a just judge, he would have to be omnipresent (everywhere) to see who is doing right and wrong. If He is everywhere, he see everything. If he sees everything, his power leads Him as the supreme force to judge. What are the two places that he says will separate those that obey and those that do not? Those places are heaven and hell. The Bible says that man looks on the outward appearance while God looks at the heart. He knows what is in all of our hearts. He knows whose hearts are vulnerable and those that are fully guarded. What about your heart? Is it guarded or left vulnerable?

Our hearts need gates to insure that not just anything can enter in. What should those gates be?

The Ten Commandments represent the gates that God desires to guard the heart. The commandments will insure that nothing outside their bounds will enter the heart. They will also ensure that whatever is allowed to enter the heart must flow through the standards of the Ten Commandments.

The Ten Commandments are found in Exodus 20.

*More information on the 10 Commandments in my first Book UNPLUGGED

God desires that these laws be on our hearts to guard against intrusion and cultivate love within the heart so that all motives and intentions are genuine and pure. If one of these commands is transgressed or broken, it immediately separates us from God. God and Sin cannot mix. Each commandment is interwoven together so that if one is broken, then the others are broken. For example, if a person has multiple gods in their life, such as sports, actors or money, then immediately Commandments 2-10 are broken. Now that thing has taken the place of God, so commandments 1-3 are broken because these refer to God being supreme in a person's life. The others refer to how one treats others.

If a person is overwhelmed with that thing, then that thing dictates their worldview. Now everything is dictated by the standards of that idol, which will lead in many cases to sins such as adultery, dishonoring parents, coveting, murder and bearing a false reputation. See how each commandment targets the condition of a person's heart? Each intention, whether to obey or disobey, derives from the heart. The heart cultivates these intentions and then manifests them into actions, actions that honor or dishonor God. Satan knows the Bible. He knows that power that is transferred to those that obey. He has strategically implemented, within his system, creative and deceptive ways to insure that the masses break these laws. He does not focus on the actual birthing of the acts, but he focuses on the planting of the seed, the conceptual stage. If he can get to the heart, he will plant seeds. The heart must be guarded and surrounded so that it will not drift from God. This life is not a game. We have to understand that our enemy never sleeps. We have to rely on someone who is omniscient. If not, we will fall and become vulnerable. At the moment salvation is conceived, the heart goes through immense changes. In order for God to use the whole being, our heart has to be in order. Satan wants this part of our being to be chaotic. He wants your thoughts to run rampant, your memories to haunt you and your ideas to lead you to sin and deeper into pride. He wants your perceptions of people to be bad so that you will love only yourself and not others. He wants your emotions to be unbalanced and unstable, causing you to operate form impulse and never reason. He wants you to obsess over knowledge, not wisdom, so that it controls your life. Satan knows the importance of the soul realm. He knows that if a person's heart is unstable, there life will be also. If their life is unstable, their eternity will be uncertain. Everything that is conceived has an end but within that end is eternity.

The moment we were conceived, our eternity began. When we die, our death is a prerequisite to true life. Our natural life is a shadow of our eternal life, and eternal life rests on the content of our core. If our core is off, then our whole being becomes unstable. If our lives are unstable, then our eternity will be uncertain.

The parable of the sower is a great parable that reveals the different type of hearts of humanity. Within the four examples lie the reasons and answers as to why our hearts are the way they are.

Matthew 13 says:

The Parable of the Sower

1 On the same day Jesus went out of the house and sat by the sea. 2 And great multitudes were gathered together to Him, so that He got into a boat and sat; and the whole multitude stood on the shore.
3 Then He spoke many things to them in parables, saying: "Behold, a sower went out to sow. 4 And as he sowed, some seed fell by the wayside; and the birds came and devoured them. 5 Some fell on stony places, where they did not have much earth; and they immediately sprang up because they had no depth of earth. 6 But when the sun was up they were scorched, and because they had no root they withered away. 7 And some fell among thorns, and the thorns sprang up and choked them. 8 But others fell on good ground and yielded a crop: some a hundredfold, some sixty, some thirty. 9 He who has ears to hear, let him hear!"

The Purpose of Parables Matthew 13:10-23

Let us break this down. I will be using Matthew 13:10-23 to help explain why the breast plate is needed.

10 And the disciples came and said to Him, "Why do You speak to them in parables?"

In verse 10, the question arises as to why Jesus used parables. Parables were used as stories that would reveal spiritual truths to the audience. Natural things were used to unveil spiritual meanings. The only problem with parables is that the carnal mind that is not familiar with spiritual things will not understand or reach the ultimate meaning. The carnal mind cannot discern or understand spiritual things. The disciples asked Jesus about the parables because they wondered why he would speak to them knowing that the people may not understand. Verses 11-15 answer this question.

Verse 11-12

11 He answered and said to them, "Because it has been given to you to know the mysteries of the kingdom of heaven, but to them it has not been given. 12 For whoever has, to him more will be given, and he will have abundance; but whoever does not have, even what he has will be taken away from him.

Jesus' answer in these verses clarifies that there is one message but two receivers. One hears only, and the other hears and understands what they have heard. He says that it (eternal life) has been given to you (true disciples) to know the mysteries of the kingdom of heaven. But to non-disciples, it (eternal life) has not been given. For whoever (disciples) has (salvation), more will be given, and he or she (disciples) will have abundance (eternal life). Whoever (non-disciples) does not have (eternal life), even what he has (life) will be taken from him.

There were 3 types of people that followed Jesus, the disciples, the crowd, and the Pharisees. The disciples were true supporters. The crowds were spectators, and the Pharisees were skeptics. These three types of people surround the gospel today. The parables are only understood by those who have the Spirit of God in them, for the Spirit of God will reveal the meaning behind the parable. The crowds, back in Jesus' day, were people only around Jesus for the miracles, not really for Him. They were around Him because of what he did, not necessarily for who he was or what he had to say. Those type of people could not understand the parables because their souls were fixed on expectations, not revelation. The Pharisees were skeptics and their hearts were already hard and against what Jesus had to say because it went against an established order.

There are people today who love God and their love for Him compels them to hear what He has to say and to strive to understand. There are also people who are only around the concept of Jesus, in order to benefit from what He has to offer. They serve the idea of Jesus (graven image), not who He truly is. There are also other people who are against Jesus and His message today. They orchestrate under their father, Satan, strategies and concepts to crucify the gospel message. Because Satan knows that the gospel has the power to save.

Jesus continues in verse 13-15 to say the reason why he speaks in parables;

13 Therefore I speak to them in parables, because seeing they do not see, and hearing they do not hear, nor do they understand. 14 And in them the prophecy of Isaiah is fulfilled, which says:

' Hearing you will hear and shall not understand,
And seeing you will see and not perceive;
15 For the hearts of this people have grown dull.
Their ears are hard of hearing,
And their eyes they have closed,
Lest they should see with their eyes and hear with their ears,
Lest they should understand with their hearts and turn,
So that I should heal them.'

His reason in speaking in parables was to reveal the distinction between those who are really for Him and those who are not. He says that therefore I speak to them (those that do not believe) in parables because, in seeing (natural seeing), they do not see (spiritual revelation.) In hearing (natural hearing), they do not hear (Understand what they have heard). They do not understand (fully grasp), and in they reflect the prophecy of Isaiah verses 14-15.

Hearing you will hear and shall not understand,
And seeing you will see and not perceive;
15 For the hearts of this people have grown dull.
Their ears are hard of hearing,
And their eyes they have closed,
Lest they should see with their eyes and hear with their ears,
Lest they should understand with their hearts and turn,
So that I should heal them.'

Jesus clearly reveals the natural response of the human heart towards the Gospel. He reveals that those whose hearts are not willing to change will hear the truth, but by them living a lie, they will not understand. They will see, but by their eyes being clouded, they will not perceive the truth when it is clearly visible. The reason why they will not understand the truth or see truth is due to their hearts growing dull. They are slow to respond, their souls being clogged with the cares and the concerns of this world, causing truth not to flow in. Jesus continues to say that their ears are hard of hearing and that they have closed their eyes. This is the deception of Satan. His system aims to blind the eyes of billions, causing them to fall into self-deception. This causes the self-deceived to openly and willingly harden their own ears and close their own eyes. Satan does this so that they will be in a cycle where they will never truly see with their eyes and hear with their ears, which will lead them to never enter into salvation and be healed by Jesus. Jesus lets his disciples know that self-deception was designed to keep people blind, because if they ever truly hear or truly see, they will hear, understand and begin the process of salvation. They will become healed from their sins and walk the long journey towards eternal salvation.

In verse 16-17, Jesus reveals the heart of a true believer. He says:

16 But blessed are your eyes for they see, and your ears for they hear; 17 for assuredly, I say to you that many prophets and righteous men desired to see what you see, and did not see it, and to hear what you hear, and did not hear it.

Many people, before Jesus came, were waiting to see the day when the messiah would come and defeat the stronghold of sin over humanity. All of us (who are true believers) are blessed today to know that we have ears to hear and eyes to see, because our hope is not in this earthly life but in eternity.

The Parable of the Sower Explained

The purpose of this part of the book comes down to what I am about to share. In the previous chapter, I discussed the importance of the belt of truth and how it holds everything in order so that our lives can flow. The heart is vital because it is the core of our being. It houses everything that encompasses our soul realm. From the heart everything derives. From the heart, meaning originates. The explanation of the parable given in Matthew 13 will reveal the condition of every person reading this book, and I pray that after you read it, you will do the necessary things to purge your heart.

The Bible says in Matthew 13:19-23:

18 "Therefore hear the parable of the sower: 19 When anyone hears the word of the kingdom, and does not understand it, then the wicked one comes and snatches away what was sown in his heart. This is he who received seed by the wayside. 20 but he who received the seed on stony places, this is he who hears the word and immediately receives it with joy; 21 yet he has no root in himself, but endures only for a while. For when tribulation or persecution arises because of the word, immediately he stumbles. 22 Now he who received seed among the thorns is he who hears the word, and the cares of this world and the deceitfulness of riches choke the word, and he becomes unfruitful. 23 But he who received seed on the good ground is he who hears the word and understands it, who indeed bears fruit and produces: some a hundredfold, some sixty, some thirty."

There are 4 different types of soils mentioned in this parable:

No soil
Soil with stones
Soil with thorns
Good soil

Let us take a deeper look at their meanings and where many of us line up;

(No soil)

The Bible says in verses 18-19:

18 "Therefore hear the parable of the sower: 19 When anyone hears the word of the kingdom, and does not understand it, then the wicked one comes and snatches away what was sown in his heart. This is he who received seed by the wayside.

The Bible says that anyone that hears the Word of the kingdom, which is the gospel, and does not understand it, the wicked one will come and snatch away what little was sown into that person's heart. Let us look deeper into this. The gospel of Jesus Christ is to repent and believe. Repent means to turn, change, believe, follow and obey. When this message is presented, the people will not understand, and immediately the deception that lies within their minds will disregard what has been said. These are people who have developed within themselves their own worldview that is outside or against God's. Their worldview, which has derived from Satan's grand deception, has built such a stronghold in them that when truth comes, their esteemed worldview seems greater than something so simple. It is not necessary for Satan himself to immediately snatch the seed, but it is the deception that is evident in their life that deceives them. These are people who have been brought up and nurtured in pride, lust, secret societies, false religions, distorted Christian views and denominations. These things have dictated their world view, making it hard for the Gospel to change their hearts because they have been indoctrinated by fables that will easily derail their prisoners from the truth. The seed, which is the word of God, lies outside their hearts, never to fall in. Satan has built a brilliant system of deception that programs people to willingly follow, lie and willingly ignore truth. Satan uses mind control and brainwashing to make sure that individuals stay under certain blankets of deception. Mind control is the scientific control over a person's thoughts. If he can control these areas, he will dictate a person's actions. He uses those who have sold their souls to him as puppets to keep others from believing the truth. Those who are bound under satanic mind control have produced, within their souls, personalities that gravitate and defend what has been indoctrinated in them. With this indoctrination, a person is blinded and only can see what their doctrine allows. Satan can keep the masses stagnant and dumb, forced to be dependent on his system. This is because the moment he crushes his system, all those lives will be permanently destroyed. His system is filled with scientifically engineered tools that never fix problems but worsen them. His system was designed to make the human heart immoral, lustful and prideful. It was designed to make sure that your heart will become hard and that you will heap for yourselves teachers that will continue to scratch your ears. Satan is no fool. A person that is indoctrinated is a person destined to go where their doctrine leads them. A lie never leads to the truth. This is why Jesus said that those that hear the gospel, but do not understand it, will never receive it. The strongholds of their beliefs will assure that the seed the word of God will find the exit door.

Satan knows that if a person does not fully understand what is being offered, he or she can be easily deceived. It is what you do not understand that will cost you. It is always the part of the contract that is not understood that ends up costing you. He also knows that a person that is deeply involved with the occult or just overly caught up with themselves will have questions that their inner circle cannot answer, which will lead them right to him. If you overly saturate the market with lies and barely teach the pastors or teachers the truth, what is there for those who have questions? Satan has infiltrated our seminaries and churches with the aim of watering down truth and diluting the gospel, which will dilute the power. If the message is only partially preached, there is no full power. If there is no power, there is no change. If Satan can overly saturate society with lies but make sure that no one is being taught fully in our seminaries, when the real gospel is preached, who will help explain it? Genius move by Satan. This will then lead countless people either back into the jaws of their former deception or into the jaws of a new deception. Are you that person? Are you deceived? Do you fully know what the gospel is? Examine yourself. Why are you a homosexual, an atheist, a Muslim or whatever else?

Seek the truth for yourself. Do not just automatically believe me. Because it is not what I say that will set you free; it is what He says. When you ask yourself tough questions, you will be forced to seek the answers. But if you never ask yourself why, you will remain the person deceived. The gospel, which has the power to save your eternal soul, will pass you by.

(The heart with Stones)

The Bible says in Matthew 13:20-21

20 But he who received the seed on stony places, this is he who hears the word and immediately receives it with joy; 21 yet he has no root in himself, but endures only for a while. For when tribulation or persecution arises because of the word, immediately he stumbles.

It says that he or she who receives the seed on stony places is a person who hears the Word and immediately receives it with joy. This person does not have any root or endurance in them but endures or is faithful for a while but when tribulation and persecution come, due to the Word of God that person falls away.

The altar call has been Satan's playground for years. He has instituted a tactic within today's Christianity that produces a partial gospel, which leads people to stumble. His tactic is to introduce the partial gospel through emotionalism by using music and a strong call from a minister. The minister will play on the strings of people's emotions to draw them down to make a decision on a gospel that does not save. They go down to the altar and receive the message with joy but never build a root system that will keep them anchored. Satan does not care about how often you evangelize. He cares more about the follow up of discipleship. Evangelism without discipleship is not true evangelism. Satan does not care about our events and our gatherings if no one is helping individuals build a root system that will keep them anchored. Evangelism without discipleship will have people caught up on the benefits of Christianity and not the requirements. With any job, you must first agree to fulfill the requirements before you begin. Satan does the opposite. He camouflages the truth with a lie and introduces it through unlearned ministers. This is a tactic which will draw people to the benefits of Christianity (prosperity and healing) and ignore the requirements of Christianity (repentance and obedience). When these people go to the front, they receive "the gospel" with joy. They are unaware that the minister has given them a false hope. This joy is not true joy but carnal happiness. This carnal happiness falls away when challenged. That is why Jesus said that when they face trials, tribulations or persecution, they will fall away. From the beginning, they were brought into a partial gospel that only explained the benefits and not the requirements. Satan goes to great lengths to make sure that people remain in this cycle of deception that keeps them from enduring. When a person does not take the time to understand the requirements that Jesus has mapped out, their soil remains shallow. They do not have any earth or soil, which will lead them to fall away. It is not the branches of a tree that displays strength but a trees roots. If the roots are not deep, the tree will easily fall when faced with great pressure. When we are introduced to God, we have to immediately dig deeper in Him. We have to dig deep to better understand who he is and who our enemies are. It is what you know that will keep you and what you do not know that will cost you. Satan wants us to remain ignorant about the conditions of our hearts, because the longer we remain ignorant, the longer his demons can design a storm that will blow us down. It is what you do not know about faith that will have you retreating in fear. It is what you do not know about your body that will leave you with cancer. This is why we are to focus more on what we need to know than what we desire to know. If I told you that what I had to offer you was full of benefits and promises but I did not tell you about the bad things that come with it, how would you feel? You would be confused right?

The Bible says that those that endure will be saved. Those that endure through trials, temptations and persecution will be saved, not those that fall in the middle of it and turn back. A person that hears the whole gospel knows that this life as a Christian will have trials, tribulations and persecution. They hear the requirements and the only benefit that matters to them is that they are saved from the wrath to come and have the opportunity to know their creator. Salvation never enters through emotions alone but through the balance of emotions and reasoning. When you operate your life through emotions, you will never have a solid outcome. Emotions only indicate a present mood, what you feel now. Salvation enters through reasoning and thinking. God gave us a brain so that we can understand what is being said. He gave it to us so we can ask questions and grow. A fool is a person who does anything without first taking the time to fully understand. Ask yourself,

"Am I really saved?"

Has your heart been yielded totally to God? I ask these questions because there will be trials and tribulations. Will you give up because you thought Christians do not get sick or are not poor? Would you still follow God if He never gave you a Bentley or one million dollars? Would you still follow Him if he never gave you your dream job or career? The moment you examine your heart, you will see where your heart truly lies. Nothing in this life stands true until it first comes up against testing. This is why on the road of Christianity there are a lot of tests. The testing tries the inner core of that Christian to make him or her stronger and to develop loyalty to God. If there are no test or trials, how will God know who is loyal? Are you willing to endure everything for Him, because He did endure everything for you!

Answer this question: Does your heart have any stones?

The Heart with Thorns

The Bible says in verse 22

22 Now he who received seed among the thorns is he who hears the word, and the cares of this world and the deceitfulness of riches choke the word, and he becomes unfruitful.

It says that he or she receives the seed among thorns (the cares of this world). This person hears the Word but the cares, concerns and deceitfulness of riches choke the Word, and it becomes unfruitful.

Many of us have been brought up within environments and situations that have caused us to develop a distorted worldview; a worldview that fixes our eyes on our present concerns and cares, as well as being driven to pursue happiness. Satan and his demons love to infiltrate our hearts through times of vulnerability. He knows that if no one is toiling the ground, naturally weeds will grow. Satan knows that a person who is ignorant of God does not have the Holy Spirit toiling their hearts. Satan can implement within a person's hearts a distorted view of life, and even if that person hears the gospel, the seed will get choked. Satan has built a system on the conveyer belt of patience. He is not concerned about time. He is concerned about the effectiveness of his overall plan, which is to keep the hearts and minds of people dark and ignorant. When a person hears the gospel, the first opposition that comes against the seed is the present state of the person's heart. The Bible says that the cares of this world and the deceitfulness of riches choke the Word and it becomes unfruitful. God intends that his seeds bear fruit. In order for that seed to bear fruit, the seed has to first be placed in a ground that is toiled by the Holy Spirit. Everyone that has heard the gospel has reacted to it, either with the willingness to obey or unwillingness to obey. If a person's heart is full of cares or the concerns of being rich, when they hear the gospel message that seed will be choked instantly. The person's core being is clouded with their concerns for their debt, family, job, career, mortgage, job loss, heath conditions, spouse, infidelity, bank account and business. These concerns (which more can be added) cause them not to focus or use their brains to reason the message of the gospel. They are overly concerned with the success of their business or the new way to gain more money, fame, prestige and honor which causes them not to have the time to use their brains to reason the message of the gospel. Satan has done a great job of instilling these cares and concerns in people's hearts before the person has the opportunity to fully understand the gospel message. That is why he has constructed society to advertise impulse, leading countless people into the jaws of deception. He knows that if he can develop a system that hardens hearts and plants weeds, people will lean toward temporal security and not an eternal one.

Satan's ultimate strategy is wrapped around these four things:

The World System
The Lust of the Flesh
The Lust of the Eye
The Pride of Life

Satan knows that every human being has sin in them and with that sin come's a sinful nature. Satan knows that if this nature exceeds a certain level or is dominant, then he will have an open door to grow those desires. How does he target this nature? He targets it through His world system. This system aims to do two things. One is to introduce an alternative to God. Two is to fuel and facilitate the desires of the flesh. The world system is fueled by deception and lies, causing it to prey on the naive and the ignorant. Through its lies, it targets the ignorant hearts of people and offers an alternative to the things of God. So instead of love, it offers lust. Instead of humility, it offers pride. Instead of contentment, it offers covetousness. He desires to offer you a distorted alternative of God's order. This world system then aims to facilitate the desires of the flesh, causing it to become addicted through its senses to his deception. The bridge between the flesh and the world is the eye. The eye represents the window of the soul. Whatever has the eye has the passions of the soul. He blankets society with multiple avenues of deception aimed for one thing and that is to capture the human eye, capturing it with an array of deceit. Whatever has our eye has our soul. Whatever has our soul has our efforts. Whatever has our efforts, guides our free will. The eye reveals the heart. Once the eye is captured the cares of this world and its deceitfulness flood the human heart, causing the individual to become prideful of this life. Pride is self-satisfaction.

Once we become overly satisfied with ourselves is the moment we become leaches to a decaying system. This pride is one that latches on to the temporal, so much that it alleviates the importance of eternity and the wrath to come. Satan knows that if he can blanket a person's environment with things that are tailored to their own lust, their eyes will latch on and become a bridge between their deprived soul and his world system. This will cause them to become focused or fixated on a temporal, limited life, stiff arming an eternal one. This formula builds within the human heart thorns that wrap around the human soul as a front line defense against the Gospel of Jesus Christ; if the Word is cast on this type of heart, their cares and their love for this temporal life will suffocate the potential of salvation within that individual.

We have to understand that within the human heart lies the essence of one's life. If that heart is dark, that person's life is dark. If a person's heart is full of light, then that person's life will be illuminated, not by self-proclamation but by evident fruit. This fruit can only come from the one seed, the seed of salvation. Satan has built a brilliant system that aims to make the human heart so concerned with this present life that they naturally ignore the eternal one. My question to you is, "Is your heart full of thorns? "

The Bible says in verse 23:

23 But he who received seed on the good ground is he who hears the word and understands it, who indeed bears fruit and produces: some a hundredfold, some sixty, some thirty."

The Bible says that the person who receives the seed (the seed of salvation) on good ground (a heart that has been toiled) is a person who hears the Word and understands it. They will indeed bear fruit and produce some one hundred fold, some sixty and some thirty.

Salvation does not come through emotions but through understanding. This is what separates the real from the fake. The real hear and fully understand what they have heard. With their full understanding, they are able to obey what they have heard. The fake hear but only partially understand. With partial understanding comes partial obedience. With partial obedience comes a void faith. In order for the human heart to be able to bear fruit, it has to be toiled. It has to be pressed and broken. In order for a person's heart not to be hard and filled with stones or thorns, it has to be forced through a canal that breaks off everything that is unfit for a God fearing heart. When the reality of death and the holiness of God have been introduced to a person, they have one of two options. They can become humble or they can remain prideful. Before a person can understand the forgiveness of God, they have to understand the present wrath of God. The reality of this leads to a broken and pliable heart, because the full explanation of the gospel leads them to understand reality not fluff. This is the beauty of a good heart. The good heart use to be a calloused one. It use to be a heart full of stones. It use to be a heart filled with thorns. No one has come to God with a perfect heart. It is only after the Holy Spirit works that a heart strives for perfection. We have to understand the art of God's pursuit. He uses what is in our negative environments to produce a positive outcome. He uses a broken home to produce a mended heart.

He uses lack to produce wholeness. He uses evil to produce good. Without lack, challenges, obstacles, poverty, broken homes, abuse and slander, how can the heart become humbled? Without a negative situation, there cannot be positive outcomes. God allowed evil to be so that good could be seen and revealed. Without evil, there cannot be any good. If there is no event or experience that causes brokenness in a person's life, there will be no salvation. Before there is a promise, there first has to be pain. Before there is exaltation, there first has to be humility, and humility comes with brokenness. The Holy Spirit introduces the gospel by breaking the soil of the heart, making it pliable and humble. He causes the heart to realize that nothing in this world is satisfying without God. He opens the eyes to see how dark the soul is, causing one to search for meaning and value. He leads people to search for the hope that their soul is searching for. It is only at this breaking point that a heart is able to receive the seed of salvation. Once a person hears and understands, then they obey. Only an ear that is open can hear, not one that is closed. The only way an ear is open to hear is if the heart has been broken. When a person's heart is hard towards something, their ears are not willing to listen. When a person's heart is desperate and broken, their ears are open to listen. This is why I do not waste my time trying to offer seed to a hard heart. If they show evidence that their heart is hardened towards the gospel, it is a wasted effort trying to offer them something their hearts are not willing to receive. A heart that has been broken by the Holy Spirit and has received the seed of salvation is on the road to bearing fruit, some one hundred fold, some sixty fold and some thirty fold. The amount of fruit produced is based on their individual potential and influence.

Our heart is the core of our being. If our hearts are defiled, our whole life is defiled. If our hearts are dark, our whole lives will be darkened. Satan endeavors, through his world system, to darken our hearts and have them defiled. He wants the treasures of our hearts to beat after the things of this world and neglect the things of God. He wants them to be hard, due to lack of understanding. He wants them filled with stones, due to a lack of endurance. He wants them to be filled with thorns, choking any and every opportunity of bearing righteous fruit. He wants them away from God, by any means necessary. If we fail to guard our hearts, we will surely pay the price in eternity. Like I always say, God is not going to judge us by the results of our actions but by the content of our hearts. What is in your heart? Is it guarded or are your guards down? Is your heart hardened because of ignorance? Is it filled with stones because you lack endurance? Is it filled with thorns, due to your cares for this temporal life?

***

Jesus paid the price for his righteousness to be our righteousness. When we rest in our own efforts we fall short of Gods plan. When Jesus was nailed to the cross our sins were placed on Him... and when he died and rose his righteousness was placed on us. Now we have, through Christ, access to the father and when the father looks at us he sees not our righteousness or our sins but the blood of Jesus. This protects our hearts from being too lofty or too low. We can no longer think of ourselves to lofty because we are only who we are by the grace of God and what Jesus did for us humbles us. We can no longer think of ourselves too low because through repentance and trust in Jesus we can approach the throne of grace with boldness and we can now walk in a confidence that only a God can give because we know who redeemed us. Don't trust in your own righteousness because the Bible says that it is as filthy rags. Put on the breastplate that Christ gives and rest your worries and your hearts desires on Him.

Chapter 10: Shoes for the Journey

Shoes

Shoes are a vital piece of any armor. Their ultimate use is to defend the feet against anything that will affect the journey towards battle or affect the level of focus during battle. When the Bible talks about the preparation of the Gospel of peace, it signifies a heart that is prepared to remain humbled under the gospel of Jesus Christ. This enables those who follow Christ to walk steady on this Christian journey.

Contrary to popular belief, the Christian journey is a difficult one. Satan has designed a system that aims to make this narrow road one that is extremely challenging. He wants to make this road full of delays, roadblocks, exits and potholes, with intent to cause weariness in the believer and tempting them into making a U-turn. Many people are unaware that the true Christian life is not just one that is solely full of blessings and promises but one full of potential persecution, trials, tribulations, testing and temptations.

Like I said before the partial gospel produces a mentality that embraces only the benefits of Christianity but ignores its requirements. Many of us have been brainwashed into adopting a distorted Christian worldview, a worldview that does not believe in suffering or pain but "only" in success and promises. This mental framework infuses the believer with procrastination, laziness and complacency. This produces zombies that walk around mountains and never straight to the promise land. Satan knows the difficulty of the narrow road. He knows the contrast that lies between the willing spirit and the weak flesh. He knows that the war inside is a constant one and only those that lean on God will endure, and the ones who lean on the world will fade away.

So what does Satan do? He introduces a partial gospel that only talks about a moment and never a process. He dilutes the gospel, because when anything is being diluted, it loses its potency. This makes what was once difficult to swallow now easy to swallow. This journey requires good, stable shoes that will not wear or lose traction. These spiritual shoes are the shoes that are shod with the preparation of peace.

Preparation is everything.

Success is only evident with those that are prepared. Life is surrounded by this simple formula:

Seed

Time

Harvest

Everything derives from a seed. Everything has a season or a time to develop, and everything has a result or harvest. Preparation is the mold that forms everything together. When something lacks preparation, it is destined to fail. In this life, if we choose not to prepare, we have chosen to fail miserably. L.I.F.E. is nothing to play with. You play with life; life will play with you. Under the umbrella of time lies potential. And that potential can only be tapped into if someone or something is prepared. Our accomplishments in between birth and death will depend on how prepared we are. Our accomplishments will show whether we adequately prepared for tests, exams, marriage and eternity. When everything is said and done, we will see if we were prepared. Preparation can only come from Understanding. You cannot hope to be prepared for something that you do not know anything about. This is what test reviews, marriage counseling and church services are for. They insure (hopefully) that you have understanding that will lead you to be prepared. The only problem is that how can you be prepared for the truth when you only understand lies? It is impossible to end up at the right destination with the wrong directions. It is also impossible to end up at the right destination with partial directions. This is what has been going on in our churches. False preachers are preaching lies to those who desire to seek truth, derailing them from God and making them comfortable and unprepared for what lies ahead. Satan knows what lies ahead. He knows the Bible. He knows how to dilute it and to distort it. He knows how to program us to shout and run around churches but leave the church and wallow back in our sins. This all derives from a partial gospel that allows people to walk a road with no shoes, causing them to get weary and leave the faith.

When a solider knows that tomorrow they will be marching towards battle, do you think they will forget their shoes? I doubt it. Many of us are walking this L.I.F.E. barefoot. We are walking in a state of fatigue, due to our lack of preparation. Lack of preparation will lead to a lack of endurance. Preparation requires patience. In order to be prepared, we have to be somewhat patient. Satan wants us to live a life of impulse. He wants us to be anxious about everything. When we live a life of impulsiveness and anxiousness, we open ourselves to forget and to overlook the important things in L.I.F.E.

Philippians 4:6 says:

Be careful for nothing; but in everything by prayer and supplication with thanksgiving let your Requests be made known unto God...

Philippians 4:7

And the peace of God, which passes all understanding, shall keep your hearts and minds through Christ Jesus.

Peace:

God is in control of everything. From the Alps to the slums, He is in control. He knows everything and has the final result of everyone's life already calculated. Once we understand that God is in control and that he knows what is best, then we can understand what His peace is all about. Peace is not based upon our understanding but by the wisdom of God. The Bible says for us to be careful or anxious for nothing but in everything by prayer and supplication with thanksgiving let your requests be made known unto God.

The Bible says not to be careful or anxious about anything. This present world system aims to make us all anxious and stressed, causing us to be bound. When a person is anxious, there trust is within the limits of their finite being. When a person is careful for nothing, their trust is within the limits of an infinite God. Satan has programmed us, through his world system, to be eager and driven to obtain a certain way of life. With such a drive, a person bypasses the necessary steps of maturity, causing them to burn out and fade away. This Christian journey is a long one and has critical stages that all believers must cross in order to obtain eternal life. It is a journey that cannot be done without full trust in God. When the Bible says to make Him lord and to allow Him to be the author and finisher of your faith, it refers to trusting Jesus to carry you through a life of intense pressure and fire so that you can shine as pure gold. Many people are scared of pain and the risks that come with this Christian life, because no one wants to be uncomfortable. We have failed to realize that comfort comes with trust.

The Gospel or the good news of Jesus Christ insures a peace that passes all understanding. The Bible says that the peace of God, which passes all understanding, shall keep your hearts and minds through Christ Jesus. When a believer trusts God, they understand that He sits in eternity and gazes through time. God sees and knows everything. With this thought, we have comfort knowing that nothing in our lives has caught God off guard but has been allowed for reasons that we cannot presently comprehend.

I remember times in my life when I would panic and get all stressed because I did not understand what was happening in my life. I allowed my emotions to alter my peace. Throughout my life I have gone through things that I thought no Christian should go through. But today March 22, 2010 I have realized that those things that I thought no one should go through are the exact things that have made me the man that I am today. God knows what is best, not for our temporal life but for our eternal one. He knows exactly what we need to go through to insure that He reaps a harvest from our lives. Everything that God created is calculated. He knows the number of the hairs on our heads. He knows how many birds are alive today. He knows what tree has fallen in the woods. He knows everything. Our confidence should be in Him. When you look at your life, nothing has happened by mistake. God knows what he is doing. He knows that your past mistakes or your present circumstances are needed to prepare you for his future plans. If I did not go through half of the things that I went through, I would not be adequately prepared to do what I am doing now. It is the pains of today that will prepare you for tomorrow's triumphs not your comforts. The salvation of God does not begin or end with us; it begins with God and ends with God. This is why the Bible says that he is the author and finisher of our faith. He is the one that writes it out and the one that finishes it, not us. Throughout this process, all we do is trust Him. We have lost our trust in God due to the disappointments we have experienced in life. We have paralleled the mistakes of fallen man to a holy God. Satan knows that God requires faith, and faith is trust. For a person to reach heavens gates, they have to have absolute faith and trust in Jesus. If you were Satan, what would you do? You would make a person's life a living hell so that they live in hell on earth, as well as throughout eternity. Satan knows that he has to develop a system that aims to keep a person's soul down, depressed and disappointed in order to limit their trust towards God. The Bible says that without faith, in other words trust, it is impossible to please God. The Gospel introduces with it an aura of peace to let the true believer know that God is with them, goes before them and makes their crooked places straight. He is not a God that lags behind or is surprised when something happens in your life. He is a God that knows what needs to be done to bring you closer to Him. When the Gospel is presented in the right way, it brings comfort with pain. It opens the doors to a life of pain but comfort. Pain that will make sure that repentance completes her work in you.

When we take the time to understand the message and the attributes of God, it will give us peace. Jesus on the cross broke the yokes of sin, death and the grave. He gave us liberty against the strongholds of sin and the fears of death and the grave. We understand that His victory is our victory and that we have power over sin and victory over death and the grave. With this in our minds, we will have peace. In order for us to embrace God's peace, which leads to absolute trust in Him, we have to fully understand the message. Our thoughts, memories, ideas, knowledge, emotions and perceptions have to line up with the things of God. Satan will use all of these things to alter you from obtaining God's peace. Satan and his demons will use your thoughts to take away your peace. They will plant thoughts of fear to cause you to forfeit the peace of God. They will use your past failures and mistakes to forfeit the peace of God that would lead you to a promising future. They will have your ideas so carnal that you leave the route of God to follow your ideas, false hopes and carnality. They will have you so caught up on occurred knowledge, thinking more highly than you ought to, that you jeopardize your life and lose sight of God's peace. Satan will have your emotions unbalanced and cause your life to be dictated by your emotions and not God's wisdom. This will cause you to lose peace. Satan and his demons know what they need to do to take your mind off of God. Remember Peter when he walked on the water? When he took his first step on the water, his mind was in a state of peace. He was not thinking any bad thoughts, recollecting on any bad memories, conjuring up any bad ideas, formulating any false perceptions of Jesus, experiencing any unbalanced emotions or analyzing within his occurred knowledge whether or not he should walk on the water. He walked on the water because His trust was not in his finite being but in an infinite God. What happened when he experienced the environment around him? He began to take his eyes off of Jesus and focus his attention on what may cause him to sink. When he did, he sank. Satan will bring storms in your life in hopes that you will take your eyes off of God in order for you to sink. When Peter took his eyes off of God, he took his eyes away from his source of peace and comfort in the midst of pain and the impossible. Fear is the opposite of faith, and faith brings peace. Fear aims to immediately grip the mind causing all of its components to go haywire. The moment Peter took his eyes off of his source of peace, fear griped every component of his mind and he began to sink. Our peace should not be determined by our own efforts but by the efforts of the almighty God. Satan and his demons steady await for the opportunity to have fear grip our hearts so that our marriages, families, businesses, careers and our character sinks. Fear is like cancer. It aims to take over the whole body so that we become stagnant and immobile, unfit for God's use. God loves to allow the winds to blow and the waves to form in our lives to test our trust in Him. Faith, trust, love and hope are not truly evident until they are tested. Though we fall, he will be there to pick us up and walk us back to comfort. This is why we have to learn to lean on God no matter how tough it may seem. There were times in my life where I thought I was going to die. There were times where I was so fearful that I became complacent and paranoid. There were times where I was contemplating quitting and committing suicide, all because I allowed fear to grip my heart. Many people have killed themselves because of what has not been taught in our homes and churches. Satan's partial gospel will be the sole reason countless people go to hell. No one is willing to be bold enough to thoroughly explain the message of Jesus Christ. Anything that is partially explained will result in a partial lackadaisical outcome. God's peace comes not at the end or in the middle but at the very beginning of a situation. For peace is the driving force that will motivate an individual to carry on and not give up. It is his peace that will enable us to endure this life, gripping hard to his everlasting hands. If this is not explained in our synagogues or churches, how will people endure?

When we take the time to understand the gospel of Jesus Christ, it will give us a peace within ourselves and a gentle mold that will bind together our whole being. Our soul, spirit and body will now work together in unity. Satan loves chaos. He believes the best time to capture and torment a person is after chaos. This will temporarily open the doors for him and the demonic to enter and unwind the bond between a person's soul, spirit and body. Once there is chaos on the inside, the cycle of chaos on the outside will continue. This is why we have to allow God to mend the broken cords that have been worn due to past failures and present concerns. This is why salvation is likening to the formula of seed, time and harvest. Salvation has a conceptual stage. It has a set time of development that leads to a harvest for God. Without a set time for salvation to grow, how will salvation develop in a person's life? We have to be willing to remain humble and allow God to calm the chaos in our hearts that causes our outside to be affected. God is the master surgeon who knows how to heal the deepest wounds of our lives. When we take the time to embrace his salvation work, it will bring us peace within. This causes us to fear nothing because we know what is being done and are not surprised by what is happening.

Peace with others.

Like the Bible says, we wrestle not against flesh and blood but against Satan and his demonic forces. When we fully understand this, we will not target our offences at the individual but at the spirit that is at work within them. Earlier in the book, I talked about Satan's bait, hook and cycle method. What he knows is that where there is unity, there is nothing that can stop its proposed efforts. Even God saw that at the tower of Babel. He knew that when there is unity and an understood common goal, there is nothing that will stop them. What Satan wants to do is to make us so emotional that we operate through our emotions and not reasoning. If he can build a society that operates their lives based upon how they feel and not common sense, then they can easily be triggered to explode and cause destruction, not only in their lives but also in the lives of others. So what does Satan do? He goes by this system of bait, hook and cycle. He baits us with an offence that will trigger our emotions and cause us to be hooked on that offence. This will lead to a cycle of un-forgiveness, hate and racism, all causing the human race to be at odds with each other and forfeit their rights to Satan. Satan's greatest motto is to rule out of chaos. He rules a marriage when there is chaos. He rules a family where there is chaos. He rules a country where there is chaos. Anywhere there is confusion and chaos, evil rules it. We cannot live a life easily offended. The number one reason why people are murdered is due to offences. Satan knows that if he can get people to wrestle amongst each other and remain ignorant, then no one will be focused on unifying against his work. Look at what he has done to the church. There is one message, one God and one Savior, but there are many denominations. Does this make sense? Should this be? No! Satan knows that in order to wreak havoc in this world, he must get the Christians caught up in debating and lose sight of disarming him from his satanic strategies. Nothing good comes from division. When we understand God's message of peace and reconciliation, we will not be easily offended. When we are tried, ridiculed or talked about, we should love and pray for the person as well as rebuke and bind the devil off of their life. You do have the right to be offended but not the right to act from that offence. Love has no respecter of persons. Jesus made it clear that we are to love our enemies and those who have offended us. We have to forgive. People have busted hell wide open because of un-forgiveness. This is because un-forgiveness is a fruit from the tree of hate, and the Bible says that if you hate anyone, you are bound for hell. He says "How can you say that you love me, who you cannot see, but hate your brother, who you see every day?" It is through love that goodness will be shown and draw men to God. The Bible says that it is His goodness that draws people to him not hate. Love has to be so evident in our lives that it breaks the callous molds on our offenders and gives the Holy Spirit an opportunity to gain access to their hearts. Salvation is conceived through understanding, reasoning and love. Unconditional care will get people thinking, and once they begin thinking, they will open the door to the Holy Spirit. If everyone is unforgiving and hateful, how then can people see the goodness of God?

***

The Christian life requires God's peace in order for it to produce good fruit. God's peace will have us prepared and willing to go through anything, no matter the cost. For we trust that He will carry us through, even unto death. Our shoes are important in this spiritual battle, because if we do not have them, we will grow weary and faint. We will lose strength in our knees and legs because of the pressure on our feet. Our shoes must be shod, giving us a hope of finishing this Christian journey. In this portion of the book, I am going to discuss some of the things that are on this Christian journey and something's that need to be inside of the Christian as they travel towards battle or are fighting in one.

Composure & Meekness

As Christians, we have to have a heart that is composed and an attitude that is meek. Our hearts have to be composed and balanced, not easily disturbed or moved. Composure means to have a self-controlled state of mind, a mind that is intact and mended. Every component of our mind has to be controlled under the mighty hand of God, through His Holy Spirit. If our mind is not controlled by the Holy Spirit, it will be loose and mangled, causing more harm than good. It has been said that people can control huge planes, ships and corporations but cannot control themselves. I would rather be broke, alone and poor and have self-control then to be rich and have none. True success derives from people who have self-control. God works best through people who have standards. People with standards have self-control because their standards control their actions and affiliates. Their high standards and inspired goals keep them composed and focused on the main goal. Nothing can pull them down because they are seated too high. In order for us to effectively finish this journey and win our battles inwardly and outwardly, we have to be composed and mended on the inside while displaying outward self-control. A person that is meek is a person that is humbly patient. Many people feel that a meek person is a weak person, but they are wrong. A meek person is a strong person because they understand the work of patience and the work of God. Our mentalities must be composed and meek from the beginning, because these things will insure that we effectively walk through this Christian life sensitive and humbled under God.

Temptation

The life of the believer will be full of temptations. Satan does not just let his sheep go away without a fight. He will do all that he can on this boulevard of Christianity to tempt us to be as dogs returning back to our vomits. Temptation will always be knocking on the doors of our lives, from salvations conceptions until its final work. We as believers have to understand that we still have sin in our veins. If sin is not dealt with, it will aim to connect to the baits of this world, drawing us back into certain cycles that aim to destroy our lives. Temptations are tailored to our experiences, sexual makeup, voids and vulnerabilities. Satan's demons are not in the business of wasting time. They are not going to tempt you with something that you have not experienced. They will tailor temptations to your sexual desires, voids or vulnerabilities. They aim to bring you down.

Experiences:

Satan and his demons are studious. They will study the believer to know exactly what to bring into the Christian's life that will destroy it. Whatever sins you committed in your past will be used to lure you backwards. Drugs, alcohol, sexual sins and promiscuity can all be used as lures. This is why society advertises sex and impulsiveness. These are the main things keeping people hooked in the cycle of sin.

Sexual make up:

Satan knows how we were made He knows what a man and woman desire. He knows that men desire to be successful, sexually pleased and respected. He knows that woman desire to be secure and stable. In order for him to gain entrance, he must make these things unbalanced or have your flesh exceed a safe level. For men, he will have our pride for success and our need for sexual pleasure exceed a safe level. This will have men fueled not by wisdom but by their sexual desires. For woman, he will do what he can to unbalance her emotions. This will cause her to be unstable and insecure. These things lead countless people on a journey of confusion. The Bible says that with confusion comes every evil work. When we are confused about who we are on the inside, it opens the door for the demonic to work in our lives. This will cause us to bite hard onto Satan's temptations.

Voids and vulnerabilities:

All of the negative results of our lives are due to childhood voids or ignored vulnerabilities. When a child does not have the proper upbringing, it can open a door for Satan to enter when they are young. He will use that void to destroy their life when they get older. When a person has voids, those voids are usually filled with anything but God. What a travesty! God is the only One that can fill the void of sin. He allowed such voids to be open in our lives for the sole reason of revealing himself as the only one to fill it. Anything that is missing a piece is not whole until the lost or missing piece is found. The beauty is that God's redemptive plan gave man free will, and when man sinned he created a way back to Him. This is the greatest love story of all Eternity. Vulnerabilities are those weak areas in our lives that lie wide open for Satan to use against us so that we fall into temptation. We all have vulnerabilities, some new, some old. They are usually the things that cause us to fall quickly because we are ignorant that we have them and are ignorant to the solution of our vulnerabilities. Such vulnerabilities are formed through ignorance and pride. When we are not willing to humble ourselves we are left vulnerable. What are your voids or vulnerable areas that are causing you to fall into temptation? Feel free to write them below and think about ways you can overcome those temptations. Also feel free to use the scriptures in the back to help.

_____

_____

_____

_____

_____

_____

_____

_____

The sure way to never fall into temptation is to never enter it. The person that never falls into temptation is the one who has discernment and is led by God's wisdom. Temptation is like a door. God said that with every temptation he has made a way of escape. The thing about the way of escape is that it does not move with you as you go deeper into temptation. When you walk into a door, it becomes your way of escape. The further you go into the room, does the door follow you? No it does not. Temptation is the same way. Your way of escape is right behind you when you enter into temptation. It is wise to exit as soon as possible. Temptation has layers and each layer aims to lure you deeper into the environment that makes it hard to escape. The deeper you go, the harder it is to escape. Many times before you can get to the door of escape, the addiction that came with the temptation has already latched onto you in the form of cancer, disease or AIDS. This is why I write so that we can see how deep this thing called life is. God's peace through the gospel will help you to recognize the deceitfulness behind Satan's crafty temptations. It is only through God and leaning on Him that we will be able to overcome temptation. If you really take the time to think, you will see that many of the things we fall for are not even worth it. We enter temptation through the impulsiveness of our heightened emotions. When those emotions die down, we regret that we even entered into temptation. The tragedy is not us entering but what we get on the way out. Many times our regret comes from what we are left with once the temptation is over. Some of us have walked out with cancer, disease, aids, pain and regrets. If you do not highlight anything in this book, make sure to highlight this, "The person that never falls into temptation is the one that never enters it!"

Testing and Trials Count it all Joy

The Bible says that when we go through trials and testing, we should count it all joy. For the trying of our life insures that we turn out pure and usable by God. No matter what it is, in this life you cannot go to the next level without a test. From Drivers-Ed to a desired job, we have to be qualified for what we endeavor to achieve or obtain. From where do you think the world adopted this standard? Do you really think God would allow anyone into heaven without some form of testing? The test results are not based upon the test giver but upon the one who takes the test. The person that takes the test determines, through their time of preparation, whether or not they pass or fail. We are not to be caught up in asking why we go through testing or question the journey towards battle or the length of the battle, but we are to be joyful because we understand that the great architect of this grand creation that spans throughout eternity has a plan through this intense fire. Everyone in life has to go through pain in order for there to be growth. This Christian life will have testing and trials which God allows so that we are tested to show whether we are wheat or a tare, goat or sheep, believer or non-believer. The Bible says in 1 John 2:19:

They went out from us, but they were not of us; for if they had been of us, they would *no doubt* have continued with us: but *they went out,* that they might be made manifest that they were not all of us.

This Scripture clearly shows the results of those that profess to be saved but are not. The Bible says that they (those that are not really saved) went out from us (went with us) but they were not of us (they were not true believers), for if they had been of us (true believers), they would no doubt have continued (endured) with us. They went out (gave up or did not endure) that they might be made manifest that they were not all (everyone that say they are saved) of us. This verse shows the result of those who follow the partial gospel. The main virtue that comes with true Christianity is the willingness to endure. The true test shows endurance, and for those that do not endure, it will be clearly shown when they fall away back to the clubs and back to their old lifestyle.

Those who were not truly saved had a burst of energy to follow but not the heart to finish.

Testing, trials and temptations were instituted on this road to make a clear distinction between those that believe and those that do not. Are you willing to endure?

Exits- Detours – Delays – road blocks- Pot holes- and other drivers

Christianity was never advertised throughout the scriptures as something easy. The moment you sign the dotted line, believe that Satan has planned to make your life a living hell. He will attack your family, finances and anything that would hinder you from a future of destiny. Satan will do all he can to see to it that you have the opportunities to quit. This Christian life is full of exits, detours, delays, pot holes and crazy drivers. As long as we have our GPS (God's positioning System –book coming soon), we will reach our destiny. Satan loves giving us the opportunities to reconsider our decision to follow wholeheartedly after God. His demons will tell you anything that will make sense to make you forfeit everything and gain nothing in the end. He will make this journey difficult and strenuous to the point of sifting us as wheat.

He will tempt you to take exits that will cause you to waste time in growing and drift you away from the main road. He will want you to be so caught up on why you have to take a detour that you overlook why God intended for you to take those roads. Many of us complain on this Christian journey when it seems like we keep hitting road blocks, when it seems like we are not progressing as fast as we would like. It is vital that we have detours because. What if there was not a detour sign? A detour sign helps you to avoid something that could cost you your life. What if God did not warn us before we made many of our turns? Many of us would have been dead years ago, and many that died ignored the detour signs and kept driving without any caution. Delays and road blocks are beneficial in our Christian lives. Satan wants us impatient and impulsive, to the point that we consider taking over the wheel of our own lives. We may be delayed but we are not denied. God's delays are the best because, by him being the father, he watches out for his own so that we safely arrive at our final destination. Pot holes are those things that aim to hinder our travel and slow us down. These are little opportunities to fall back into old sins. The more potholes that he can put down, the greater the chance that you will get a flat tire. He also wants us focused on other drivers, accomplishments of other Christians. He wants us to compare ourselves. God says that those that compare themselves are not wise, mainly because you are telling God that he made a mistake with you. When we compare ourselves, it distracts us from focusing on the main goal and staying in our own lane. When we take our eyes off of the road, it can result in an accident. We all have a lane that we are to drive in. It is within that lane that we become the most successful in bringing more into the kingdom of God. This journey will have all of these hardships on them. It is the peace of God that comes from the gospel of Jesus that will help us ignore exits, understand why we have delays, detours and road blocks and help us to avoid potholes and comparing ourselves to others. If we successfully allow his peace to guide us, we will make it to our destiny.

Presentation: Understanding Evangelism

On this Christian journey comes the responsibility of sharing the gospel of Jesus Christ, which will bring hope and peace to those with open hearts. Just like salvation has to be understood before receiving, the same is true for bringing the salvation message, evangelism. Whether you know it or not, if you are a believer, you are constantly evangelizing. The greatest form of evangelism is not verbal it is through your lifestyle. People watch more than they listen. People collect more data through their eyes then with their ears. There is an old saying that says that actions speak louder than words. They do. With this in mind, we have to fully understand the importance of living a life that parallels with the gospel message we say we are sharing. A life that is contrary to the message it proclaims dilutes the effectiveness of the gospel. The vessel is now tainted and gives a false representation of Jesus Christ. This happens every day. People's hearts grow hard due to those who evangelize with an unchanged heart. Satan knows that if he gets the masses deceived into thinking they are saved, they will continue a cycle of unbelievers. People will ask, why follow Jesus if His followers are not? For those with that question, let me answer you. There is a difference between those that are real and those that are counterfeit. Satan knows exactly what to do to make you excuse why you are not humbled under the message of Jesus Christ. There is a huge difference between those that follow God and those that say they follow Him. Those that follow Him are not perfect but are striving and want to be made clean. Those that are not following him are not willing to be made clean unto perfection. Our lives have to speak louder for God than our own words. Our lives have to match the message we proclaim in order to help aid those that are looking for hope. If they see that you are enduring, it gives them hope to endure. If they keep seeing you, a Christian, constantly stumbling, it will advertise a false gospel. This false gospel of inclusion says that everyone is welcome. If this is true, then why did Jesus have to die if humanity had no requirements of changing? The gospel of peace will prepare us to humbly present the gospel in word and deed.

Evangelism without Discipleship is not True Evangelism

Evangelism without discipleship is not true evangelism; it is just mere conversation. Effective evangelism is one that has with it discipleship, a way to encourage the new believer in their journey with God. No army goes out, recruits and immediately throws the new inductees onto the battle fields! No! There is a thing called boot camp that prepares them for the battle ahead. Modern day evangelist do not disciple. They get new inductees but throw them right back into the jaws of Satan. Men and woman that are in the ministry can become prideful, and with this pride comes the desire of numbers instead of conversions. They want to herald more of how many have been saved under their ministry instead of the full gospel of Jesus Christ. They love to see the herds of people flock to them but leave with their hearts still not change. Satan knows that if he can get a young minister caught up on numbers, they will practice presenting the partial gospel in order to infuse their pride. What I am about to write; please take the time to understand. No one knows who is truly saved. A convert is revealed during discipleship. All these pastors and evangelist that say they got hundreds or thousands of people saved are just prideful, wanting you to look to them as the source of salvation not God. Next time you hear a preacher say some non-sense like that, ask them for the proof. Ask them for the form of discipleship that they are using to prove that what they are saying is true. A prayer alone at an evangelistic meeting does not prove salvation but the process under the umbrella of discipleship does.

In 2008, I was under the same mentality that many are under today. This mentality was that salvation begins and ends with a prayer. I had a rude awakening at my first AMPED concert in Tulsa OK. We had a benefit concert for a group of inner city kids in Tulsa to help raise money and support for the ministry there. We had a great event. We had live bands, flashing lights and loud speakers; you name it. But what we did not have was any discipleship resources.

Yes that night we had a great event. The message was preached. People came to the alter, but I did not have one disciple. Sometime after that evening, I began to think. Was that event really affective? Are those kids that were at my event on May 1st 2008, still on fire for God today, March 23, 2010? I hope but I doubt it. Across America and around the world we are advertising a product without any follow up or discipleship to see whether or not these people are enduring. If we are all about events and the sea of people that stand at our weak evangelistic concerts and conferences but do not have any discipleship, can we say we really care about their eternal souls? Do we just care about the pride that is rotting our own souls? I will never, ever do another event without MULTIPLE forms of discipleship. When you really care about the work of God, you will make sure that those that God has graced to be under your ministry, in your family or in your neighborhood really want to follow God. You will have what they need to build their faith and to understand the full Gospel of our Lord Jesus Christ. This is why I write books and do videos. I want to die empty and leave countless resources that will help disciple people years after I am gone.

A general will never train a soldier to fail. He will train them with fervent intensity so that when in battle, they will survive and be able to come home alive.

***

Evangelism and discipleship is like a theme park. Within a theme park there are tour guides, tourist attractions, tourist and tours. The tour guide represents an evangelist (which we all are).

The tourist attraction represents God. The tourist represents one who is interested in God. The tour guide represents the evangelist. The tour represents the form of discipleship. All 4 have to work together in order to gain an eternal result. The tour guide or the evangelist has to be one that thoroughly knows the tourist attraction in order to accurately give the tour. What is the purpose of bringing a tourist to a tourist attraction and not give the tour. That is pointless. This is what many of us are doing today. We are bringing people to God but not helping them understand who He is and what He requires. This leaves people still ignorant or babes. A babe does not grow into maturity without assistance.

The tourist attraction or the act of evangelism is pointless without any explanation of what it is. God requires that we are patient enough to explain exactly who God is. Satan loves for tour guides to bring plenty of people to God but leave them there with no assistance. Tourists are people that are being drawn by the Holy Spirit to events, church meetings and conferences. This is so that their natural ears can hear what their spiritual hearts have already heard so that their souls can receive the mighty Word of God. The Bible says in Romans 10:13-17

13 For "everyone who calls on the name of the Lord will be saved." 14 How then will they call on him in whom they have not believed? And how are they to believe in him of whom they have never heard? And how are they to hear without someone preaching? 15 And how are they to preach unless they are sent? As it is written, "How beautiful are the feet of those who preach the good news!" 16 But they have not all obeyed the gospel. For Isaiah says, "Lord, who has believed what he has heard from us?" 17 So faith comes from hearing, and hearing through the word of Christ.

Verse 13 shares the results of the following verses. He says that whoever calls on the name of the Lord shall be saved, but before they can call Him lord and enter into salvation, the acts of the following verses have to be complete. The Bible says in verse 14, "How then shall they call on him who they have not believed," meaning how can they call upon Jesus for salvation if they do not believe or know who He is? This shows that understanding precedes salvation. Before you can say you believe anything, you have to fully understand it. It continues to say, "How can they believe in Him who they have not heard," meaning how can they believe if they say what is in verse 13. if they have not heard who he is and have not understood what he has done, they cannot understand the message He has proclaimed. Paul continues to say that how can they hear without a preacher or tour guide.

Verse 15 says, "How can they preach unless they are sent?"

"Many people go but few are sent."

There are a lot of people who go but have not been sent. They cast dysfunctional seeds onto callous hearts that end up bearing no fruit. It is important to be sent and to be humble enough to go exactly when and where God desires. He knows the state of the hearts of those that will listen. He knows the right time for the message to be sown into their hearts. Many of us have been preaching to the wrong crowds, wasting precious time. God equals efficiency. He will not waste seed; he will not waste time or energy on any one that he knows will never receive him. If God is not a God that wastes time on sinners who are unwilling to change, then why should we? We have to be sent. We have to be humbled under the leading of the Holy Spirit to use wisdom not zeal. It is ok to be zealous about the things of God, but it must be governed by the Wisdom of God. If it is not, it will cause more damage than good and harden hearts instead of soften them. This is evident at family reunions, colleges, and a lot of door to door witnessing. People with zeal pound the message of Jesus to a heart that has not been toiled by God, trying to force feed the gospel to a person that is not presently willing to eat of it. **This is not evangelism**.

Evangelism starts and ends with Him not us. We are just the vessels that are used by Him at the right place and at the right time. God will never send you out without the equipment necessary for discipleship. Jesus told his disciples when he met them, "Follow me and I will make you **fishers of men**." He did not just say, "Hey, look at me. I am Jesus. You need to be saved." No. He said to follow Him and He will show you how to become fishers of men. Those disciples immediately cast down their nets and followed Him not because of zeal on Jesus part but his timing. Verse 15 says, "How beautiful are the feet of those that preach the gospel of peace and bring good tidings or the Gospel." This Christian journey is a beautiful one. It is a journey filled with tests and trials, but with those testing and trials come the endurance to walk towards the battle and remain steady. Verse 17 says that faith comes by hearing and hearing by the Word of God. In order for verse 13 to be done, the formula in verse 17 has to be done. The formula is hearing (understanding) by or through the Word of God preached by his messengers. It is not us that convict the hearts of men but the Word of God. Imagine where our world would be today if all those that profess to be saved walked with endurance, willingness and boldness to proclaim the whole Gospel? Those that preach any other gospel than the full one are insecure and have a serious price to pay when they step into eternity. This journey of peace is not one for us to hold on to but one to share. The peace comes through the proper presentation of the gospel of Jesus Christ. If you have been brought under a partial gospel, you will not survive this Christian journey.

If you have not taken the time to examine your heart to see what its present condition is, then you are under a partial gospel. If you have taken the time to write down your sins and to repent of them with evidence of turning from them, you are under a partial gospel. Before you can understand the forgiveness of God, you have to understand his wrath which remains on those that do not obey him. Just because your earthly life may seem good does not mean your eternal one will be. Be aware of the deceptive ways of Satan, and take the time, while you have it, to think about your life. I would rather think about it now and make some changes now then to be in hell, wishing I had time to make those changes.

Take the time to think about your life. Use the space below to write from your heart and tell God what you need to help you endure this Christian walk. If you have concerns about whether or not you are saved, take time to allow the Holy Spirit to minister to your heart. He is the greatest evangelist and will lead you to God.

_____
_____
_____
_____
_____
_____
_____
_____
_____
_____
_____
_____
_____
_____
_____
_____
_____
_____
_____
_____
_____
_____
_____
_____
_____
_____
_____
_____
_____
_____

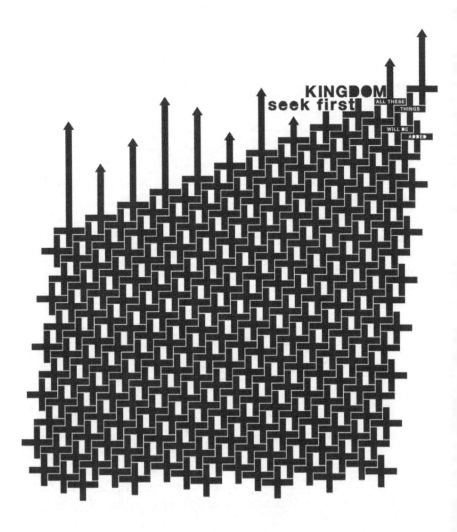

Chapter 11: Faith vs. Fear

A shield is important in battle. Without it, we are vulnerable to weaponry. A breastplate may be able to guard against some things but not all. What a shield becomes is an extension of the shield that is on the body. Faith is the same; it is an extension of our lives. It is an extension of what is going on the inside, our trust in God. What Satan wants to do is dilute your faith so that he can send darts your way to pierce through the armor that is guarding your heart. He aims to have you unbalanced. He knows that faith is a shield that will keep everything within safe. The greatest thing that brings down our shield is fear within our hearts. This can include our phobias, concerns and scars. Satan loves to target those un-dealt with fears and use them to bring down our faith and trust in God. This leads to no endurance in completing the war within and the war against Satan. Fear aims to suffocate the power of faith. Faith is a strong force, because the Bible says that faith is the substance of things hoped for and the evidence of things not seen. It is the tangible unseen substance of the hope to become one with God and the evidence (assurance) we have within our hearts that Jesus will be the author and finisher of our faith.

The unique thing about faith and fear is that they both have humble beginnings. They both are instituted during a state of vulnerability or openness. God uses things to humble us so that we can receive faith and truth. Satan aims to use things to make us vulnerable and to be controlled by fear. The Bible says that fear has torment, and its ways of torment aim to keep us from ever walking in faith. You cannot hope to walk in faith while standing in fear. Fear paralyzes and faith mobilizes. The sin is not experiencing fear but acting from it. When we act from fear, we show God that we do not trust or have faith in Him to bring us through. We choose to either be complacent or lazy, resulting in being no good to God. We love to make excuses when it comes to doing what we know we need to do. We fear growth. We fear change or anything that is not normal to what we have decided to formulate in our little worlds. Satan knows that fear paralyzes. He knows that if his demonic system can gain access to the mind, through thoughts, emotions or memories, he can gain control of a person's will and move them from ever walking in faith. This is happening daily. People are afraid to move with God. They are afraid to answer the call due to the demonic excuses and thoughts that formulate in their minds. The best way to have a person not walk in faith is to show them the risk involved. Following God requires risk. Faith equals risk. God will always lead you to the impossible, because it is only through Him making the impossible possible that He gets the glory. Satan's system is comfortable.

Fear loves comfort.

If anything shakes our nest, we retreat. We love to be comfortable and to never take divine risk (keyword divine) that come from God. Whenever God says go, we should go, trusting Him with the directions and the details. Faith requires trusting in God. This is why the Bible says that without faith it is impossible to please God. When we lack faith, we lack trust. Satan will do all that he can to bombard your mind with reasons why you should not have faith. He knows the impact of anything that comes through faith.

Fear is a natural emotion. It is an emotion that God allows for us to experience in order to see if we trust him. God will always put something in our lives that contrasts with any of his attributes in order to test us. If he did not do this, there would be no true evidence of whether or not a person trusts him. What we have to understand is that none of the gifts of God or the attributes of God are evident until they are tested. Love is not proven till it is tested. Faith is not proven until it is tested. Hope in God is not evident until it is tested. Fear was allowed to be made because it proves if a person really has faith. Faith is not proven in comfort but in chaos, when all hell is breaking loose. Anyone can have faith when every bill is paid or when everything is good. But can you have faith when you have no way of paying your bills? This is why the children of Israel had to go through the wilderness. It was through the wilderness that God could see who believed and who did not. Only few, instead of all, made it into the promise land. Pain comes with faith. Frustration comes with faith. Questions come with faith. Does the Bible say that we are the author and finishers of our faith, or does it say Jesus is? When we move from the driver seat to sit shotgun, then we will understand that it is within Him we live, move and have our being. It is in Him that we should trust, not in ourselves or in this falling world system. When famine comes to America and the world, we will see who you have faith in. Faith purges. Faith is a journey that purges us to prove us worthy of God. This is why Satan loves to impose fear. Fear will torment us and corner us so that we forfeit from this Christian journey. Fear wants us to latch onto its system that will program us to trust it and not God.

The Bible says that perfect love casts out all fear. God is perfect and He is love. It is only through Him that fear can be cast out. We have to humble our minds under Him and allow Him to cast out all fear. When we lean on Him and trust in Him, He will become our personal physician. He can remove all of the fears caused by the events and experiences of yesterday. He can remove all of the anxieties that we face today and remove all fear of tomorrow.

The Bible says in 1 Corinthians 13:13:

So now faith, hope and love abide, these three, but the greatest of these is love.

The Christian life is surrounded by three things:

- Love
- Faith
- Hope

Each of these are woven together but held by the greater cord of love. Throughout this Christian life, each of these are evident and must be united, in order for us to reach Heaven. I will use the seedtime and Harvest formula to show how this works. The conceptual stage of this Christian life is about understanding the Gospel of Jesus Christ. It causes us to examine our hearts and become humble to receive Him as Lord and Savior. Once this takes place, the peace of God covers the individual. They are lead down a path that is filled with faith, hope and love, propelling us to remain fixed and focused on the common goal of reuniting with God. Love is the conceptual stage. Love has to replace lust. Once love is in position, the individuals' heart begins to go through renovations and causes the heart to love instead of being bound by lust. All of us have lust and it must be removed and replaced with love. Love is the first and the greatest. Just like pride is the mother to all sin, love is the mother to all godly character. Instead of hating ourselves, we now love ourselves. Instead of hating, coveting and being defiled by un-forgiveness, we now love others with an unconditional love. Instead of hating God through our deprived hearts, we begin to love and reposition Him from being number 2, 5 or 7 on our top 10 list to being number one. It is only through love that all things begin.

Faith is the developmental or time stage where love grows and is nurtured unto ripeness. Faith begins to formulate and to increase. It can only increase if it is being fed from the proper source, which is through God and His Word. Satan's system aims to take you and me from God and His Word at any cost. If your faith is not being fed, your love diminishes and begins to become contaminated by lust and selfishness. Every stage requires focus and consistency. If there is no focus, there will be no consistency or growth. Satan wants us so caught up on being moved by fear that we begin to build for ourselves safety nets and question everything that God wants us to do. Look at all the great people of the Bible. They all had to move in faith. Look at their results. A truly successful life starts with love and is nurtured by faith which grows into a harvest where our hope is fulfilled.

The Bible says that hope deferred makes the heart sick meaning that when our hopes are stretched and never answered it makes the heart sick and weary. Death is a process and it begins with the condition of the spiritual heart. If the spiritual heart is always disappointed or always up and down then it affects the natural one beginning the push of an early death. Satan loves for us to gravitate to false hopes, gravitating to his pawns, his governments, his system because these things will lead to ditches. Our hope should be in God and in God alone because he is the only one that is consistent everything else will disappoint you even those closest to you. When love is conceived in the heart it is nurtured by faith which leads to our hope in God being fulfilled.

Our shield of faith is the extension of our faith in our hearts. It aims to make sure that everything in our heart is mended and balanced, blocking out the negative. Without our shield, we are vulnerable to Satanic and demonic darts that are thrown at us constantly through his system. This could be through our environment or the multiple streams of media. We have to continuously sharpen our lives with the Word of God. We need to train hard with our General the Holy Spirit so that our arms will never grow weary in holding up our shields. Just imagine all the people who have left their shields at home. Image all the people that may have some of their armor but do not have their extension of their faith on the inside. If you have no shield of faith, Satan will try to dilute the faith that is working in you.

And remember that our faith is not geared to obtaining a way of life but driven with the hope of being reunited with our Lord!

***

I love the scripture that says; and without faith it is impossible to please God, for whoever would draw near to God must believe that he exists and that he rewards those who diligently seek him.

God says that it is impossible to please him if you don't have faith or trust in him. Before we endeavor to draw near to God and to be pleasing to him we must first know he exist and that he rewards those who diligently seek Him.

Now I'm sure (unless you are an atheist) believe that God exist but do you believe he exist for your specific situation? Do you believe he will reward you in his due timing? Satan loves to drift us from God due to a lack of Faith. His demons love to prey on us when they know we HAVE to walk in faith. They want us comfortable they want us not exceeding in faith because they know that God works BEST in the arena of faith.

God wants to do great things in and through you but you have to trust him. He wants you to know He exist for every situation you face and that he can turn any bad situation around for your good. He wants you to believe that if you are willing to give him your whole heart and diligently seek him he will reward you not just of himself but with the desires of your heart.

But if your faith is not being developed and your shield is down all the darts (thoughts) that those demons that are assigned to you have to challenge you will take root in your mind, grow and manifest in your natural life.

Do what it takes to constantly develop your faith and the only way to develop it is through the word of God.

Chapter 12: The Greatest Weapon

Each and every one of us is at war with ourselves and with darkness. Each and every one of us can look within our lives and see the affects that this war is having on our lives. Countless people are suffering due to ignorance and are being constantly tormented in their minds. Satan has constructed a system with the main objective of limiting the masses of their access to the truth. He knows that if you know how to fight this war, he will be defenseless. Many of us are losing the war. Many of us are walking like sheep to the slaughter house, with no idea that we are being led to our deaths. God is about purpose and is about His original plan. His plan is to redeem man back to Him. He desires that we cast aside all sin and distractions in order to focus on the sole purpose of our life, which is to give Him glory. With that purpose comes the boldness and the courage to remain focused as we fight in this war called Life. Life is serious. If we take it seriously, it will take us seriously. If we take advantage of it, it will take advantage of us. Satan wants to disarm us. Satan, through ignorance and confusion, wants to keep us distracted and defenseless. He wants to leave countless doors open in our lives for the demonic to have access. He wants for us to drift away from God and His Word. The Bible is a unique piece of literature. Its uniqueness comes from its ability to accurately define the condition of the human heart. Within its pages, it accurately reveals the plans of darkness and the solutions of life. Within its covers lies the blueprint to success, which is through Jesus Christ.

Satan knows the power that lies within the pages of the Bible. He knows the divine inspiration that flows from Genesis to Revelations. He knows that anyone who is serious about God and his Word will know the blueprint of living a successful and victorious life. The Bible is called the Sword of the Spirit. It is our weapon. It is our solution to the answers of life. It is the weapon to use to renew the mind, clean the heart, prepare our feet for the Christian journey and maintain our faith. It is through the Word of God that we defeat the plans and plots of Satan. It is called the Sword of the Spirit because its inspiration came from the Spirit of God, and its content is void if the Spirit is not inspiring it. The Word works, and it only works when it is inspired by the Holy Spirit. What do I mean by this? God only answers the prayers and endorse the work of those who speak his Word from a heart that has been inspired by His Holy Spirit. His Word will only work in the lives of those who have humbled themselves under the Gospel of Jesus Christ and whose hearts have been changed. That change is evident in their lives. Many people are using the Word of God, but that Word has no power because the vessel that is speaking that Word is empty in his or her soul. The Word brings conviction which then leads to change. No conviction; no change. Both conviction and change must have power backing them because only the Word of God that is divinely inspired can spark change. Satan knows that if he can defile the human heart and confuse the human mind, even if they try to use the Word of God, it will come back void. For the motive and intention of the hearts towards the use of God's Word were not pure. God will never answer back his Word if the person that is using it uses it in a manner to reap for themselves selfishly.

A soldier that does not know how to use his weapon is a useless soldier. What is the use of having a gun or a sword if you do not know how to use it? Satan does not care how you hold your Bible or how you read it. If it is not inspired by the Holy Spirit, It will not work. You will be like a soldier holding a gun or a sword but not knowing how to use it. Many of us have been deceived. Many of us have been strategically manipulated to drift away from God and His Word. If we are going to win this battle, we have to know how to use our weapons. Before a soldier goes into battle, he spends countless hours training on how to use his weapon. He spends days and months constantly sharpening his skills. Because he knows that his training will fare well in battle. Every day we have to sharpen our lives with the Word of God. Every day we have to train ourselves to use our weapon, because when a battle comes in our lives, we will know how to respond. Repetition is the greatest form of teaching. The more you repeat something, the more you will remember it; it will become a part of your life. The tragic thing about this is that many of us have been repeating things that will not help us in life. We repeat more sexual acts, addictive hobbies and selfishness than we do the things of God. Do we really expect to win this war called life if we do not know how to use our weapon? Satan knows that if he can get humanity addicted to his system, they will drift away from God, leaving them defenseless against the whiles of the enemy. Look around you. Look at your family. Look at your friends. Look at society. Look at your own life. Can you not see what is going on? Can you not see this machine at work? Satan has no power over us unless we give him power.

Satan's agenda is simple when it comes to drifting the masses away from God's Word. It is found in this simple formula:

Bait

Hook

Cycle

The bait is the temptations to be overly consumed with the affairs of life. He wants us to believe the lie that we have no use for God and His Word. Satan's first tactic when approaching us is to infuse us with pride, to elevate our sense of self-reliance. He knows that pride opens the heart to multiple sins that will defile it. He baits us to be self-reliant, independent, and B.U.S.Y (Being under Satan's Yoke). Think about your life. What are some things that are presently drifting you away from God and His Word? Is it your job, hobbies or friends? What is in your life that keeps you away from His Word? Satan knows how to distort our natural cravings and desires for the things of the world over the things of God. He knows exactly what to bring into your life that will have the best chances of drifting you from God. He will put the right type of men and women in your life. He will put the right job and opportunities in your life. He will put the right hobby or substance in your life. He knows what to bring within your environment that will bait the voids and the sins in your heart. He knows that the only thing he has to do is to present something before the eye to grab its attention. He will begin to paint within the mind a picture that will draw you into making a choice which will lead you to become addicted or captive. This will then lead you to be conformed into the way he wants you. He knows that a heart that is not being worked on by the Holy Spirit or guarded by the Word will fall. God orchestrated the work of the Bible to reveal to us the condition and the solution of our deprived hearts. He foreknew that his products would need a manual to ensure that they remained focused and renewed. Without a manual the product would be worthless. This is why Satan will do anything to lure you away from reading the Bible. How often do you read your Bible? Compare the time you spend on your social networking sites, at the club or with friends to the Bible? What excites your heart? What sparks it? Is it the world or the Word of God? When you answer this question, you will know which one is the generator of your heart.

Once he baits us, he aims to hook us with self-deception. He wants us to deceive ourselves into living life for earthly gain. His master deception will lead us to self-deception. He baits us to be self-reliant and then hooks us into a stream that makes us reliant on great jobs, great opportunities, and satisfying addictions. He wants to lure us into being motivated by self and not God, causing us to be defenseless. When salvation is presented, it is first presented by the conviction that comes from the Word of God inspired by the Holy Spirit. When it is accurately presented, it sparks light within a dark soul. As the light begins to spread, it reveals the sins that lay dark behind the different components of the mind. It aims to renew the mind. All of this is sparked by the Word of God. The Word is like a single match that lands on something dry. It will catch fire, and what was so small will fuel a blaze that cannot be put out. The world system aims to make sure that this does not happen. It aims to fuel people's hearts to pursue temporal happiness and forfeit the journey towards eternal security. Satan wants us to deceive ourselves into thinking that we do not need God.

This will lead us to never have a heart that will catch fire from the convicting Word of God. This self-deception has had countless people leave their Bible on the shelves as they build their careers and their selfish lives, not knowing that they are leaving themselves open to the things of the demonic. Satan knows that if he can bait and hook them to be self-reliant, he will then bring something tragic into their lives like cancer or a death in the family. Those people will not know how to respond and will be left in a cycle of confusion and depression. The main thing with Satan is setting us up to fall. He will bring things into our life with the intent of using them to destroy us. He will bring men and woman into our lives to give us STD's. He will bring friends and hobbies into our lives to make us addicted to substances or become distracted. He will bring great jobs and careers and take them away, leaving us depressed and suicidal. He loves pulling the rug out from under us, because once the rug is pulled, there will be nothing there to hinder us from hitting the ground.

The Word of God is our only weapon against the devil and his demons.

The Bible says in 2 Corinthians 10:4

(For the weapons of our warfare *are* not carnal, but mighty through God to the pulling down of strong holds).

The Bible says that our weapons of this present warfare are not carnal (fleshy) but mighty through God to the pulling down of strongholds. The Bible says that it is only through God that our weapons will work and will have the power to pull down strongholds. We have to understand that anything away from God and His Word will not last but will remain to rot. The Word of God is a representation of Him and who He is. His attributes are interwoven throughout its 66 books. Its how we ought to live. It is the only tool we have that will pull down the strongholds in our lives. A stronghold by definition is a well-fortified place, a place that serves as the center of a group. Many of us have sinful strongholds, things that have fortified themselves in our lives. They house within them demonic influences that aim to not be torn down. Many of us have sexual, lying and manipulative strongholds. These strongholds have been fortified by demons to destroy your life. We have to understand that Jesus came to set the captives free. He came to tear down those strongholds, but he needs a willing heart that is willing to allow the Word of God to fight the demons and this world's system. We cannot hope to win the battle that is against us if we have not won the battle that is within us.

Salvation begins with the conviction of the Word of God that is carried by the power of the Holy Spirit. When it enters the heart, it conceives with the intent to birth eternal life. The Word of God is like a seed. Once it is planted, it has to be nurtured and taken care of. If not, it will not bear any fruit. The word of God serves as the fertilizer to make sure that faith, love, hope, peace, longsuffering, meekness, and self-control will grow. It will be clearly seen that God is at work in a person's heart. The only and predominate thing that should be in our hearts is the Word of God so that when we are attacked in our health, finances and families, we will be more than conquerors every time. Starting today, take time every day to sharpen your mind with the Word of God. Take time to learn how to use your greatest weapon. This spiritual battle cannot be won with natural resources; it can only be won by spiritual ones, the ones that are inspired by the Holy Spirit.

The devil knows the power that is packaged within the Word of God. He knows the effects it has against his kingdom. This is why he goes to great lengths to make sure that you stay away from it. Just imagine where your life would be today if you fortified your life in the Word of God? Imagine the level of confidence you would have? Imagine how defeated the devil would be in your life? The Bible says to resist the devil and he will flee. In order to resist something, you have to have something that is doing the resisting. The Word of God is what will be effective in resisting him. Satan is a strategist, and his demons are relentless. They will scheme and devise bigger plans to tear you down. If you are wise in God and humble, there will be no weapon that the enemy forms against you that will prosper. The Word is powerful and effective.

How to increase your weaponry

1. Target the areas that you know you have strongholds in. Write them down and look up scriptures that are tailored to those issues such as sex, addictions, etc.
2. Set aside time every day to study and meditate on those scriptures, and plant them in your spirit. Remember that repetition is the greatest form of learning.
3. Form a solid accountability team. Notice I said team. One person is not able to account for all the main issues in your life. Find people that you know are solid and wise enough to keep you accountable to stay on track. Satan loves isolation and wants you away from those that can help you. He will surround you with people that will aid your aliments.
4. Begin to use the Word of God against Satan. After you have built yourself up and increased your faith in God's Word, target your sword against those areas the demons are attacking. Before you know it, that issue will be resolved. Remember that a soldier has to take time with his weapon. He has to learn it and learn how to use it so that it can be effective in war. Here is what I did when I was going through intense spiritual warfare. I would carry a book of Bible verses based on topics (similar to what's in the back of this book). Every time I was being attacked in a certain area, I would find the area of attack and read those

scriptures over and over again. If I had a sexual thought or was tempted to look at a girl, I would open the book to the section that talked about sex and lust and use those few minutes to renew my thoughts. It is going to take work, but it will be worth it in the end. Also remember what Jesus did in the wilderness when He was tempted by Satan. He won the battles against Satan's temptations only through his use of the word of God.

5. Fight relentlessly. Increase your tenacity to the point that you will not stop until you get the victory. This is not for quitters. This is for people who are tired of losing and falling back into sins that they should have already conquered. Everything in life takes time, and it is within that set time that progress occurs. You have to want to win. Winning does not start when the game is over; it begins in the weight rooms and tracks. It begins in the heart. Does your heart want to win?

No weapons; No war won.

***

Chapter 13: The Power of Prayer

Communication is everything. Without it, our worlds will collapse. When it comes to communication, there are 3 parts:

The Sender

The Message

The Receiver

each work together to form communication. Communication is important. Without communication, there would always be confusion and chaos. If I have important information for you but never relay the message, it can cost you. Many of the results in our lives are due to miscommunication. Each of the three components of communication is extremely important. If there is no sender, there is no message. If there is no message, there is no need of a sender or receiver.

Sender:

The sender is where the message is formulated. This is where the message is conceived and developed into a package for delivery. The sender has the control over his or her message. It is the sole responsibility of the sender that the message is accurately sent and received by the person they desire to hear the message. If the message is not relayed properly, it is not the message or the receivers fault but the sender.

Message

Every message has a meaning, and that meaning is determined by the sender. Every message, from giving directions to giving encouragement, has some type of meaning. The message is extremely important. If it never reaches the receiver, it can cost them. Many of us have been damaged by miscommunication. Many of us have built distorted worldviews due to not receiving the correct message. All of us receive messages, but the problem with the message in our world today is that it is corrupted by lies and deceit. The lies and deceit are meant to keep the receiver limited in what the sender knows.

Every day, we receive messages from the media. Usually, those messages aim to make sure that we are derailed from truth and hindered from receiving the true message.

Receiver

All of us are receivers. Every day, we all receive messages from our parents, friends and the media. The receiver is usually the one that is affected the most because many times they receive the wrong message or a partial message. This leaves the receiver at a disadvantage. Both the sender and the message are affected by the receiver. How the receiver receives and responds to the message can hurt the sender. For example, if the sender wants the receiver to do A and not B but the receiver does B, the receiver will receive the opposite of what was intended.

The gospel of Jesus Christ is the ultimate message that our hearts need to receive. Many of us are either receiving the wrong message or a partial one. Satan knows the importance of communication, for communication helps us to receive the right directions and instructions. Anyone that has the right directions and the right instructions reaches the right destination and completes the right task. Prayer is vital. This is why the Bible says to pray always with all prayer and supplication in the spirit. This verse from Ephesians is powerful because it gives us the blueprint on how to always be on guard and connected to God. It says to pray always, not sometimes. The reason why it says always is because we are to always be connected and in tune with God, for we are at war. A soldier's ears are always attentive to the words of his general because the general knows the game plan of the Commander and Chief. The Holy Spirit is our General, and God is our Commander in Chief. God knew that man would fall and he would have to redeem man's soul. The only way to redeem the soul was to ignite within man His spirit that would serve as His antenna to relay His messages. The problem is that many people think they are connected but they are not. My question to you is, "Are you on His frequency?"

Satan has done a great job of drifting us away from connecting and communicating with God. He knows that God is constantly relaying messages, and with that message comes the solutions to the problems Satan is causing. With this in mind, Satan has built a system that continuously occupies the human soul so that the human soul will never hear important messages. He entertains our souls with media, sports, social networks, movies, music, careers, and false doctrine so that there is no time or any room in the soul to clearly hear from God. Look at your life. How often do you pray? Countless people have been brainwashed and have forfeited their right to connect with God. Connection with God is vital. If we are not connected to Him, we are affected. God is the sender. He is constantly sending, and His message is the Gospel of Jesus Christ that holds within it the salvation for our defiled hearts. God's message comes with the ability to clean out all the junk that is in our hearts. The problem is that Satan's system has made sure that countless people are clogged in their hearts and in their minds. He has made sure that we have strategically been programmed to latch on to the different tentacles of his system so that our hearts will yearn more for this life and not for the life to come. This is why salvation is a process; it undoes the negative programming. We have been deceived to believe that the ultimate process which is salvation can be summed up in a single moment.

Praying always is like the fuel that keeps the engine running. No fuel or oil means no properly functioning vehicle. No prayer means no proper functioning individual. Once we enter into the salvation process, we are targeted by Satan to insure that the gospel does not bear fruit in our lives. The only way salvation can bear fruit is if it is constantly being nurtured. Consistency in prayer nurtures the seed of salvation. We are constantly humbled and in contact with God, receiving messages daily. Salvation is like any natural seed. Its growth is dependent upon what comes down from the sky (sunlight and rain) in order for it to bring forth fruit. Satan wants us out of the cycle of seed time and harvest. If he can break this cycle in our lives and distort our understanding of how this applies to our lives, it will break us. A seed cannot grow in the wrong conditions. Prayer is our connection with God, the believer's source. Prayer is our source for directions and instruction on winning the war within and this war called life. Imagine where your life would be today if you and God spoke often? Where would you be today? Many of the problems of our world and in our lives are due to our separation from God. Sin causes separation and with that separation comes death and its components. Death has components that aim to latch on to our lives and slowly dry our soul until we are helpless in hell. We will be forever separated from God, both in our earthly and eternal life. This is why the Bible says that the wages of sin is death. The wage or the return of sin will be death and this death is eternal damnation in hell. Has death latched on to you? God promises the believer one thing and that is salvation from the wrath of God. That one promise holds multiple promises that are only given in stages due to maturity. He instituted prayer so that the soul of man would be connected to the Spirit of God and would lead our soul to all truth. It should be our deepest desire and concern that we have the blueprint, not only for our lives but for every day. Many of us are so wrapped up on receiving the call of God for our future that we forget to seek the call of God for today. For when we answer the call for today, it will lead us towards the call for tomorrow. How can we endeavor to accomplish the grand call of our lives if we are too lazy to adhere to what God has called for us to do today? This is why many of us never tap into our full potential or our purpose. We have been programmed to be so focused on the overall picture that we overlook the individual pieces that formulates the overall picture. Life is not summed up by its totality but by its individual moments.

Satan knows that no communication with God equals a deprived heart, a heart that is withheld from the necessary things that it needs for survival. Like our natural heart, if our spiritual heart is deprived due to a clog, it will lead to a heart attack. If our spiritual heart or soul is deprived of a clear connection with God due to arteries clogged with the cares of this world and the deceitfulness of riches, it will lead to chaos. Satan wants us to be blocked from God's message, because we will be left temporarily satisfied but eternally damned. Is your heart clogged?

The Prayer Deception

It is more prevalent to pray the deceptive way than it is the right way. The deceptive way is more so about self and self-gratification. The right or godly way is to constantly pray the will of God. In our modern day Christian circles or churches, we have been programmed to pray the will of man not the will of God. We have been derailed to believe that praying is more about things, houses, and spouses than it is about the purging of our souls and the souls of others. We have been baited and tempted to pray our will be done not the will of God, and we wonder why our prayers have not been answered. When we pray, we are to pray the will of God. Many people want to know the will of God.

The will of God is about him and him alone. It is about his purpose in your life not your own decided purpose. It is about living a holy and pleasing life that is acceptable to Him. It is about feeding the hungry, giving water to the thirsty and putting clothes on the backs of the naked. It is self-examination and spiritual discipline. It is about Him and not about us.

We have to understand that life is fulfilled one day at a time. It is not about housing the glory for ourselves but making sure that God gets the glory. Satan knows that a prayer that is prayed from a selfish heart will never receive anything from God. He knows that if he can deceive the masses into praying selfish and lustful prayers, their prayers will never be answered. This will lead countless people into viewing God in a negative way. It will produce people that complain instead of those that are content. Satan knows that if people continue to pray false prayers with no response from God, the lack of response will build hate towards God in the long run. God always does things to clearly reveal the real from the fake, the sheep from the goats and the believer from the unbeliever. It all begins with truth.

Satan has done a great job of making sure that we think we are saved as we pray prayers that do not get answered and build false hopes. Prayer works only if it comes from a pure heart with genuine motives. God wants us to pray His will from a heart that pants after Him. One scripture that many people have taken out of context is Psalms 37:4, "Delight yourself in the Lord and he will give you the desires of your heart." Many people take this scripture out of context and believe that God is talking about all desires. He is solely talking about those desires that he has formed within the heart, not those that are carnal and lustful. Delight means a high degree of pleasure or joy. Do you really have delight in God or what he has to offer? Many people do not delight in God, because if they did, their prayers would be aimed towards things that honor him and give Him glory. God looks at the heart and its motives. He will never answer any prayers that have motives to accentuate pride or lust. What are the motives behind your prayers?

Prayer was meant to be used for venting, interceding and to gain wisdom and revelation. It was aimed to communicate with God to build a solid and strong relationship with Him. He wants us to vent, release our frustrations and cast all our cares on Him. He wants us to use our prayer time to intercede for people.

He wants us to intercede for the salvation of those that are lost in our family. He wants us to pray earnestly for wisdom and to gain revelation. He wants us to constantly desire to communicate with him in order to build on our relationship. God wants a relationship with His creation, and there is no relationship where there is no communication. How often do you communicate with God? If you rarely talk to Him, could you say that you have a solid relationship with Him?

Strategy:

The Bible says that we ought to pray always, without ceasing and fervently. Why? This is because our enemy never sleeps. We sleep but the demons that follow us do not. They constantly roam to find loop holes in our lives so that we can end up breaching our commitments to God. Many people view prayer as a burden or as something religious or ritualistic when it should not be viewed that way. God does not want robots that come every day saying the same thing. He wants a people to pray with a joyful heart, a heart that yearns to talk to God about anything. Prayer was never meant to be an obligation but a desire. It should be a desire that drives us to wants to talk to God and to be His friend. Let me ask. When you communicate with your close family and friends, do you talk to them only at a certain time of the day or do you consistently talk to them? As a believer we have access to Him, and we can literally talk to him anytime we want for as long as we want. I would rather pray throughout my day then only once. I would rather talk to God about everything throughout my day so that I can always be connected to Him. I always start my day with God in prayer, but it does not end there.

I vent throughout the day when life frustrates me. When people pop into my spirit, I intercede for them on the drop of a dime. I pray when I need wisdom or revelation. While I am processing thoughts, I ask God for clarity. I do this throughout my day. This helps to keep the signal flowing throughout our soul and spirit. It keeps us sensitive and alert to God enabling us to be His sheep that know his voice and a stranger they will not follow. If you are being led astray today, you have to ask yourself if you know the Shepherd's voice. Many times we entertain countless voices but not the supreme voice. Whose voice should we make sure we hear? Should it be men and women's voices who are tainted or God's? If we know God's voice, character and attributes, we will know the differences of demonicly inspired opinions and God inspired solutions. God can care less about how long you pray if it does not come from a genuine heart. One word that cries from a broken and humbled heart will be heard by God over a ritualistic two hour long prayer from a hypocrite. For some people, long prayers are fine and we should want to be at that level, but we should not be burdened by or forced to be like someone else out of a religious spirit.

We as humans are at a disadvantage. Since the fall we have fallen away from our place in God and have spiraled down to a place where we were never intended to be. Everything in our lives is surrounded by three things:

1. God
2. Us
3. Satan

God

God is omniscient. He knows everything which places Him at the pinnacle of everything.

US

We are limited due to our present conditions and ignorance. We are limited because we are bound by time, while all spiritual forces spans through eternity. With our limitations, we are at a disadvantage because we are constantly being affected by spiritual things.

Satan

Satan knows more than us seeing that he has been around humanity from the beginning. We cannot stand alone against him. However, Satan is not all knowing like God. This means that those that are constantly connected to God will be in the advantage against Satan. This is why Satan wants you deceived and focused on vanity. Vanity will keep you limited in what you know. Many people know a lot of things, but the things they know are useless when it comes to this war called life. It is what you do not know about your enemy that will cost you in war. What is your strategy? Are you connected to God constantly or are you just wondering throughout life being deceived with many L's (losses) but few wins?

We can either remain ignorant and at a disadvantage or connect to the One who knows everything, putting Satan at a disadvantage.

In any war what are the two things that an army wants to destroy or have power over? They want to destroy their enemy's form of intelligence and their power or weaponry. Now look at our lives. What are the two things we rarely do? Pray and read our Bible.

***

Prayer is essential.

I can tell you from personal experiences on how prayer has changed not only my circumstances but me as well. I'm currently working on a book on prayer that I can't wait to release because I think a lot of people in my generation don't quite understand the importance of communicating with God through prayer.

I want to take some time now to share with you how I pray. Nothing spectacular just simple.

I follow these 3 R's; Rejoice, Repent and Request.

I love the scripture that says in Psalms 100:4; Enter his gates with thanksgiving, and his courts with praise! Give thanks to him; bless his name!

Before I even get to repent or to request I enter his presence with thanksgiving. I begin to look around me and find things to thank him for. I begin to thank him for a roof over my head. I begin to thank him for blessing me with the ability to see, hear, smell taste, and walk. I begin to thank him for my lungs my heart my spleen even. I just get so caught up in entering his presence with thanksgiving that it overshadows my need to request. Once I have finished thanking him and praising him I begin to repent of all my current sins. Sins I know about and sins I may not know about.

When you go before God with rejoicing it humbles you because you begin to realize just how bless you really are. Ladies and gentleman there are people in 3rd world countries that are more thankful with less than what we have. And with that thought sinking so deep within my soul during prayer my heart can't help but repent of all the things I've done wrong. It motivates me not to say God I'm Sorry but to say God IM DONE.

Bout time I've finished rejoicing and repenting my request become more Godly and Biblical because as the Holy Spirit is governing my time in Prayer and I'm praying in the spirit I begin to ask for HIS WILL. It goes from Father take this from me or father add this to me to Father not my will but thine will be done.

And my request will then be backed by faith, knowing that God will come through for me and a faith that will trust in His timing.

I promise when you make a habit of Rejoicing, Repenting and Requesting according to his will your prayer life will deepen and your relationship with will grow like never before.

I love you all and my heart is for you to know His. Take some time now to talk with God. Cut on your favorite worship song or go to where you and God always meet and take some to worship him.

The Finale: Watch

We are at war within our hearts and with darkness. This war is not over until death. There are two ultimate realities that we all will have to face, death and God's judgment. How would you fare after death? Life is nothing to play with. It is too delicate for you to live recklessly. Life spans between the day you were born and the day you die, something like (19** - 20**). The main thing within that bracket is the dash (-). What are you doing with that time? We have been warned to watch and pray. We have been warned about the condition of our hearts. We have been warned about the devil, but how many of us are adhering to the warnings? When a soldier is asleep, he is at a disadvantage versus when he is awake and watching. The army that is currently awake is the army that is at an advantage; the army that is comfortable and sleeps is not. Are you awake or are you asleep? Look in your heart and ask yourself is it guarded. Is your mind balanced? What about your faith? Is it strong or is it nonexistent? Are your feet weary on this Christian journey? Are you familiar with how to use your weapon? How many scriptures do you know verses rap lyricsor lines in a movie? These are questions you have to ask yourself. It will let you know where you stand in this war. Many people say Satan is defeated but are clueless on the defeats in their lives, finances, health and homes. L.I.F.E. is serious because of what happens at the end of it. There is a judgment coming and how you fare in this war will determine where you will go.

The Bible says in Matthew 26:41 to watch and pray that you may not enter into temptation. The Spirit is willing but the flesh is weak. Jesus was warning His disciples and us to watch and pray that we may not enter into temptation. He warns us that there will be temptations that will be aimed at turning our hearts away from salvation. The Bible tells us that the spirit is willing but the flesh is weak. Our spirits are willing to endure, but it is our flesh that wants to be lazy, complacent and entertained. It is up to us to lean on our spirits and decapitate our carnal flesh. Which one is alive? Is your flesh thriving and your spirit deprived, or is your flesh dead and your spirit alive?

Watch and pray so that you will not fall into temptation. For temptation will come.

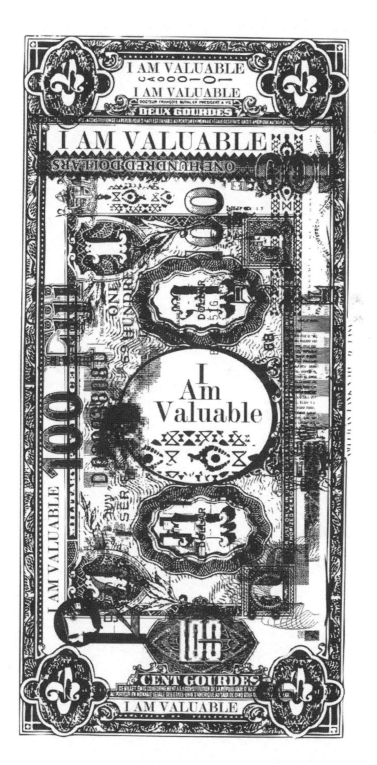

List of Scriptures

Table of Contents

Accountability – Page 143

A Child's Duty – Page 144

A Parent's Duty – Page 146

Appearance – Page 148

Anger/Rage – Page 149

Bad Habits – Page 151

Beauty – Page 153

Belief – Page 154

Blessing – Page 155

Children – Page 158

Comfort – Page 159

Conceit/Pride – Page 161

Contentment – Page 163

Courage – Page 164

Death – Page 165

Enemies – Page 167

Envy – Page 170

Eternal Life – Page 172

Faith – Page 176

Fasting – Page 178

Fear/Worry – Page 181

Food & Clothes – Page 184

Forgiveness – Page 185

Freedom from sin – Page 186

Fruitfulness – Page 187

Giving – Page 188

God's Correction – Page 191

God's Protection – Page 192

Gossip/Rumors – Page 194

Growing in grace – Page 195

Guidance – Page 197

Healing – Page 198

Help In Troubles – Page 201

Holy Spirit – Page 204

Honesty – Page 207

Hope – Page 209

Humiliation – Page 211

Humility – Page 212

Increased Life – Page 213

Joy/Happiness – Page 215

Kindness – Page 218

Laziness – Page 219

Loneliness – Page 222

Love – Page 223

Loving God – Page 227

Lust – Page 229

Lying – Page 232

Marriage – Page 234

Meekness – Page 236

Mercy – Page 237

Money – Page 239

Obedience – Page 242

Patience – Page 245

Peace – Page 246

Poverty – Page 247

Prayer – Page 249

Prisoners – Page 253

Prosperity – Page 254

Remorse – Page 256

Repentance – Page 259

Righteousness – Page 260

Salvation – Page 262

Seeking God – Page 264

Self-Denial – Page 266

Selfishness – Page 267

Self-Righteousness – Page 268

Sexual Sins – Page 270

Shame – Page 272

Sickness/Disease – Page 273

Slander – Page 274

Submission – Page 275

The Love of God – Page 277

The Word Of God – Page 279

Trust – Page 282

Wisdom – Page 284

Scriptures on Accountability

2 Corinthians 5:10

"For we must all appear before the judgment seat of Christ that every one may receive the things done in his body, according to what he hath done, whether it be good or bad."

Romans 14:12

"So then each of us shall give account of himself to God."

Proverbs 27:17

"As iron sharpens iron, So a man sharpens the countenance of his friend."

Matthew 12:36-37

"But I say to you that for every idle word men may speak, they will give account of it in the Day of Judgment. For by your words you will be justified, and by your words you will be condemned."

Hebrews 13:17

"Obey those who rule over you, and be submissive, for they watch out for your souls, as those who must give account..."

Luke 16:1-2

"He also said to His disciples: "There was a certain rich man who had a steward, and an accusation was brought to him that this man was wasting his goods. So he called him and said to him, 'What is this I hear about you? Give an account of your stewardship..."

Ezekiel 33:8-9

"When I say to the wicked, 'O wicked man, you shall surely die!' and you do not speak to warn the wicked from his way, that wicked man shall die in his iniquity; but his blood I will require at your hand. Nevertheless if you warn the wicked to turn from his way, and he does not turn from his way, he shall die in his iniquity; but you have delivered your soul.

A Children's Duty

Ephesians 6:1-3

"Children, obey your parents in the Lord, for this is right. "Honor your father and mother," which is the first commandment with promise: "that it may be well with you and you may live long on the earth."

Colossians 3:20

"Children, obey your parents in all things, for this is well pleasing to the Lord."

Deuteronomy 27:16

"Cursed is the one who treats his father or his mother with contempt."

Leviticus 19:3

"Every one of you shall revere his mother and his father... I am the Lord your God."

Deuteronomy 5:16

"Honor your father and your mother, as the Lord your God has commanded you, that your days may be long, and that it may be well with you..."

Proverbs 6:20

"My son, keep your father's command, and do not forsake the law of your mother."

Proverbs 13:1

"A wise son heeds his father's instruction, but a scoffer does not listen to rebuke."

Proverbs 15:5

"A fool despises his father's instruction, but he who receives correction is prudent."

Proverbs 20:11

"Even a child is known by his deeds, whether what he does is pure and right."

Proverbs 10:1

"A wise son makes a glad father, but a foolish son is the grief of his mother."

Proverbs 28:7

"Whoever keeps the law is a discerning son, but a companion of gluttons shames his father."

Proverbs 8: 32, 33

"Now therefore, listen to me, my children, For blessed are those who keep my ways. Hear instruction and be wise, And do not disdain it."

Proverbs 23:15, 16

"My son, if your heart is wise, my heart will rejoice—indeed, I myself; yes, my inmost being will rejoice when your lips speak right things."

Proverbs 23:22

"Listen to your father who begot you, and do not despise your mother when she is old."

Proverbs 23:24-26

"The father of the righteous will greatly rejoice, and he who begets a wise child will delight in him. Let your father and your mother be glad, and let her who bore you rejoice. My son, give me your heart, and let your eyes observe my ways."

Scriptures on a Parents duty

Proverbs 22:6

"Train up a child in the way he should go, and when he is old he will not depart from it."

Colossians 3:21

"Fathers, do not provoke your children, lest they become discouraged."

Proverbs 29:17

"Correct your son, and he will give you rest; Yes, he will give delight to your soul."

Deuteronomy 11:19

"You shall teach them to your children, speaking of them when you sit in your house, when you walk by the way, when you lie down, and when you rise up."

Psalms 78:4-7

"Telling to the generation to come the praises of the Lord, and His strength and His wonderful works that He has done. For He established a testimony in Jacob, and appointed a law in Israel, which He commanded our fathers, that they should make them known to their children; That the generation to come might know them, the children who would be born, that they may arise and declare them to their children, that they may set their hope in God, and not forget the works of God, but keep His commandments..."

Genesis 18:19

"For I have known him, in order that he may command his children and his household after him, that they keep the way of the Lord, to do righteousness and justice, that the Lord may bring to Abraham what He has spoken to him."

Exodus 13:8

"And you shall tell your son in that day, saying, 'This is done because of what the Lord did for me when I came up from Egypt"

Deuteronomy 4:9,10

"Only take heed to yourself, and diligently keep yourself, lest you forget the things your eyes have seen, and lest they depart from your heart all the days of your life. And teach them to your children and your grandchildren, especially concerning the day you stood before the Lord your God in Horeb, when the Lord said to me, 'Gather the people to Me, and I will let them hear My words, that they may learn to fear Me all the days they live on the earth, and that they may teach their children"

Ephesians 6:4

"And you, fathers, do not provoke your children to wrath, but bring them up in the training and admonition of the Lord."

Scriptures of Appearance

John 7:24

"Do not judge according to appearance, but judge with righteous judgment."

1 Samuel 16:7

"... the Lord does not see as man sees; for man looks at the outward appearance, but the Lord looks at the heart."

2 Corinthians 5:12

"For we do not commend ourselves again to you, but give you opportunity to boast on our behalf, that you may have an answer for those who boast in appearance and not in heart."

1 Peter 3: 3-4

"Do not let your adornment be merely outward – arranging the hair, wearing gold, or putting on fine apparel – rather let it be the hidden person of the heart, with the incorruptible beauty of a gentle and quiet spirit, which is very precious in the sight of God."

Matthew 6:16

"Moreover, when you fast, do not be like the hypocrites, with a sad countenance. For they disfigure their faces that they may appear to men to be fasting. Assuredly, I say to you, they have their reward."

1 Thessalonians 5:22

"Abstain from every form (appearance reads the KJV) of evil

Scriptures on Anger/ Rage

James 1:19, 20

"So then, my beloved brethren, let every man be swift to hear, slow to speak, slow to wrath; for the wrath of man does not produce the righteousness of God."

Ephesians 4:31, 32

"Let all bitterness, wrath, anger, clamor, and evil speaking be put away from you, with all malice. And be kind to one another, tenderhearted, forgiving one another, even as God in Christ forgave you."

Psalms 145:8

"The Lord is gracious and full of compassion, slow to anger and great in mercy."

Nehemiah 9:17

"...You are God, Ready to pardon, Gracious and merciful, Slow to anger, Abundant in kindness..."

Psalms 30:5

"For His anger is but for a moment, His favor is for life; Weeping may endure for a night, But joy comes in the morning. "

Ecclesiastes 7:9

"Do not hasten in your spirit to be angry, for anger rests in the bosom of fools."

Proverbs 16:32

"He who is slow to anger is better than the mighty, and he who rules his spirit than he who takes a city."

Proverbs 15:18

"A wrathful man stirs up strife, but he who is slow to anger allays contention."

Proverbs 29:22

"An angry man stirs up strife, and a furious man abounds in transgression."

Psalms 37:8

"Cease from anger, and forsake wrath; do not fret – it only causes harm."

Proverbs 22:24, 25

"Make no friendship with an angry man, and with a furious man do not go, lest you learn his ways and set a snare for your soul. "

Proverbs 15:1

"A soft answer turns away wrath, but a harsh word stirs up anger."

Colossians 3:21

"Fathers, do not provoke your children, lest they become discouraged."

Proverbs 19:11

"The discretion of a man makes him slow to anger, and his glory is to overlook a transgression. "

Proverbs 21:19

"Better to dwell in the wilderness, than with a contentious and angry woman."

Matthew 5:22

"But I say to you that whoever is angry with his brother without a cause shall be in danger of the judgment..."

Romans 12:19, 21

"Beloved, do not avenge yourselves, but rather give place to wrath; for it is written, "Vengeance is Mine, I will repay," says the Lord. Therefore 'If your enemy is hungry, feed him; If he is thirsty, give him a drink; For in so doing you will heap coals of fire on his head.' Do not be overcome by evil, but overcome evil with good."

Proverbs 25:21, 22

"If your enemy is hungry, give him bread to eat; and if he is thirsty, give him water to drink; for so you will heap coals of fire on his head, and the Lord will reward you."

Colossians 3:8

"But now you yourselves are to put off all these: anger, wrath, malice, blasphemy, filthy language out of your mouth."

Proverbs 14:17

"A quick-tempered man acts foolishly, and a man of wicked intentions is hated."

Scriptures on Bad Habits

2 Timothy 2:16

"But shun profane and idle babblings, for they will increase to more ungodliness."

Galatians 5:19-21

"Now the works of the flesh are evident, which are: adultery, fornication, uncleanness, lewdness, idolatry, sorcery, hatred, contentions, jealousies, outbursts of wrath, selfish ambitions, dissensions, heresies, envy, murders, drunkenness, revelries, and the like; of which I tell you beforehand, just as I also told you in time past, that those who practice such things will not inherit the kingdom of God."

Proverbs 17:20

"He who has a deceitful heart finds no good, and he who has a perverse tongue falls into evil."

Proverbs 12:19-22

The truthful lip shall be established forever, but a lying tongue is but for a moment. Deceit is in the heart of those who devise evil, but counselors of peace have joy. No grave trouble will overtake the righteous, but the wicked shall be filled with evil. Lying lips are an abomination to the Lord, but those who deal truthfully are His delight.

James 4:7

Therefore submit to God. Resist the devil and he will flee from you

Scriptures on Beauty

Proverbs 31:30

"Charm is deceitful and beauty is passing, but a woman who fears the Lord, she shall be praised."

Proverbs 11:22

"As a ring of gold in a swine's snout, so is a lovely woman who lacks discretion."

1 Peter 3:3-4

"Do not let your adornment be merely outward – arranging the hair, wearing gold, or putting on fine apparel – rather let it be the hidden person of the heart, with the incorruptible beauty of a gentle and quiet spirit, which is very precious in the sight of God."

Ecclesiastes 3:11

"He has made everything beautiful in its time..."

Matthew 23:27,28

"Woe to you, scribes and Pharisees, hypocrites! For you are like whitewashed tombs which indeed appear beautiful outwardly, but inside are full of dead men's bones and all uncleanness. Even so you also outwardly appear righteous to men, but inside you are full of hypocrisy and lawlessness."

Proverbs 20:29

"The glory of young men is their strength, and the splendor of old men is their gray head."

Philippians 4:8

"Finally, brethren, whatever things are true, whatever things are noble, whatever things are just, whatever things are pure, whatever things are lovely, whatever things are of good report, if there is any virtue and if there is anything praiseworthy—meditate on these things

Scriptures on Belief:

John 3:16

"For God so loved the world that He gave His only begotten Son, that whoever believes in Him should not perish but have everlasting life."

Acts 10:43

"To Him all the prophets witness that, through His name, whoever believes in Him will receive remission of sins."

John 1:12

"But as many as received Him, to them He gave the right to become children of God, to those who believe in His name:"

John 3:18

"He who believes in Him is not condemned; but he who does not believe is condemned already, because he has not believed in the name of the only begotten Son of God."

John 3:36

"He who believes in the Son has everlasting life; and he who does not believe the Son shall not see life, but the wrath of God abides on him."

Acts 16:31

"So they said, "Believe on the Lord Jesus Christ, and you will be saved, you and your household."

John 12:46

"I have come as a light into the world, that whoever believes in Me should not abide in darkness."

John 6:35

"And Jesus said to them, 'I am the bread of life. He who comes to Me shall never hunger, and he who believes in Me shall never thirst.' "

Mark 9:23

"Jesus said to him, 'If you can believe, all things are possible to him who believes.' "

John 20:29

"Jesus said to him, 'Thomas, because you have seen Me, you have believed. Blessed are those who have not seen and yet have believed' "

John 6:47

"Most assuredly, I say to you, he who believes in Me has everlasting life."

Scriptures on Blessing

Psalm 21: 6

"For You have made him most blessed forever; You have made him exceedingly glad with Your presence."

James 3:10

"Out of the same mouth proceed blessing and cursing. My brethren, these things ought not to be so."

Psalm 21: 3

"For You meet him with the blessings of goodness; You set a crown of pure gold upon his head."

Zechariah 8: 13

"And it shall come to pass that just as you were a curse among the nations, O house of Judah and house of Israel, so I will save you, and you shall be a blessing. Do not fear, let your hands be strong."

Galatians 3: 14

"that the blessing of Abraham might come upon the Gentiles in Christ Jesus, that we might receive the promise of the Spirit through faith."

Psalm 109: 17

"As he loved cursing, so let it come to him; As he did not delight in blessing, so let it be far from him."

Deuteronomy 11: 26-27

"Behold, I set before you today a blessing and a curse: 27 the blessing, if you obey the commandments of the LORD your God which I command you today;"

Deuteronomy 23: 5

"Nevertheless the LORD your God would not listen to Balaam, but the LORD your God turned the curse into a blessing for you, because the LORD your God loves you."

1 Corinthians 10: 16

"The cup of blessing which we bless, is it not the communion of the blood of Christ? The bread which we break, is it not the communion of the body of Christ?"

Ephesians 1: 3

"Blessed be the God and Father of our Lord Jesus Christ, who has blessed us with every spiritual blessing in the heavenly places in Christ"

Proverbs 10: 6

"Blessings are on the head of the righteous, but violence covers the mouth of the wicked."

Proverbs 10: 7

"The memory of the righteous is blessed, but the name of the wicked will rot."

Psalm 41: 1

"For You, O LORD, will bless the righteous; With favor You will surround him as with a shield."

Psalm 106: 3

"Blessed are those who keep justice, and he who does righteousness at all times!"

Hebrews 6:7

"For the earth which drinks in the rain that often comes upon it, and bears herbs useful for those by whom it is cultivated, receives blessing from God;"

Revelation 5: 12

"...Worthy is the Lamb who was slain To receive power and riches and wisdom, And strength and honor and glory and blessing!"

Scriptures on Children

Proverbs 17:6

"Children's children are the crown of old men, And the glory of children is their father. "

Acts 16:31

"For the promise is to you and to your children, and to all who are afar off, as many as the Lord our God will call."

Acts 16:31

"So they said, 'Believe on the Lord Jesus Christ, and you will be saved, you and your household.' "

Isaiah 54:13

"All your children shall be taught by the Lord, and great shall be the peace of your children."

Isaiah 44:3

"For I will pour water on him who is thirsty, and floods on the dry ground; I will pour My Spirit on your descendants, and My blessing on your offspring;"

Mark 10:14-16

"But when Jesus saw it, He was greatly displeased and said to them, 'Let the little children come to Me, and do not forbid them; for of such is the kingdom of God. Assuredly, I say to you, whoever does not receive the kingdom of God as a little child will by no means enter it.' And He took them up in His arms, laid His hands on them, and blessed them."

Psalms 127:3-5

"Behold, children are a heritage from the Lord, The fruit of the womb is a reward. Like arrows in the hand of a warrior, So are the children of one's youth. Happy is the man who has his quiver full of them; They shall not be ashamed, But shall speak with their enemies in the gate."

Psalms 128:3

"Your wife shall be like a fruitful vine In the very heart of your house, Your children like olive plants All around your table."

Psalms 107:41

"Yet He sets the poor on high, far from affliction, And makes their families like a flock."

Job 21:11

"They send forth their little ones like a flock, And their children dance.

Scriptures on Comfort

Psalms 46:1- 3

"God is our refuge and strength, A very present help in trouble. Therefore we will not fear, Even though the earth be removed, And though the mountains be carried into the midst of the sea; Though its waters roar and be troubled, Though the mountains shake with its swelling."

Psalms 138:7

"Though I walk in the midst of trouble, You will revive me; You will stretch out Your hand Against the wrath of my enemies, And Your right hand will save me."

Psalms 18:2

"The Lord is my rock and my fortress and my deliverer; My God, my strength, in whom I will trust; My shield and the horn of my salvation, my stronghold."

Psalms 22:24

"For He has not despised nor abhorred the affliction of the afflicted; Nor has He hidden His face from Him; But when He cried to Him, He heard."

Psalms 37:24

"Though he fall, he shall not be utterly cast down; For the Lord upholds him with His hand."

Nahum 1:7

"The Lord is good, A stronghold in the day of trouble; And He knows those who trust in Him."

Psalms 37:39

"But the salvation of the righteous is from the Lord; He is their strength in the time of trouble."

Psalms 55:22

"Cast your burden on the Lord, And He shall sustain you; He shall never permit the righteous to be moved. "

John 16:33

" 'These things I have spoken to you, that in Me you may have peace. In the world you will have tribulation; but be of good cheer, I have overcome the world.' "

Matthew 11:28

"Come to Me, all you who labor and are heavy laden, and I will give you rest."

2 Corinthians 1:5

"For as the sufferings of Christ abound in us, so our consolation also abounds through Christ."

Psalms 9:9

"The Lord also will be a refuge for the oppressed, A refuge in times of trouble."

Lamentations 3:31- 33

"For the Lord will not cast off forever. Though He causes grief, Yet He will show compassion According to the multitude of His mercies. For He does not afflict willingly, Nor grieve the children of men. "

Psalms 27:14

"Wait on the Lord; Be of good courage, And He shall strengthen your heart; Wait, I say, on the Lord!

Scriptures on Conceit and pride

Proverbs 21:4

"A haughty look, a proud heart, And the plowing of the wicked are sin."

Proverbs 14:3

"In the mouth of a fool is a rod of pride, But the lips of the wise will preserve them."

Proverbs 27:2

"Let another man praise you, and not your own mouth; A stranger, and not your own lips."

Proverbs 28:25,26

"He who is of a proud heart stirs up strife, But he who trusts in the Lord will be prospered. He who trusts in his own heart is a fool, But whoever walks wisely will be delivered."

Isaiah 5:21

"Woe to those who are wise in their own eyes, And prudent in their own sight!"

Job 40:12

"Look on everyone who is proud, and bring him low; Tread down the wicked in their place."

Proverbs 26:12

"Do you see a man wise in his own eyes? There is more hope for a fool than for him."

Proverbs 16:18

"Pride goes before destruction, And a haughty spirit before a fall."

Psalms 119:21

"You rebuke the proud – the cursed, Who stray from Your commandments."

Luke 16:15

"And He said to them, 'You are those who justify yourselves before men, but God knows your hearts. For what is highly esteemed among men is an abomination in the sight of God.' "

Proverbs 8:13

"The fear of the Lord is to hate evil; Pride and arrogance and the evil way And the perverse mouth I hate. "

John 5:44

"How can you believe, who receive honor from one another, and do not seek the honor that comes from the only God?"

Mark 9:35

"And He sat down, called the twelve, and said to them, 'If anyone desires to be first, he shall be last of all and servant of all.' "

2 Corinthians 10:17,18

"But 'he who glories, let him glory in the Lord.' For not he who commends himself is approved, but whom the Lord commends."

Scriptures on Contentment

Proverbs 17:22

"A merry heart does good, like medicine, But a broken spirit dries the bones."

Hebrews 13:5

"Let your conduct be without covetousness; be content with such things as you have. For He Himself has said, 'I will never leave you nor forsake you.' "

Proverbs 15:15

"All the days of the afflicted are evil, But he who is of a merry heart has a continual feast."

Proverbs 14:30

"A sound heart is life to the body, But envy is rottenness to the bones."

1 Timothy 6:6

"Now godliness with contentment is great gain."

Proverbs 23:17, 18

"Do not let your heart envy sinners, But be zealous for the fear of the Lord all the day; For surely there is a hereafter, And your hope will not be cut off.

Scriptures on Courage:

Psalms 27:14

"Wait on the Lord; Be of good courage, And He shall strengthen your heart; Wait, I say, on the Lord!"

Psalms 37:28

"For the Lord loves justice, And does not forsake His saints; They are preserved forever, But the descendants of the wicked shall be cut off."

Isaiah 43:1

" But now, thus says the Lord, who created you, O Jacob, And He who formed you, O Israel: ' Fear not, for I have redeemed you; I have called you by your name; you are Mine. '

2 Kings 6:16

"So he answered, 'Do not fear, for those who are with us are more than those who are with them.' "

Psalms 37:3

"Trust in the Lord, and do good; Dwell in the land, and feed on His faithfulness."

Isaiah 40:29

"He gives power to the weak, And to those who have no might He increases strength."

Psalms 31:24

"Be of good courage, And He shall strengthen your heart, All you who hope in the Lord."

Philippians 4:12, 13

"I know how to be abased, and I know how to abound. Everywhere and in all things I have learned both to be full and to be hungry, both to abound and to suffer need. I can do all things through Christ who strengthens me."

Scriptures on Death

Romans 8:38,39

"For I am persuaded that neither death nor life, nor angels nor principalities nor powers, nor things present nor things to come, nor height nor depth, nor any other created thing, shall be able to separate us from the love of God which is in Christ Jesus our Lord."

Psalms 23:4

"Yea, though I walk through the valley of the shadow of death, I will fear no evil; For You are with me; Your rod and Your staff, they comfort me."

John 8:51

"Most assuredly, I say to you, if anyone keeps My word he shall never see death."

Psalms 48:14

"For this is God, Our God forever and ever, He will be our guide even to death."

1 Corinthians 15:55

"O Death, where is your sting? O Hades, where is your victory?"

Proverbs 14:32

"The wicked is banished in his wickedness, But the righteous has a refuge in his death."

Romans 5:9

"Much more then, having now been justified by His blood, we shall be saved from wrath through Him."

Hebrews 2:14, 15

"Inasmuch then as the children have partaken of flesh and blood, He Himself likewise shared in the same, that through death He might destroy him who had the power of death, that is, the devil, and release those who through fear of death were all their lifetime subject to bondage."

Psalms 73:26

"My flesh and my heart fail; But God is the strength of my heart and my portion forever. "

Psalms 49:15

"But God will redeem my soul from the power of the grave, For He shall receive me. Selah "

Isaiah 25:8

"He will swallow up death forever, And the Lord God will wipe away tears from all faces; The rebuke of His people He will take away from all the earth; For the Lord has spoken. "

Hosea 13:14

"I will ransom them from the power of the grave; I will redeem them from death. O Death, I will be your plagues! O Grave, I will be your destruction! Pity is hidden from My eyes."

Psalms 37:37

"Mark the blameless man, and observe the upright; For the future of that man is peace."

2 Corinthians 4:16

"Therefore we do not lose heart. Even though our outward man is perishing, yet the inward man is being renewed day by day."

John 3:15

"that whoever believes in Him should not perish but have eternal life."

Scriptures on Enemies

Psalms 37:40

"And the Lord shall help them and deliver them; He shall deliver them from the wicked, And save them, Because they trust in Him."

Job 8:22

"Those who hate you will be clothed with shame, And the dwelling place of the wicked will come to nothing."

Deuteronomy 28:7

"The Lord will cause your enemies who rise against you to be defeated before your face; they shall come out against you one way and flee before you seven ways."

Deuteronomy 20:4

"for the Lord your God is He who goes with you, to fight for you against your enemies, to save you."

Job 5:20

"In famine He shall redeem you from death, And in war from the power of the sword."

Psalms 60:12

"Through God we will do valiantly, For it is He who shall tread down our enemies."

Isaiah 54:17

" ' No weapon formed against you shall prosper, And every tongue which rises against you in judgment You shall condemn. This is the heritage of the servants of the Lord, And their righteousness is from Me," Says the Lord.' "

Psalms 118:7

"The Lord is for me among those who help me; Therefore I shall see my desire on those who hate me."

Luke 1:74

"To grant us that we, Being delivered from the hand of our enemies, Might serve Him without fear,"

Psalms 125:3

"For the scepter of wickedness shall not rest On the land allotted to the righteous, Lest the righteous reach out their hands to iniquity."

Psalms 27:5, 6

"For in the time of trouble He shall hide me in His pavilion; In the secret place of His tabernacle He shall hide me; He shall set me high upon a rock. And now my head shall be lifted up above my enemies all around me; Therefore I will offer sacrifices of joy in His tabernacle; I will sing, yes, I will sing praises to the Lord. "

Proverbs 16:7

"When a man's ways please the Lord, He makes even his enemies to be at peace with him. "

Psalms 112:8

"His heart is established; He will not be afraid, Until he sees his desire upon his enemies. "

Luke 18:7

"And shall God not avenge His own elect who cry out day and night to Him, though He bears long with them?"

Isaiah 54:15

"Indeed they shall surely assemble, but not because of Me. Whoever assembles against you shall fall for your sake."

Psalms 97:10

"You who love the Lord, hate evil! He preserves the souls of His saints; He delivers them out of the hand of the wicked."

Jeremiah 39:17, 18

" 'But I will deliver you in that day,' says the Lord, 'and you shall not be given into the hand of the men of whom you are afraid. For I will surely deliver you, and you shall not fall by the sword; but your life shall be as a prize to you, because you have put your trust in Me,' says the Lord."

2 Kings 17:39

"But the Lord your God you shall fear; and He will deliver you from the hand of all your enemies."

2 Kings 6:16

"So he answered, 'Do not fear, for those who are with us are more than those who are with them.' "

Proverbs 3:25, 26

"Do not be afraid of sudden terror, Nor of trouble from the wicked when it comes; For the Lord will be your confidence, And will keep your foot from being caught. "

Isaiah 41:11, 12

"Behold, all those who were incensed against you shall be ashamed and disgraced; They shall be as nothing, And those who strive with you shall perish. You shall seek them and not find them – Those who contended with you. Those who war against you shall be as nothing, As a nonexistent thing."

Luke 1:71

"That we should be saved from our enemies And from the hand of all who hate us, "

Acts 18:10

"for I am with you, and no one will attack you to hurt you; for I have many people in this city."

Hebrews 13:6

"So we may boldly say: ' The Lord is my helper; I will not fear. What can man do to me?' " (see Psalm 118:6)

Scriptures on Envy

Proverbs 23:17,18

"Do not let your heart envy sinners, But be zealous for the fear of the Lord all the day! For surely there is a hereafter, And your hope will not be cut off. "

Proverbs 14:30

"A sound heart is life to the body, But envy is rottenness to the bones. "

James 4:5

"Or do you think that the Scripture says in vain, 'The Spirit who dwells in us yearns jealously?' "

Deuteronmy 5:2

"You shall not covet your neighbor's wife; and you shall not desire your neighbor's house, his field, his male servant, his female servant, his ox, his donkey, or anything that is your neighbor's."

James 3:16

"For where envy and self-seeking exist, confusion and every evil thing are there."

Psalms 37:7

"Rest in the Lord, and wait patiently for Him; Do not fret because of him who prospers in his way, Because of the man who brings wicked schemes to pass."

Psalms 10:3

"For the wicked boasts of his heart's desire; He blesses the greedy and renounces the Lord."

Proverbs 3:31

"Do not envy the oppressor, And choose none of his ways; "

Proverbs 24:1

"Do not be envious of evil men, Nor desire to be with them; "

Proverbs 27:4

"Wrath is cruel and anger a torrent, But who is able to stand before jealousy? "

Galatians 5:26

"Let us not become conceited, provoking one another, envying one another."

Luke 12:22,23

"Then He said to His disciples, 'Therefore I say to you, do not worry about your life, what you will eat; nor about the body, what you will put on. Life is more than food, and the body is more than clothing.' "

James 3:14

"But if you have bitter envy and self-seeking in your hearts, do not boast and lie against the truth."

1 Corinthians 10:24

"Let no one seek his own, but each one the other's well-being."

Ecclesiates 4:4

"Again, I saw that for all toil and every skillful work a man is envied by his neighbor. This also is vanity and grasping for the wind."

Scriptures on Eternal Life

John 6:47

"Most assuredly, I say to you, he who believes in Me has everlasting life."

John 11:25, 26

"Jesus said to her, 'I am the resurrection and the life. He who believes in Me, though he may die, he shall live. And whoever lives and believes in Me shall never die. Do you believe this?' "

1 Corinthians 15:51-54

"Behold, I tell you a mystery: We shall not all sleep, but we shall all be changed in a moment, in the twinkling of an eye, at the last trumpet. For the trumpet will sound, and the dead will be raised incorruptible, and we shall be changed. For this corruptible must put on incorruption, and this mortal must put on immortality. So when this corruptible has put on incorruption, and this mortal has put on immortality, then shall be brought to pass the saying that is written: 'Death is swallowed up in victory.' "

1 John 2:25

"And this is the promise that He has promised us – eternal life."

1 Corinthians 15:21

"For since by man came death, by Man also came the resurrection of the dead."

1 John 5:13

"These things I have written to you who believe in the name of the Son of God, that you may know that you have eternal life, and that you may continue to believe in the name of the Son of God."

John 5:28 , 29

"Do not marvel at this; for the hour is coming in which all who are in the graves will hear His voice and come forth – those who have done good, to the resurrection of life, and those who have done evil, to the resurrection of condemnation."

1 Thessalonians 4:16

"For the Lord Himself will descend from heaven with a shout, with the voice of an archangel, and with the trumpet of God. And the dead in Christ will rise first."

Revelation 7:15-17

"Therefore they are before the throne of God, and serve Him day and night in His temple. And He who sits on the throne will dwell among them. They shall neither hunger anymore nor thirst anymore; the sun shall not strike them, nor any heat; for the Lamb who is in the midst of the throne will shepherd them and lead them to living fountains of waters. And God will wipe away every tear from their eyes"

John 3:16

"For God so loved the world that He gave His only begotten Son, that whoever believes in Him should not perish but have everlasting life."

1 Corinthians 15:42 – 44

"So also is the resurrection of the dead. The body is sown in corruption, it is raised in incorruption. It is sown in dishonor, it is raised in glory. It is sown in weakness, it is raised in power. It is sown a natural body, it is raised a spiritual body. There is a natural body, and there is a spiritual body."

Romans 8:11

"But if the Spirit of Him who raised Jesus from the dead dwells in you, He who raised Christ from the dead will also give life to your mortal bodies (emphasis added) through His Spirit who dwells in you."

Revelation 21:4

"And God will wipe away every tear from their eyes; there shall be no more death, nor sorrow, nor crying. There shall be no more pain, for the former things have passed away."

Romans 6:23

"For the wages of sin is death, but the gift of God is eternal life in Christ Jesus our Lord."

Job 19:26 , 27

"And after my skin is destroyed, this I know, That in my flesh I shall see God, Whom I shall see for myself, And my eyes shall behold, and not another. How my heart yearns within me!"

Galatians 6:8

"For he who sows to his flesh will of the flesh reap corruption, but he who sows to the Spirit will of the Spirit reap everlasting life."

Daniel 12:2

"And many of those who sleep in the dust of the earth shall awake, Some to everlasting life, Some to shame and everlasting contempt."

Isaiah 26:19

"Your dead shall live; Together with my dead body they shall arise. Awake and sing, you who dwell in dust; For your dew is like the dew of herbs, And the earth shall cast out the dead."

Psalms 16:10

"For You will not leave my soul in Sheol, Nor will You allow Your Holy One to see corruption."

2 Timothy 1:10

"but has now been revealed by the appearing of our Savior Jesus Christ, who has abolished death and brought life and immortality to light through the gospel"

1 John 5:11

"And this is the testimony: that God has given us eternal life, and this life is in His Son."

2 Corinthians 5:1

"For we know that if our earthly house, this tent, is destroyed, we have a building from God, a house not made with hands, eternal in the heavens."

John 14:2, 3

"In My Father's house are many mansions; if it were not so, I would have told you. I go to prepare a place for you. And if I go and prepare a place for you, I will come again and receive you to Myself; that where I am, there you may be also."

John 6:39, 40

"This is the will of the Father who sent Me, that of all He has given Me I should lose nothing, but should raise it up at the last day. And this is the will of Him who sent Me, that everyone who sees the Son and believes in Him may have everlasting life; and I will raise him up at the last day."

Luke 20:35, 36

"But those who are counted worthy to attain that age, and the resurrection from the dead, neither marry nor are given in marriage; nor can they die anymore, for they are equal to the angels and are sons of God, being sons of the resurrection."

John 10:27, 28

"My sheep hear My voice, and I know them, and they follow Me. And I give them eternal life, and they shall never perish; neither shall anyone snatch them out of My hand."

John 6:54

"Whoever eats My flesh and drinks My blood has eternal life, and I will raise him up at the last day." (Metaphoric meaning)

Scriptures on Faith

Psalms 31:23

"Oh, love the Lord, all you His saints! For the Lord preserves the faithful, And fully repays the proud person."

Matthew 17:20

So Jesus said to them, 'Because of your unbelief; for assuredly, I say to you, if you have faith as a mustard seed, you will say to this mountain, 'Move from here to there,' and it will move; and nothing will be impossible for you.' "

Hebrews 11:1

"Now faith is the substance of things hoped for, the evidence of things not seen."

Romans 10:17

"So then faith comes by hearing, and hearing by the word of God."

Galatians 5:6

"For in Christ Jesus neither circumcision nor uncircumcision avails anything, but faith working through love."

2 Corinthians 5:7

"For we walk by faith, not by sight."

Mark 11:23,24

"For assuredly, I say to you, whoever says to this mountain, 'Be removed and be cast into the sea,' and does not doubt in his heart, but believes that those things he says will be done, he will have whatever he says. Therefore I say to you, whatever things you ask when you pray, believe that you receive them, and you will have them."

Hebrews 11:6

"But without faith it is impossible to please Him, for he who comes to God must believe that He is, and that He is a rewarder of those who diligently seek Him. "

James 1:5,6

"If any of you lacks wisdom, let him ask of God, who gives to all liberally and without reproach, and it will be given to him. But let him ask in faith, with no doubting, for he who doubts is like a wave of the sea driven and tossed by the wind."

Colossians 2:6,7

"As you therefore have received Christ Jesus the Lord, so walk in Him, rooted and built up in Him and established in the faith, as you have been taught, abounding in it with thanksgiving. "

Ephesians 2:8

"For by grace you have been saved through faith, and that not of yourselves; it is the gift of God,"

Galatians 3:26

"For you are all sons of God through faith in Christ Jesus."

2 Timothy 3:14,15

"But you must continue in the things which you have learned and been assured of, knowing from whom you have learned them, and that from childhood you have known the Holy Scriptures, which are able to make you wise for salvation through faith which is in Christ Jesus."

1 Corinthians 16:13

"Watch, stand fast in the faith, be brave, be strong."

Galatians 5:22

"But the fruit of the Spirit is love, joy, peace, longsuffering, kindness, goodness, faithfulness,"

Galatians 2:20

"I have been crucified with Christ; it is no longer I who live, but Christ lives in me; and the life which I now live in the flesh I live by faith in the Son of God, who loved me and gave Himself for me."

Ephesians 3:17-19

"that Christ may dwell in your hearts through faith; that you, being rooted and grounded in love, may be able to comprehend with all the saints what is the width and length and depth and height – to know the love of Christ which passes knowledge; that you may be filled with all the fullness of God."

Hebrews 12:1,2

"Therefore we also, since we are surrounded by so great a cloud of witnesses, let us lay aside every weight, and the sin which so easily ensnares us, and let us run with endurance the race that is set before us, looking unto Jesus, the author and finisher of our faith, who for the joy that was set before Him endured the cross, despising the shame, and has sat down at the right hand of the throne of God."

Scriptures on Fasting

Matthew 6:16

"Moreover, when you fast, do not be like the hypocrites, with a sad countenance. For they disfigure their faces that they may appear to men to be fasting. Assuredly, I say to you, they have their reward."

Matthew 6:17, 18

"But you, when you fast, anoint your head and wash your face, so that you do not appear to men to be fasting, but to your Father who is in the secret place; and your Father who sees in secret will reward you openly."

Isaiah 58:4-11

"Indeed you fast for strife and debate, And to strike with the fist of wickedness. You will not fast as you do this day, To make your voice heard on high.

Is it a fast that I have chosen, A day for a man to afflict his soul? Is it to bow down his head like a bulrush, And to spread out sackcloth and ashes? Would you call this a fast, And an acceptable day to the Lord?

'Is this not the fast that I have chosen: To loose the bonds of wickedness, To undo the heavy burdens, To let the oppressed go free, And that you break every yoke?

Is it not to share your bread with the hungry, And that you bring to your house the poor who are cast out; When you see the naked, that you cover him, And not hide yourself from your own flesh?

Then your light shall break forth like the morning, Your healing shall spring forth speedily, And your righteousness shall go before you; The glory of the Lord shall be your rear guard.

Then you shall call, and the Lord will answer; You shall cry, and He will say, 'Here I am.' 'If you take away the yoke from your midst, The pointing of the finger, and speaking wickedness,

If you extend your soul to the hungry And satisfy the afflicted soul, Then your light shall dawn in the darkness, And your darkness shall be as the noonday.

The Lord will guide you continually, And satisfy your soul in drought, And strengthen your bones; You shall be like a watered garden, And like a spring of water, whose waters do not fail."

Jeremiah 36:6

"You go, therefore, and read from the scroll which you have written at my instruction, the words of the Lord, in the hearing of the people in the Lord's house on the day of fasting. And you shall also read them in the hearing of all Judah who come from their cities."

Nehemiah 9:1

"Now on the twenty-fourth day of this month the children of Israel were assembled with fasting, in sackcloth, and with dust on their heads."

Daniel 9:3

"Then I set my face toward the Lord God to make request by prayer and supplications, with fasting, sackcloth, and ashes."

Joel 2:12

"Now, therefore," says the Lord, Turn to Me with all your heart, With fasting, with weeping, and with mourning."

Luke 2:37

"and this woman was a widow of about eighty-four years, who did not depart from the temple, but served God with fastings and prayers night and day."

Acts 13:2

"As they ministered to the Lord and fasted, the Holy Spirit said, "Now separate to Me Barnabas and Saul for the work to which I have called them."

Acts 14:23

"So when they had appointed elders in every church, and prayed with fasting, they commended them to the Lord in whom they had believed."

Scriptures on Fear and Worry

Romans 8:37- 39

"Yet in all these things we are more than conquerors through Him who loved us. For I am persuaded that neither death nor life, nor angels nor principalities nor powers, nor things present nor things to come, nor height nor depth, nor any other created thing, shall be able to separate us from the love of God which is in Christ Jesus our Lord."

Psalms 27:1

"The Lord is my light and my salvation; Whom shall I fear? The Lord is the strength of my life; Of whom shall I be afraid?"

Psalms 27:3

"Though an army may encamp against me, My heart shall not fear; Though war may rise against me, In this I will be confident. "

Isaiah 41:13

"For I, the Lord your God, will hold your right hand, Saying to you, 'Fear not, I will help you.'"

Proverbs 1:33

"But whoever listens to me will dwell safely, And will be secure, without fear of evil."

Luke 12:32

"Do not fear, little flock, for it is your Father's good pleasure to give you the kingdom."

Matthew 10:28

"And do not fear those who kill the body but cannot kill the soul. But rather fear Him who is able to destroy both soul and body in hell."

Proverbs 3:25,26

"Do not be afraid of sudden terror, Nor of trouble from the wicked when it comes; For the Lord will be your confidence, And will keep your foot from being caught."

2 Timothy 1:7

"For God has not given us a spirit of fear, but of power and of love and of a sound mind."

Isaiah 14:3

"It shall come to pass in the day the Lord gives you rest from your sorrow, and from your fear and the hard bondage in which you were made to serve,"

Proverbs 3:24

"When you lie down, you will not be afraid; Yes, you will lie down and your sleep will be sweet. "

1 Peter 3:12-14

"For the eyes of the Lord are on the righteous, And His ears are open to their prayers; But the face of the Lord is against those who do evil. And who is he who will harm you if you become followers of what is good? But even if you should suffer for righteousness' sake, you are blessed. And do not be afraid of their threats, nor be troubled."

Isaiah 54:14

"In righteousness you shall be established; You shall be far from oppression, for you shall not fear; And from terror, for it shall not come near you."

Hebrews 13:6

"So we may boldly say: 'The Lord is my helper; I will not fear. What can man do to me?' "

Psalms 46:1

"God is our refuge and strength, A very present help in trouble."

Proverbs 29:25

"The fear of man brings a snare, But whoever trusts in the Lord shall be safe."

Psalms 91:4-6

"He shall cover you with His feathers, And under His wings you shall take refuge; His truth shall be your shield and buckler. You shall not be afraid of the terror by night, Nor of the arrow that flies by day, Nor of the pestilence that walks in darkness, Nor of the destruction that lays waste at noonday."

Isaiah 54:4

"Do not fear, for you will not be ashamed; Neither be disgraced, for you will not be put to shame; For you will forget the shame of your youth, And will not remember the reproach of your widowhood anymore. "

Isaiah 43:2

"When you pass through the waters, I will be with you; And through the rivers, they shall not overflow you. When you walk through the fire, you shall not be burned, Nor shall the flame scorch you. "

John 14:27

"Peace I leave with you, My peace I give to you; not as the world gives do I give to you. Let not your heart be troubled, neither let it be afraid."

Psalms 23:4,5

"Yea, though I walk through the valley of the shadow of death, I will fear no evil; For You are with me; Your rod and Your staff, they comfort me. You prepare a table before me in the presence of my enemies; You anoint my head with oil; My cup runs over."

Luke 12:7

"But the very hairs of your head are all numbered. Do not fear therefore; you are of more value than many sparrows."

Luke 8:50

"But when Jesus heard it, He answered him, saying, "Do not be afraid; only believe, and she will be made well.""

Scriptures on Food and Clothing

Joel 2:26

"You shall eat in plenty and be satisfied, And praise the name of the Lord your God, Who has dealt wondrously with you; And My people shall never be put to shame."

Psalms 147:14

"He makes peace in your borders, And fills you with the finest wheat. "

Psalms 111:5

"He has given food to those who fear Him; He will ever be mindful of His covenant."

Proverbs 13:25

"The righteous eats to the satisfying of his soul, But the stomach of the wicked shall be in want."

Psalms 132:15

" I will abundantly bless her provision; I will satisfy her poor with bread."

Matthew 6:31- 34

"Therefore do not worry, saying, 'What shall we eat?' or 'What shall we drink?' or 'What shall we wear?' For after all these things the Gentiles (heathen) seek. For your heavenly Father knows that you need all these things. But seek first the kingdom of God and His righteousness, and all these things shall be added to you. Therefore do not worry about tomorrow, for tomorrow will worry about its own things. Sufficient for the day is its own trouble."

Scriptures on Forgiveness

Matthew 5:44,45

"But I say to you, love your enemies, bless those who curse you, do good to those who hate you, and pray for those who spitefully use you and persecute you, that you may be sons of your Father in heaven; for He makes His sun rise on the evil and on the good, and sends rain on the just and on the unjust."

1 John 1:9

" If we confess our sins, He is faithful and just to forgive us our sins and to cleanse us from all unrighteousness."

Mark 11:25,26

"And whenever you stand praying, if you have anything against anyone, forgive him, that your Father in heaven may also forgive you your trespasses. But if you do not forgive, neither will your Father in heaven forgive your trespasses."

Matthew 6:14

"For if you forgive men their trespasses, your heavenly Father will also forgive you."

Romans 12:20

"Therefore ' If your enemy is hungry, feed him; If he is thirsty, give him a drink; For in so doing you will heap coals of fire on his head."

Luke 6:35-38

"But love your enemies, do good, and lend, hoping for nothing in return; and your reward will be great, and you will be sons of the Most High. For He is kind to the unthankful and evil. Therefore be merciful, just as your Father also is merciful. Judge not, and you shall not be judged. Condemn not, and you shall not be condemned. Forgive, and you will be forgiven. Give, and it will be given to you: good measure, pressed down, shaken together, and running over will be put into your bosom. For with the same measure that you use, it will be measured back to you."

Proverbs 20:22

"Do not say, "I will recompense evil"; Wait for the Lord, and He will save you."

Scriptures on Freedom from Sin

Ezekiel 36:25,26

"Then I will sprinkle clean water on you, and you shall be clean; I will cleanse you from all your filthiness and from all your idols. I will give you a new heart and put a new spirit within you; I will take the heart of stone out of your flesh and give you a heart of flesh."

Acts 10:43

"To Him all the prophets witness that, through His name, whoever believes in Him will receive remission of sins."

Romans 6:6,7

"knowing this, that our old man was crucified with Him, that the body of sin might be done away with, that we should no longer be slaves of sin. For he who has died has been freed from sin."

2 Corinthians 5:17

"Therefore, if anyone is in Christ, he is a new creation; old things have passed away; behold, all things have become new."

Romans 6:1,2

"What shall we say then? Shall we continue in sin that grace may abound? Certainly not! How shall we who died to sin live any longer in it?"

Romans 6:11

"Likewise you also, reckon yourselves to be dead indeed to sin, but alive to God in Christ Jesus our Lord."

Romans 6:14

"For sin shall not have dominion over you, for you are not under law but under grace."

Scriptures on Fruitfulness

John 15:1- 5

"I am the true vine, and My Father is the vinedresser. Every branch in Me that does not bear fruit He takes away; and every branch that bears fruit He prunes, that it may bear more fruit. You are already clean because of the word which I have spoken to you. Abide in Me, and I in you. As the branch cannot bear fruit of itself, unless it abides in the vine, neither can you, unless you abide in Me. I am the vine, you are the branches. He who abides in Me, and I in him, bears much fruit; for without Me you can do nothing."

Matthew 7:15-17

"Beware of false prophets, who come to you in sheep's clothing, but inwardly they are ravenous wolves. You will know them by their fruits. Do men gather grapes from thornbushes or figs from thistles? Even so, every good tree bears good fruit, but a bad tree bears bad fruit."

Psalms 1:3

"He shall be like a tree Planted by the rivers of water, That brings forth its fruit in its season, Whose leaf also shall not wither; And whatever he does shall prosper."

Psalms 92:14

"They shall still bear fruit in old age; They shall be fresh and flourishing,"

Hosea 14:5

"I will be like the dew to Israel; He shall grow like the lily, And lengthen his roots like Lebanon."

2 Peter 1:8

"For if these things are yours and abound, you will be neither barren nor unfruitful in the knowledge of our Lord Jesus Christ."

Jeremiah 31:12

"Therefore they shall come and sing in the height of Zion, Streaming to the goodness of the Lord – For wheat and new wine and oil, For the young of the flock and the herd; Their souls shall be like a well-watered garden, And they shall sorrow no more at all."

Scriptures for Giving

Psalms 41:1,2

"Blessed is he who considers the poor; The Lord will deliver him in time of trouble. The Lord will preserve him and keep him alive, And he will be blessed on the earth; You will not deliver him to the will of his enemies."

Proverbs 19:17

"He who has pity on the poor lends to the Lord, And He will pay back what he has given."

Luke 14:13,14

"But when you give a feast, invite the poor, the maimed, the lame, the blind. And you will be blessed, because they cannot repay you; for you shall be repaid at the resurrection of the just."

Luke 12:33

"Sell what you have and give alms; provide yourselves money bags which do not grow old, a treasure in the heavens that does not fail, where no thief approaches nor moth destroys."

Proverbs 14:21

"He who despises his neighbor sins; But he who has mercy on the poor, happy is he."

Ecclesiastes 11:1

"Cast your bread upon the waters, For you will find it after many days."

Psalms 112:9

"He has dispersed abroad, He has given to the poor; His righteousness endures forever; His horn will be exalted with honor."

Proverbs 22:9

"He who has a generous eye will be blessed, For he gives of his bread to the poor."

Luke 6:38

"Give, and it will be given to you: good measure, pressed down, shaken together, and running over will be put into your bosom. For with the same measure that you use, it will be measured back to you."

Proverbs 28:27

"He who gives to the poor will not lack, But he who hides his eyes will have many curses."

2 Corinthians 9:7

"So let each one give as he purposes in his heart, not grudgingly or of necessity; for God loves a cheerful giver."

Proverbs 11:24,25

"There is one who scatters, yet increases more; And there is one who withholds more than is right, But it leads to poverty. The generous soul will be made rich, And he who waters will also be watered himself."

Psalms 37:25,26

"I have been young, and now am old; Yet I have not seen the righteous forsaken, Nor his descendants begging bread. He is ever merciful, and lends; And his descendants are blessed."

Isaiah 58:10

"If you extend your soul to the hungry And satisfy the afflicted soul, Then your light shall dawn in the darkness, And your darkness shall be as the noonday."

1 Timothy 6:17,18

"Command those who are rich in this present age not to be haughty, nor to trust in uncertain riches but in the living God, who gives us richly all things to enjoy. Let them do good, that they be rich in good works, ready to give, willing to share..."

Isaiah 58:7,8

"Is it not to share your bread with the hungry, And that you bring to your house the poor who are cast out; When you see the naked, that you cover him, And not hide yourself from your own flesh? Then your light shall break forth like the morning, Your healing shall spring forth speedily, And your righteousness shall go before you; The glory of the Lord shall be your rear guard."

Deuteronomy 14:29

"And the Levite, because he has no portion nor inheritance with you, and the stranger and the fatherless and the widow who are within your gates, may come and eat and be satisfied, that the Lord your God may bless you in all the work of your hand which you do."

Mark 10:21

"Then Jesus, looking at him, loved him, and said to him, 'One thing you lack: Go your way, sell whatever you have and give to the poor, and you will have treasure in heaven; and come, take up the cross, and follow Me.' "

Matthew 6:1- 4

"Take heed that you do not do your charitable deeds before men, to be seen by them. Otherwise you have no reward from your Father in heaven. Therefore, when you do a charitable deed, do not sound a trumpet before you as the hypocrites do in the synagogues and in the streets, that they may have glory from men. Assuredly, I say to you, they have their reward. But when you do a charitable deed, do not let your left hand know what your right hand is doing, that your charitable deed may be in secret; and your Father who sees in secret will Himself reward you openly."

Scriptures on God's Correction

Proverbs 3:12

"For whom the Lord loves He corrects, Just as a father the son in whom he delights."

Job 5:17, 1

"Behold, happy is the man whom God corrects; Therefore do not despise the chastening of the Almighty. For He bruises, but He binds up; He wounds, but His hands make whole."

Psalms 94:12, 13

"Blessed is the man whom You instruct, O Lord, And teach out of Your law, That You may give him rest from the days of adversity, Until the pit is dug for the wicked."

1 Corinthians 11:32

"But when we are judged, we are chastened by the Lord, that we may not be condemned with the world."

2 Corinthians 4:16 ,17

"Therefore we do not lose heart. Even though our outward man is perishing, yet the inward man is being renewed day by day. For our light affliction, which is but for a moment, is working for us a far more exceeding and eternal weight of glory,"

Hebrews 12:6, 7

"For whom the Lord loves He chastens, And scourges every son whom He receives. If you endure chastening, God deals with you as with sons; for what son is there whom a father does not chasten?"

Hebrews 12:10, 11

"For they indeed for a few days chastened us as seemed best to them, but He for our profit, that we may be partakers of His holiness. Now no chastening seems to be joyful for the present, but painful; nevertheless, afterward it yields the peaceable fruit of righteousness to those who have been trained by it.

Scriptures on God's Protection

Psalms 27:1- 5

"The Lord is my light and my salvation; Whom shall I fear? The Lord is the strength of my life; Of whom shall I be afraid? When the wicked came against me To eat up my flesh, My enemies and foes, They stumbled and fell. Though an army may encamp against me, My heart shall not fear; Though war may rise against me, In this I will be confident.

One thing I have desired of the Lord, That will I seek: That I may dwell in the house of the Lord All the days of my life, To behold the beauty of the Lord, And to inquire in His temple.

For in the time of trouble He shall hide me in His pavilion; In the secret place of His tabernacle He shall hide me; He shall set me high upon a rock."

Proverbs 3:24

"When you lie down, you will not be afraid; Yes, you will lie down and your sleep will be sweet."

Proverbs 18:10

"The name of the Lord is a strong tower; The righteous run to it and are safe."

Job 5:22

"You shall laugh at destruction and famine, And you shall not be afraid of the beasts of the earth."

Psalms 112:7

"He will not be afraid of evil tidings; His heart is steadfast, trusting in the Lord."

Psalms 91:9,10

"Because you have made the Lord, who is my refuge, Even the Most High, your dwelling place, No evil shall befall you, Nor shall any plague come near your dwelling;"

Isaiah 43:1,2

"...Fear not, for I have redeemed you; I have called you by your name; You are Mine. When you pass through the waters, I will be with you; And through the rivers, they shall not overflow you. When you walk through the fire, you shall not be burned, Nor shall the flame scorch you."

Ezekiel 34:28

"And they shall no longer be a prey for the nations, nor shall beasts of the land devour them; but they shall dwell safely, and no one shall make them afraid."

Proverbs 1:33

"But whoever listens to me will dwell safely, And will be secure, without fear of evil."

Job 11:18,19

"And you would be secure, because there is hope; Yes, you would dig around you, and take your rest in safety. You would also lie down, and no one would make you afraid; Yes, many would court your favor."

Psalms 121:7,8

"The Lord shall preserve you from all evil; He shall preserve your soul. The Lord shall preserve your going out and your coming in From this time forth, and even forevermore."

1 Peter 3:13

"And who is he who will harm you if you become followers of what is good?"

Deuteronomy 33:12

"Of Benjamin he said: 'The beloved of the Lord shall dwell in safety by Him, Who shelters him all the day long; And he shall dwell between His shoulders."

Psalms 4:8

"I will both lie down in peace, and sleep; For You alone, O Lord, make me dwell in safety."

Scriptures on Gossip and Rumors

Leviticus 19:16

"You shall not go about as a talebearer among your people; nor shall you take a stand against the life of your XXXeighbor: I am the Lord."

Proverbs 18:8

"The words of a talebearer are like tasty trifles (wounds), And they go down into the inmost body."

Proverbs 20:19

"He who goes about as a talebearer reveals secrets; Therefore do not associate with one who flatters with his lips."

Proverbs 11:13

"A talebearer reveals secrets, But he who is of a faithful spirit conceals a matter."

Proverbs 16:28

"A perverse man sows strife, And a whisperer separates the best of friends."

Psalms 52:2

"Your tongue devises destruction, Like a sharp razor, working deceitfully."

Proverbs 25:23

"The north wind brings forth rain, And a backbiting tongue an angry countenance."

Proverbs 26:20,21

"Where there is no wood, the fire goes out; And where there is no talebearer, strife ceases. As charcoal is to burning coals, and wood to fire, So is a contentious man to kindle strife."

Psalms 34:13

"Keep your tongue from evil, And your lips from speaking deceit."

Scriptures on Growing in Grace

John 15:8

"By this My Father is glorified, that you bear much fruit; so you will be My disciples."

Philippians 1:9

"And this I pray, that your love may abound still more and more in knowledge and all discernment,"

2 Thessalonians 1:3

"We are bound to thank God always for you, brethren, as it is fitting, because your faith grows exceedingly, and the love of every one of you all abounds toward each other,"

1 Thessalonians 4:1

"Finally then, brethren, we urge and exhort in the Lord Jesus that you should abound more and more, just as you received from us how you ought to walk and to please God;"

Philippians 1:11

"being filled with the fruits of righteousness which are by Jesus Christ, to the glory and praise of God."

2 Peter 1:5

"But also for this very reason, giving all diligence, add to your faith virtue, to virtue knowledge,"

Job 17:9

"Yet the righteous will hold to his way, And he who has clean hands will be stronger and stronger."

2 Corinthians 3:18

"But we all, with unveiled face, beholding as in a mirror the glory of the Lord, are being transformed into the same image from glory to glory, just as by the Spirit of the Lord."

Psalms 138:8

"The Lord will perfect that which concerns me; Your mercy, O Lord, endures forever; Do not forsake the works of Your hands."

Colossians 1:6

"which has come to you, as it has also in all the world, and is bringing forth fruit, as it is also among you since the day you heard and knew the grace of God in truth;"

Philippians 3:14-16

"I press toward the goal for the prize of the upward call of God in Christ Jesus. Therefore let us, as many as are mature, have this mind; and if in anything you think otherwise, God will reveal even this to you. Nevertheless, to the degree that we have already attained, let us walk by the same rule, let us be of the same mind"

Proverbs 4:18

"But the path of the just is like the shining sun, That shines ever brighter unto the perfect day."

Scriptures on Guidance

Isaiah 30:21

"Your ears shall hear a word behind you, saying, 'This is the way, walk in it,' Whenever you turn to the right hand Or whenever you turn to the left."

Psalms 48:14

"For this is God, Our God forever and ever; He will be our guide Even to death."

Proverbs 16:9

"A man's heart plans his way, But the Lord directs his steps."

Psalms 37:23

"The steps of a good man are ordered by the Lord, And He delights in his way."

Isaiah 28:26

"For He instructs him in right judgment, His God teaches him."

Proverbs 11:5

"The righteousness of the blameless will direct his way aright, But the wicked will fall by his own wickedness."

Proverbs 3:6

"In all your ways acknowledge Him, And He shall direct your paths."

Isaiah 42:16

"I will bring the blind by a way they did not know; I will lead them in paths they have not known. I will make darkness light before them, And crooked places straight. These things I will do for them, And not forsake them."

Psalms 73:23,24

"Nevertheless I am continually with You; You hold me by my right hand. You will guide me with Your counsel, And afterward receive me to glory. "

Psalms 32:8

"I will instruct you and teach you in the way you should go; I will guide you with My eye."

Scriptures on Healing

James 5:14-16

"Is anyone among you sick? Let him call for the elders of the church, and let them pray over him, anointing him with oil in the name of the Lord. And the prayer of faith will save the sick,and if he has committed sins, he will be forgiven."

Psalm 105:37

"He also brought them out with silver and gold, And there was none feeble among his tribes."

1 Peter 2:24

"Who himself bore our sins in his own body on the tree, that we, having died to sins, might live for righteousness-by whose stripes you were healed."

Isaiah 53:4-5

"Surely he has borne our griefs and carried our sorrows; Yet we esteemed him stricken, smitten by God, and afflicted. But he was wounded for our transgressions, He was crushed for our iniquities; The chastisement for our peace was upon him, And by his stripes we are healed."

Jeremiah 30:17

"For I will restore health to you and heal you of your wounds, says the Lord."

Psalm 118:17

"I shall not die but live and declare the works of the Lord."

Proverbs 4:20-24

"My son, give attention to my words; Incline your ear to my sayings. Do not let them depart from your eyes; Keep them in the midst of your heart; For they are life to those who find them, And health to all their flesh. Keep your heart with all diligence, for out of it spring the issues of life. And put away from you a deceitful mouth, and out perverse lips far from you."

Psalm 107:19-21

"Then they cried out to the Lord in their trouble, and he saved them out of their distresses. He sent his word and healed them from their destruct ions Oh that men would give thanks to the Lord for his goodness, and for his wonderful works to the children of men."

3 John 2

"Beloved I pray that you may prosper in all things and be in health, just as your soul prospers."

Deuteronomy 30:19-20

"I call heaven and earth as witnesses today against you, that I have set before you life and death, blessings and cursing; therefore choose life, that both you and your descendants may live; that you may love the lord your God, that you may obey him, for he is your life and the length of your days; and that you may dwell in the land which the Lord swore to your fathers, to Abraham, Isaac, and Jacob, to give them."

Deuteronomy 7:14-15

"You shall be blessed above all peoples; there shall not be a male or female barren among you or among your livestock. And the Lord will take away from you all sickness, and will afflict you with none of the terrible diseases of Egypt which you have known, but will lay them on a;; those who hate you."

Exodus 15:26

"If you diligently heed the voice of the Lord your God and do what is right in his sight, give ear to his commandments and keep all his statutes, I will put none of the diseases on you which I have brought on the Egyptians. For I am the Lord who heals you."

Exodus 23:25

"So you shall serve the Lord you God and he will bless your bread and your water. And I will take sickness away from the midst of you."

Matthew:8:16-17

"When evening had come, they brought to him many who were demon-possessed. And he cast out the spirits with a word, and healed all who were sick, that it might be fulfilled which was spoken by Isaiah the prophet,, saying "He himself took our infirmities and bore our sicknesses"

Scriptures on Help in Trouble

John 16:33

"These things I have spoken to you, that in Me you may have peace. In the world you will have tribulation; but be of good cheer, I have overcome the world."

Psalms 37:39

"But the salvation of the righteous is from the Lord; He is their strength in the time of trouble."

Psalms 146:8

"The Lord opens the eyes of the blind; The Lord raises those who are bowed down; The Lord loves the righteous."

Nahum 1:7

"The Lord is good, A stronghold in the day of trouble; And He knows those who trust in Him. "

Psalm 37:24

"Though he fall, he shall not be utterly cast down; For the Lord upholds him with His hand. "

Psalms 32:7

"You are my hiding place; You shall preserve me from trouble; You shall surround me with songs of deliverance. Selah"

Psalms 71:20

"You, who have shown me great and severe troubles, Shall revive me again, And bring me up again from the depths of the earth."

Psalms 42:11

"Why are you cast down, O my soul? And why are you disquieted within me? Hope in God; For I shall yet praise Him, The help of my countenance and my God."

Psalms 73:26

"My flesh and my heart fail; But God is the strength of my heart and my portion forever."

Psalms 91:10, 11

"No evil shall befall you, Nor shall any plague come near your dwelling; For He shall give His angels charge over you, To keep you in all your ways."

Psalms 126:5, 6

"Those who sow in tears Shall reap in joy. He who continually goes forth weeping, Bearing seed for sowing, Shall doubtless come again with rejoicing, Bringing his sheaves with him."

Psalms 31:23

"Oh, love the Lord, all you His saints! For the Lord preserves the faithful, And fully repays the proud person."

Psalms 68:13

"Though you lie down among the sheepfolds, You will be like the wings of a dove covered with silver, And her feathers with yellow gold."

Job 8:20, 21

"Behold, God will not cast away the blameless, Nor will He uphold the evildoers. He will yet fill your mouth with laughing, And your lips with rejoicing."

Psalms 22:24

"For He has not despised nor abhorred the affliction of the afflicted; Nor has He hidden His face from Him; But when He cried to Him, He heard. "

Job 5:19 – 23

"He shall deliver you in six troubles, Yes, in seven no evil shall touch you. In famine He shall redeem you from death, And in war from the power of the sword. You shall be hidden from the scourge of the tongue, And you shall not be afraid of destruction when it comes. You shall laugh at destruction and famine, And you shall not be afraid of the beasts of the earth. For you shall have a covenant with the stones of the field, And the beasts of the field shall be at peace with you."

Psalms 22:24

"For He has not despised nor abhorred the affliction of the afflicted; Nor has He hidden His face from Him; But when He cried to Him, He heard."

Psalms 9:9

"The Lord also will be a refuge for the oppressed, A refuge in times of trouble."

Psalms 138:7

"Though I walk in the midst of trouble, You will revive me; You will stretch out Your hand Against the wrath of my enemies, And Your right hand will save me."

Psalm 18:28

"For You will light my lamp; The Lord my God will enlighten my darkness."

Psalms 34:19

"Many are the afflictions of the righteous, But the Lord delivers him out of them all."

Lamentations 3:31- 33

"For the Lord will not cast off forever. Though He causes grief, Yet He will show compassion According to the multitude of His mercies. For He does not afflict willingly, Nor grieve the children of men."

Psalms 18:2

"The Lord is my rock and my fortress and my deliverer; My God, my strength, in whom I will trust; My shield and the horn of my salvation, my stronghold."

Micah 7:8,9

"Do not rejoice over me, my enemy; When I fall, I will arise; When I sit in darkness, The Lord will be a light to me. I will bear the indignation of the Lord, Because I have sinned against Him, Until He pleads my case And executes justice for me. He will bring me forth to the light; I will see His righteousness."

Scriptures on the Holy Spirit

John 14:16,17

"And I will pray the Father, and He will give you another Helper, that He may abide with you forever – the Spirit of truth, whom the world cannot receive, because it neither sees Him nor knows Him; but you know Him, for He dwells with you and will be in you."

John 7: 38,39

"He who believes in Me, as the Scripture has said, out of his heart will flow rivers of living water. But this He spoke concerning the Spirit, whom those believing in Him would receive; for the Holy Spirit was not yet given, because Jesus was not yet glorified."

John 16:13

"However, when He, the Spirit of truth, has come, He will guide you into all truth; for He will not speak on His own authority, but whatever He hears He will speak; and He will tell you things to come."

Isaiah 59:21

" 'As for Me,' says the Lord, 'this is My covenant with them: My Spirit who is upon you, and My words which I have put in your mouth, shall not depart from your mouth, nor from the mouth of your descendants, nor from the mouth of your descendants' descendants,' says the Lord, 'from this time and forevermore. ' "

Luke 11:13

"If you then, being evil, know how to give good gifts to your children, how much more will your heavenly Father give the Holy Spirit to those who ask Him."

John 4:14

"but whoever drinks of the water that I shall give him will never thirst. But the water that I shall give him will become in him a fountain of water springing up into everlasting life."

Ezekiel 36:27

"I will put My Spirit within you and cause you to walk in My statutes, and you will keep My judgments and do them."

Galatians 3:14

"that the blessing of Abraham might come upon the Gentiles in Christ Jesus, that we might receive the promise of the Spirit through faith."

1 John 2:27

"But the anointing which you have received from Him abides in you, and you do not need that anyone teach you; but as the same anointing teaches you concerning all things, and is true, and is not a lie, and just as it has taught you, you will abide in Him."

Romans 8:26,27

"Likewise the Spirit also helps in our weaknesses. For we do not know what we should pray for as we ought, but the Spirit Himself makes intercession for us with groanings which cannot be uttered. Now He who searches the hearts knows what the mind of the Spirit is, because He makes intercession for the saints according to the will of God."

Romans 14:17

"for the kingdom of God is not eating and drinking, but righteousness and peace and joy in the Holy Spirit."

1 Corinthians 2:12

"Now we have received, not the spirit of the world, but the Spirit who is from God, that we might know the things that have been freely given to us by God."

Romans 8:15

"For you did not receive the spirit of bondage again to fear, but you received the Spirit of adoption by whom we cry out, 'Abba, Father.' "

Scriptures on Homosexuality

1 Corinthians 6:9, 10

"Do you not know that the unrighteous will not inherit the kingdom of God? Do not be deceived. Neither fornicators, nor idolaters, nor adulterers, nor homosexuals, nor sodomites, nor thieves, nor covetous, nor drunkards, nor revilers, nor extortioners will inherit the kingdom of God."

1 John 1:9

"If we confess our sins, He is faithful and just to forgive us our sins and to cleanse us from all unrighteousness."

Romans 1:26, 27

"For this reason God gave them up to vile passions. For even their women exchanged the natural use for what is against nature. Likewise also the men, leaving the natural use of the woman, burned in their lust for one another, men with men committing what is shameful, and receiving in themselves the penalty of their error which was due."

Jude 1:7

"as Sodom and Gomorrah, and the cities around them in a similar manner to these, having given themselves over to sexual immorality and gone after strange flesh, are set forth as an example, suffering the vengeance of eternal fire."

Mark 10:6-9

"But from the beginning of the creation, God 'made them male and female. 'For this reason a man shall leave his father and mother and be joined to his wife, and the two shall become one flesh'; then they are no longer two, but one flesh. Therefore what God has joined together, let not man separate."

Leviticus 18:22

"You shall not lie with a male as with a woman. It is an abomination."

Leviticus 20:13

"If a man lies with a male as he lies with a woman, both of them have committed an abomination. They shall surely be put to death. Their blood shall be upon them."

Genesis 19:4-8

"Now before they lay down, the men of the city, the men of Sodom, both old and young, all the people from every quarter, surrounded the house. And they called to Lot and said to him, 'Where are the men who came to you tonight? Bring them out to us that we may know them carnally.' So Lot went out to them through the doorway, shut the door behind him, and said, 'Please, my brethren, do not do so wickedly! See now, I have two daughters who have not known a man; please, let me bring them out to you, and you may do to them as you wish; only do nothing to these men, since this is the reason they have come under the shadow of my roof.' "

Scriptures on Honesty

Leviticus 19:11

"You shall not steal, nor deal falsely, nor lie to one another."

Micah 6:10-12

"Are there yet the treasures of wickedness In the house of the wicked, And the short measure that is an abomination? Shall I count pure those with the wicked scales, And with the bag of deceitful weights? For her rich men are full of violence, Her inhabitants have spoken lies, And their tongue is deceitful in their mouth."

Leviticus 19:35

"You shall do no injustice in judgment, in measurement of length, weight, or volume."

Proverbs 11:1

"Dishonest scales are an abomination to the Lord, But a just weight is His delight."

Deuteronomy 25:15,16

"You shall have a perfect and just weight, a perfect and just measure, that your days may be lengthened in the land which the Lord your God is giving you. For all who do such things, all who behave unrighteously, are an abomination to the Lord your God." 1

Thessalonians 4:6,7

"that no one should take advantage of and defraud his brother in this matter, because the Lord is the avenger of all such, as we also forewarned you and testified. For God did not call us to uncleanness, but in holiness."

Colossians 3:9,10

"Do not lie to one another, since you have put off the old man with his deeds, and have put on the new man who is renewed in knowledge according to the image of Him who created him,"

Psalms 37:21

"The wicked borrows and does not repay, But the righteous shows mercy and gives."

Proverbs 3:27

" Do not withhold good from those to whom it is due When it is in the power of your hand to do so."

Leviticus 25:14

"And if you sell anything to your neighbor or buy from your neighbor's hand, you shall not oppress one another."

Leviticus 25:17

"Therefore you shall not oppress one another, but you shall fear your God; for I am the Lord your God."

Proverbs 16:8

"Better is a little with righteousness, Than vast revenues without justice."

Isaiah 33:15,16

"He who walks righteously and speaks uprightly, He who despises the gain of oppressions, Who gestures with his hands, refusing bribes, Who stops his ears from hearing of bloodshed, And shuts his eyes from seeing evil: He will dwell on high; His place of defense will be the fortress of rocks; Bread will be given him, His water will be sure."

Scriptures on Hope

Psalms 42:11

"Why are you cast down, O my soul? And why are you disquieted within me? Hope in God; For I shall yet praise Him, The help of my countenance and my God."

1 Peter 1:21

"who through Him believe in God, who raised Him from the dead and gave Him glory, so that your faith and hope are in God."

1 Peter 1:13

"Therefore gird up the loins of your mind, be sober, and rest your hope fully upon the grace that is to be brought to you at the revelation of Jesus Christ;"

1 John 3:3

"And everyone who has this hope in Him purifies himself, just as He is pure."

Proverbs 14:32

"The wicked is banished in his wickedness, But the righteous has a refuge in his death. "

Colossians 1:5

"because of the hope which is laid up for you in heaven, of which you heard before in the word of the truth of the gospel"

Psalms 71:5

"For You are my hope, O Lord God; You are my trust from my youth."

1 Peter 1:3

"Blessed be the God and Father of our Lord Jesus Christ, who according to His abundant mercy has begotten us again to a living hope through the resurrection of Jesus Christ from the dead"

Proverbs 13:12

Hope deferred makes the heart sick, But when the desire comes, it is a tree of life.

Scriptures on Humiliation

Romans 10:11

"For the Scripture says, 'Whoever believes on Him will not be put to shame.' "

Psalms 119:6

"Then I would not be ashamed, When I look into all Your commandments."

Romans 5:5

"Now hope does not disappoint, because the love of God has been poured out in our hearts by the Holy Spirit who was given to us."

2 Timothy 1:12

"For this reason I also suffer these things; nevertheless I am not ashamed, for I know whom I have believed and am persuaded that He is able to keep what I have committed to Him until that Day."

Romans 9:33

"Behold, I lay in Zion a stumbling stone and rock of offense, And whoever believes on Him will not be put to shame." (Also see Isaiah 28:16 & Isaiah 8:14)

2 Timothy 2:15

"Be diligent to present yourself approved to God, a worker who does not need to be ashamed, rightly dividing the word of truth."

Psalms 119:80

"Let my heart be blameless regarding Your statutes, That I may not be ashamed."

1 Peter 4:16

"Yet if anyone suffers as a Christian, let him not be ashamed, but let him glorify God in this matter."

Scriptures on Humility

Proverbs 22:4

"By humility and the fear of the Lord Are riches and honor and life."

Matthew 18:4

"Therefore whoever humbles himself as this little child is the greatest in the kingdom of heaven."

Psalms 10:17

"Lord, You have heard the desire of the humble; You will prepare their heart; You will cause Your ear to hear"

Proverbs 29:23

"A man's pride will bring him low, But the humble in spirit will retain honor."

1 Peter 5:6

"Therefore humble yourselves under the mighty hand of God, that He may exalt you in due time"

Matthew 23:12

"And whoever exalts himself will be humbled, and he who humbles himself will be exalted."

Job 22:29

"When they cast you down, and you say, 'Exaltation will come!' Then He will save the humble person."

Proverbs 16:19

"Better to be of a humble spirit with the lowly, Than to divide the spoil with the proud."

Proverbs 3:34

"Surely He scorns the scornful, But gives grace to the humble."

Psalms 9:12

"When He avenges blood, He remembers them; He does not forget the cry of the humble."

James 4:6

"But He gives more grace. Therefore He says: 'God resists the proud, But gives grace to the humble.' "

Proverbs 15:33

"The fear of the Lord is the instruction of wisdom, And before honor is humility."

Scriptures on Increased Life

Psalms 91:16

"With long life I will satisfy him, And show him My salvation."

Proverbs 10:27

"The fear of the Lord prolongs days, But the years of the wicked will be shortened."

Deuteronomy 6:2

"that you may fear the Lord your God, to keep all His statutes and His commandments which I command you, you and your son and your grandson, all the days of your life, and that your days may be prolonged."

Proverbs 20:29

"The glory of young men is their strength, And the splendor of old men is their gray head."

Isaiah 46:4

"Even to your old age, I am He, And even to gray hairs I will carry you! I have made, and I will bear; Even I will carry, and will deliver you."

Job 11:17

"And your life would be brighter than noonday. Though you were dark, you would be like the morning."

Titus 2:1- 5

"But as for you, speak the things which are proper for sound doctrine: that the older men be sober, reverent, temperate, sound in faith, in love, in patience; the older women likewise, that they be reverent in behavior, not slanderers, not given to much wine, teachers of good things – that they admonish the young women to love their husbands, to love their children, to be discreet, chaste, homemakers, good, obedient to their own husbands, that the word of God may not be blasphemed."

Psalms 71:17,18

"O God, You have taught me from my youth; And to this day I declare Your wondrous works. Now also when I am old and grayheaded, O God, do not forsake me, Until I declare Your strength to this generation, Your power to everyone who is to come."

Job 12:12,13

"Wisdom is with aged men, And with length of days, understanding. 'With Him are wisdom and strength, He has counsel and understanding.' "

Job 5:26

"You shall come to the grave at a full age, As a sheaf of grain ripens in its season."

Psalms 71:9

"Do not cast me off in the time of old age; Do not forsake me when my strength fails."

Psalms 39:4,5

"Lord, make me to know my end, And what is the measure of my days, That I may know how frail I am. Indeed, You have made my days as handbreadths, And my age is as nothing before You; Certainly every man at his best state is but vapor. Selah "

Proverbs 9:11

"For by me your days will be multiplied, And years of life will be added to you."

Deuteronomy 5:33

"You shall walk in all the ways which the Lord your God has commanded you, that you may live and that it may be well with you, and that you may prolong your days in the land which you shall possess."

Proverbs 3:1,2

"My son, do not forget my law, But let your heart keep my commands; For length of days and long life And peace they will add to you."

Scriptures on Joy and Happiness

Psalms 126:5,6

"Those who sow in tears shall reap in joy. He who continually goes forth weeping, bearing seed for sowing, shall doubtless come again with rejoicing, bringing his sheaves with him."

Psalms 64:10

"The righteous shall be glad in the Lord, and trust in Him. And all the upright in heart shall glory."

Psalms 63:5

"My soul shall be satisfied as with marrow and fatness, And my mouth shall praise You with joyful lips."

Isaiah 55:12

"For you shall go out with joy, And be led out with peace; The mountains and the hills Shall break forth into singing before you, And all the trees of the field shall clap their hands."

Psalms 118:15

"The voice of rejoicing and salvation Is in the tents of the righteous; The right hand of the Lord does valiantly."

Psalms 4:7

"You have put gladness in my heart, More than in the season that their grain and wine increased."

Psalms 89:15,16

"Blessed are the people who know the joyful sound! They walk, O Lord, in the light of Your countenance. In Your name they rejoice all day long, And in Your righteousness they are exalted."

Psalms 97:11,12

"Light is sown for the righteous, And gladness for the upright in heart. Rejoice in the Lord, you righteous, And give thanks at the remembrance of His holy name."

Job 22:26

"For then you will have your delight in the Almighty, And lift up your face to God."

John 15:11

"These things I have spoken to you, that My joy may remain in you, and that your joy may be full."

Habakkuk 3:18

"Yet I will rejoice in the Lord, I will joy in the God of my salvation."

Isaiah 51:11

"So the ransomed of the Lord shall return, And come to Zion with singing, With everlasting joy on their heads. They shall obtain joy and gladness; Sorrow and sighing shall flee away."

Psalms 33:21

"For our heart shall rejoice in Him, Because we have trusted in His holy name."

1 Peter 1:8

"whom having not seen you love. Though now you do not see Him, yet believing, you rejoice with joy inexpressible and full of glory"

Isaiah 41:16

"You shall winnow them, the wind shall carry them away, And the whirlwind shall scatter them; You shall rejoice in the Lord, And glory in the Holy One of Israel."

Psalms 68:3

"But let the righteous be glad; Let them rejoice before God; Yes, let them rejoice exceedingly."

John 16:22

"Therefore you now have sorrow; but I will see you again and your heart will rejoice, and your joy no one will take from you."

Isaiah 61:10

"I will greatly rejoice in the Lord, My soul shall be joyful in my God; For He has clothed me with the garments of salvation, He has covered me with the robe of righteousness, As a bridegroom decks himself with ornaments, And as a bride adorns herself with her jewels."

Nehemiah 8:10

"Then he said to them, 'Go your way, eat the fat, drink the sweet, and send portions to those for whom nothing is prepared; for this day is holy to our Lord. Do not sorrow, for the joy of the Lord is your strength.' "

Scriptures on Kindness

2 Corinthians 8:13,14

"For I do not mean that others should be eased and you burdened; but by an equality, that now at this time your abundance may supply their lack, that their abundance also may supply your lack – that there may be equality."

Romans 12:13

"distributing to the needs of the saints, given to hospitality."

1 Peter 4:9,10

"Be hospitable to one another without grumbling. As each one has received a gift, minister it to one another, as good stewards of the manifold grace of God."

Matthew 25:35,36

"for I was hungry and you gave Me food; I was thirsty and you gave Me drink; I was a stranger and you took Me in; I was naked and you clothed Me; I was sick and you visited Me; I was in prison and you came to Me."

Hebrews 13:2

"Do not forget to entertain strangers, for by so doing some have unwittingly entertained angels."

James 2:15,16

"If a brother or sister is naked and destitute of daily food, and one of you says to them, "Depart in peace, be warmed and filled," but you do not give them the things which are needed for the body, what does it profit?"

Mark 9:41

"For whoever gives you a cup of water to drink in My name, because you belong to Christ, assuredly, I say to you, he will by no means lose his reward."

Acts 20:35

"I have shown you in every way, by laboring like this, that you must support the weak. And remember the words of the Lord Jesus, that He said, 'It is more blessed to give than to receive.' "

1 John 3:17

"But whoever has this world's goods, and sees his brother in need, and shuts up his heart from him, how does the love of God abide in him?"

Scriptures on Laziness

Proverbs 10:4,5

"He who has a slack hand becomes poor, But the hand of the diligent makes rich. He who gathers in summer is a wise son; He who sleeps in harvest is a son who causes shame."

Proverbs 20:13

"Do not love sleep, lest you come to poverty; Open your eyes, and you will be satisfied with bread."

1 Thessalonians 4:11,12

"that you also aspire to lead a quiet life, to mind your own business, and to work with your own hands, as we commanded you, that you may walk properly toward those who are outside, and that you may lack nothing."

Proverbs 15:19

"The way of the lazy man is like a hedge of thorns, But the way of the upright is a highway."

Proverbs 21:5

"The plans of the diligent lead surely to plenty, But those of everyone who is hasty, surely to poverty."

Romans 12:11

"not lagging in diligence, fervent in spirit, serving the Lord;"

Proverbs 28:19

"He who tills his land will have plenty of bread, But he who follows frivolity will have poverty enough!"

Proverbs 13:4

"The soul of a lazy man desires, and has nothing; But the soul of the diligent shall be made rich."

Proverbs 13:18

"Poverty and shame will come to him who disdains correction, But he who regards a rebuke will be honored."

2 Thessalonians 3:10-12

"For even when we were with you, we commanded you this: If anyone will not work, neither shall he eat. For we hear that there are some who walk among you in a disorderly manner, not working at all, but are busybodies. Now those who are such we command and exhort through our Lord Jesus Christ that they work in quietness and eat their own bread."

Proverbs 27:23

"Be diligent to know the state of your flocks, And attend to your herds;"

Proverbs 27:27

"You shall have enough goats' milk for your food, For the food of your household, And the nourishment of your maidservants."

Ecclesiastes 5:18,19

"Here is what I have seen: It is good and fitting for one to eat and drink, and to enjoy the good of all his labor in which he toils under the sun all the days of his life which God gives him; for it is his heritage. As for every man to whom God has given riches and wealth, and given him power to eat of it, to receive his heritage and rejoice in his labor – this is the gift of God."

Proverbs 13:23

"Much food is in the fallow ground of the poor, And for lack of justice there is waste." 2

Timothy 2:6

"The hardworking farmer must be first to partake of the crops."

Ephesians 4:28

"Let him who stole steal no longer, but rather let him labor, working with his hands what is good, that he may have something to give him who has need."

Proverbs 24:30-34

"I went by the field of the lazy man, And by the vineyard of the man devoid of understanding; And there it was, all overgrown with thorns; Its surface was covered with nettles; Its stone wall was broken down. When I saw it, I considered it well; I looked on it and received instruction: A little sleep, a little slumber, A little folding of the hands to rest; So shall your poverty come like a prowler, And your need like an armed man."

Proverbs 12:11

"He who tills his land will be satisfied with bread, But he who follows frivolity is devoid of understanding."

Scriptures on Loneliness

2 Corinthians 6:18

"I will be a Father to you, And you shall be My sons and daughters, Says the Lord Almighty." (Also see 2 Samuel 7:14)

Genisis 28:15

"Behold, I am with you and will keep you wherever you go, and will bring you back to this land; for I will not leave you until I have done what I have spoken to you."

Colossians 2:10

"and you are complete in Him, who is the head of all principality and power."

John 14:18

"I will not leave you orphans; I will come to you."

Isaiah 58:9

"Then you shall call, and the Lord will answer; You shall cry, and He will say, 'Here I am.'..."

Isaiah 43:4

"Since you were precious in My sight, You have been honored, And I have loved you; Therefore I will give men for you, And people for your life."

Psalms 40:17

"But I am poor and needy; Yet the Lord thinks upon me. You are my help and my deliverer; Do not delay, O my God."

Scriptures on Love

1 Corinthians 13:4 – 7

"Love suffers long and is kind; love does not envy; love does not parade itself, is not puffed up; does not behave rudely, does not seek its own, is not provoked, thinks no evil; does not rejoice in iniquity, but rejoices in the truth; bears all things, believes all things, hopes all things, endures all things."

Matthew 5:44 – 48

"But I say to you, love your enemies, bless those who curse you, do good to those who hate you, and pray for those who spitefully use you and persecute you, that you may be sons of your Father in heaven; for He makes His sun rise on the evil and on the good, and sends rain on the just and on the unjust. For if you love those who love you, what reward have you? Do not even the tax collectors do the same? And if you greet your brethren only, what do you do more than others? Do not even the tax collectors do so? Therefore you shall be perfect, just as your Father in heaven is perfect."

Matthew 19:19

"...You shall love your neighbor as yourself."

Matthew 22:37 – 39

"Jesus said to him, 'You shall love the Lord your God with all your heart, with all your soul, and with all your mind.' This is the first and great commandment. And the second is like it: 'You shall love your neighbor as yourself.' "

Luke 7:47

"Therefore I say to you, her sins, which are many, are forgiven, for she loved much. But to whom little is forgiven, the same loves little."

John 3:16

"For God so loved the world that He gave His only begotten Son, that whoever believes in Him should not perish but have everlasting life."

John 14:15

" 'If you love Me, keep My commandments.' "

John 13:34, 35

"A new commandment I give to you, that you love one another; as I have loved you, that you also love one another. By this all will know that you are My disciples, if you have love for one another."

John 15:13

"Greater love has no one than this, than to lay down one's life for his friends."

Romans 12:9 – 21

"Let love be without hypocrisy. Abhor what is evil. Cling to what is good. Be kindly affectionate to one another with brotherly love, in honor giving preference to one another; not lagging in diligence, fervent in spirit, serving the Lord; rejoicing in hope, patient in tribulation, continuing steadfastly in prayer; distributing to the needs of the saints, given to hospitality. Bless those who persecute you; bless and do not curse. Rejoice with those who rejoice, and weep with those who weep. Be of the same mind toward one another. Do not set your mind on high things, but associate with the humble. Do not be wise in your own opinion. Repay no one evil for evil. Have regard for good things in the sight of all men. If it is possible, as much as depends on you, live peaceably with all men. Beloved, do not avenge yourselves, but rather give place to wrath; for it is written, 'Vengeance is Mine, I will repay,' says the Lord. Therefore 'If your enemy is hungry, feed him; If he is thirsty, give him a drink; For in so doing you will heap coals of fire on his head.' Do not be overcome by evil, but overcome evil with good.' "

Romans 13:8

"Owe no one anything except to love one another, for he who loves another has fulfilled the law."

Romans 13:10

"Love does no harm to a neighbor; therefore love is the fulfillment of the law."

Galatians 5:22

"But the fruit of the Spirit is love, joy, peace, longsuffering, kindness, goodness, faithfulness"

Ephesians 5:25

"Husbands, love your wives, just as Christ also loved the church and gave Himself for her"

Colossians 3:19

" Husbands, love your wives and do not be bitter toward them."

1 Timothy 6:10

"For the love of money is a root of all kinds of evil, for which some have strayed from the faith in their greediness, and pierced themselves through with many sorrows."

2 Timothy 1:7

"For God has not given us a spirit of fear, but of power and of love and of a sound mind." Hebrews 13:1

"Let brotherly love continue."

1 John 2:10

"He who loves his brother abides in the light, and there is no cause for stumbling in him."

1 John 2:25

"And this is the promise that He has promised us – eternal life."

1 John 3:11

"For this is the message that you heard from the beginning, that we should love one another,"

1 John 3:14

"We know that we have passed from death to life, because we love the brethren. He who does not love his brother abides in death."

1 John 3:18

"My little children, let us not love in word or in tongue, but in deed and in truth."

1 John 4:8

"He who does not love does not know God, for God is love."

1 John 4:12

"No one has seen God at any time. If we love one another, God abides in us, and His love has been perfected in us."

1 John 4:18

"There is no fear in love; but perfect love casts out fear, because fear involves torment. But he who fears has not been made perfect in love."

1 John 4:19

"We love Him because He first loved us."

Ephesians 5:1, 2

"Therefore be imitators of God as dear children. And walk in love, as Christ also has loved us and given Himself for us, an offering and a sacrifice to God for a sweet-smelling aroma."

Scriptures on Loving God

Matthew 22:27,28

"You shall love the Lord your God with all your heart, with all your soul, and with all your mind. This is the first and great commandment."

Deuteronomy 11:13-15

"And it shall be that if you earnestly obey My commandments which I command you today, to love the Lord your God and serve Him with all your heart and with all your soul, then I will give you the rain for your land in its season, the early rain and the latter rain, that you may gather in your grain, your new wine, and your oil. And I will send grass in your fields for your livestock, that you may eat and be filled."

John 14:21

"He who has My commandments and keeps them, it is he who loves Me. And he who loves Me will be loved by My Father, and I will love him and manifest Myself to him."

Deuteronomy 7:9

"Therefore know that the Lord your God, He is God, the faithful God who keeps covenant and mercy for a thousand generations with those who love Him and keep His commandments"

Proverbs 8:17

"I love those who love me, And those who seek me diligently will find me."

Psalms 145:20

"The Lord preserves all who love Him, But all the wicked He will destroy."

Psalms 91:14

"Because he has set his love upon Me, therefore I will deliver him; I will set him on high, because he has known My name."

Proverbs 8:21

"That I may cause those who love me to inherit wealth, That I may fill their treasuries."

Psalms 37:4

"Delight yourself also in the Lord, And He shall give you the desires of your heart. "

1 Corinthians 2:9

"But as it is written: 'Eye has not seen, nor ear heard, Nor have entered into the heart of man The things which God has prepared for those who love Him.' "

Ephesians 6:24

"Grace be with all those who love our Lord Jesus Christ in sincerity. Amen."

Scriptures on Lust

Romans 6:11- 13

"Likewise you also, reckon yourselves to be dead indeed to sin, but alive to God in Christ Jesus our Lord. Therefore do not let sin reign in your mortal body, that you should obey it in its lusts. And do not present your members as instruments of unrighteousness to sin, but present yourselves to God as being alive from the dead, and your members as instruments of righteousness to God."

Proverbs 6:25 – 29

"Do not lust after her beauty in your heart, Nor let her allure you with her eyelids. For by means of a harlot A man is reduced to a crust of bread; And an adulteress will prey upon his precious life. Can a man take fire to his bosom, And his clothes not be burned? Can one walk on hot coals, And his feet not be seared? So is he who goes in to his neighbor's wife; Whoever touches her shall not be innocent."

James 4:7,8

"Therefore submit to God. Resist the devil and he will flee from you. Draw near to God and He will draw near to you. Cleanse your hands, you sinners; and purify your hearts, you double-minded."

James 4:1 – 4

"Where do wars and fights come from among you? Do they not come from your desires for pleasure that war in your members? You lust and do not have. You murder and covet and cannot obtain. You fight and war. Yet you do not have because you do not ask. You ask and do not receive, because you ask amiss, that you may spend it on your pleasures. Adulterers and adulteresses! Do you not know that friendship with the world is enmity with God? Whoever therefore wants to be a friend of the world makes himself an enemy of God." 1 John 2:16,17

"For all that is in the world – the lust of the flesh, the lust of the eyes, and the pride of life – is not of the Father but is of the world. And the world is passing away, and the lust of it; but he who does the will of God abides forever."

Matthew 5:27,28

"You have heard that it was said to those of old, 'You shall not commit adultery.'But I say to you that whoever looks at a woman to lust for her has already committed adultery with her in his heart."

1 Peter 2:11

"Beloved, I beg you as sojourners and pilgrims, abstain from fleshly lusts which war against the soul,"

1 Peter 1:14 – 16

"as obedient children, not conforming yourselves to the former lusts, as in your ignorance; but as He who called you is holy, you also be holy in all your conduct, because it is written, 'Be holy, for I am holy.' "

2 Timothy 2:22

"Flee also youthful lusts; but pursue righteousness, faith, love, peace with those who call on the Lord out of a pure heart."

Titus 3:3 – 5

"For we ourselves were also once foolish, disobedient, deceived, serving various lusts and pleasures, living in malice and envy, hateful and hating one another. But when the kindness and the love of God our Savior toward man appeared, not by works of righteousness which we have done, but according to His mercy He saved us, through the washing of regeneration and renewing of the Holy Spirit,"

Jude 1:18 – 21

"how they told you that there would be mockers in the last time who would walk according to their own ungodly lusts. These are sensual persons, who cause divisions, not having the Spirit. But you, beloved, building yourselves up on your most holy faith, praying in the Holy Spirit, keep yourselves in the love of God, looking for the mercy of our Lord Jesus Christ unto eternal life."

Galatians 5:16,16

"I say then: Walk in the Spirit, and you shall not fulfill the lust of the flesh."

2 Peter 1:4

"by which have been given to us exceedingly great and precious promises, that through these you may be partakers of the divine nature, having escaped the corruption that is in the world through lust."

Ephesians 2:3 – 6

"among whom also we all once conducted ourselves in the lusts of our flesh, fulfilling the desires of the flesh and of the mind, and were by nature children of wrath, just as the others. But God, who is rich in mercy, because of His great love with which He loved us, even when we were dead in trespasses, made us alive together with Christ (by grace you have been saved), and raised us up together, and made us sit together in the heavenly places in Christ Jesus,"

Titus 2:11,12

"For the grace of God that brings salvation has appeared to all men, teaching us that, denying ungodliness and worldly lusts, we should live soberly, righteously, and godly in the present age,"

Galatians 5:24

"And those who are Christ's have crucified the flesh with its passions and desires."

James 1:13

"Let no one say when he is tempted, 'I am tempted by God'; for God cannot be tempted by evil, nor does He Himself tempt anyone.

Scriptures on Lying

Deuteronomy 19:16 – 19

"If a false witness rises against any man to testify against him of wrongdoing,then both men in the controversy shall stand before the Lord, before the priests and the judges who serve in those days. And the judges shall make careful inquiry, and indeed, if the witness is a false witness, who has testified falsely against his brother, then you shall do to him as he thought to have done to his brother; so you shall put away the evil from among you."

Revelation 21:8

"But the cowardly, unbelieving, abominable, murderers, sexually immoral, sorcerers, idolaters, and all liars shall have their part in the lake which burns with fire and brimstone, which is the second death."

Colossians 3:9,10

"Do not lie to one another, since you have put off the old man with his deeds, and have put on the new man who is renewed in knowledge according to the image of Him who created him"

Leviticus 19:12

"And you shall not swear by My name falsely, nor shall you profane the name of your God: I am the Lord."

Proverbs 25:18

"A man who bears false witness against his neighbor Is like a club, a sword, and a sharp arrow."

Zechariah 8:17

"Let none of you think evil in your heart against your neighbor; And do not love a false oath. For all these are things that I hate,' Says the Lord."

Proverbs 14:5

"A faithful witness does not lie, But a false witness will utter lies."

1 Kings 22:16

"So the king said to him, 'How many times shall I make you swear that you tell me nothing but the truth in the name of the Lord?' "

Proverbs 19:5

"A false witness will not go unpunished, And he who speaks lies will not escape."

Proverbs 24:28

"Do not be a witness against your neighbor without cause, For would you deceive with your lips?"

Psalms 58:3

"The wicked are estranged from the womb; They go astray as soon as they are born, speaking lies."

Exodus 23:1

"You shall not circulate a false report. Do not put your hand with the wicked to be an unrighteous witness."

James 3:14

"But if you have bitter envy and self-seeking in your hearts, do not boast and lie against the truth."

Proverbs 12:19

"The truthful lip shall be established forever, But a lying tongue is but for a moment."

Scriptures on Marriage

Ecclesiastes 9:9

"Live joyfully with the wife whom you love all the days of your vain life which He has given you under the sun, all your days of vanity; for that is your portion in life, and in the labor which you perform under the sun."

Proverbs 5:15

"Drink water from your own cistern, And running water from your own well."

Proverbs 5:18-20

"Let your fountain be blessed, And rejoice with the wife of your youth. As a loving deer and a graceful doe, Let her breasts satisfy you at all times; And always be enraptured with her love. For why should you, my son, be enraptured by an immoral woman, And be embraced in the arms of a seductress?"

1 Corinthians 7:3

"Let the husband render to his wife the affection due her, and likewise also the wife to her husband."

Ephesians 5:22,23

"Wives, submit to your own husbands, as to the Lord. For the husband is head of the wife, as also Christ is head of the church; and He is the Savior of the body."

Ephesians 5:25

"Husbands, love your wives, just as Christ also loved the church and gave Himself for her"

Ephesians 5:28

"So husbands ought to love their own wives as their own bodies; he who loves his wife loves himself."

Ephesians 5:31

"For this reason a man shall leave his father and mother and be joined to his wife, and the two shall become one flesh." (Also see Genesis 2:24)

Ephesians 5:33

"Nevertheless let each one of you in particular so love his own wife as himself, and let the wife see that she respects her husband."

1 Timothy 5:8

"But if anyone does not provide for his own, and especially for those of his household, he has denied the faith and is worse than an unbeliever."

Colossians 3:18,19

"Wives, submit to your own husbands, as is fitting in the Lord. Husbands, love your wives and do not be bitter toward them."

1 Peter 3:7

"Husbands, likewise, dwell with them with understanding, giving honor to the wife, as to the weaker vessel, and as being heirs together of the grace of life, that your prayers may not be hindered."

Titus 2:4,5

"that they admonish the young women to love their husbands, to love their children, to be discreet, chaste, homemakers, good, obedient to their own husbands, that the word of God may not be blasphemed."

Scriptures on Meekness

Matthew 5:5

"Blessed are the meek, For they shall inherit the earth."

Isaiah 11:4

"But with righteousness He shall judge the poor, And decide with equity for the meek of the earth; He shall strike the earth with the rod of His mouth, And with the breath of His lips He shall slay the wicked."

Psalms 22:26

"The poor shall eat and be satisfied; Those who seek Him will praise the Lord. Let your heart live forever!"

Psalms 149:4

"For the Lord takes pleasure in His people; He will beautify the humble with salvation."

Isaiah 29:19

"The humble also shall increase their joy in the Lord, And the poor among men shall rejoice In the Holy One of Israel."

Psalms 147:6

"The Lord lifts up the humble; He casts the wicked down to the ground."

Psalms 25:9

"The humble He guides in justice, And the humble He teaches His way."

Zephaniah 2:3

"Seek the Lord, all you meek of the earth, Who have upheld His justice. Seek righteousness, seek humility. It may be that you will be hidden In the day of the Lord's anger."

1 Peter 3:4

"rather let it be the hidden person of the heart, with the incorruptible beauty of a gentle and quiet spirit, which is very precious in the sight of God."

Psalms 37:11

"But the meek shall inherit the earth, And shall delight themselves in the abundance of peace."

Proverbs 15:1

"A soft answer turns away wrath, But a harsh word stirs up anger."

Scriptures on Mercy

Isaiah 30:18

"Therefore the Lord will wait, that He may be gracious to you; And therefore He will be exalted, that He may have mercy on you. For the Lord is a God of justice; Blessed are all those who wait for Him."

Job 11:6

"That He would show you the secrets of wisdom! For they would double your prudence. Know therefore that God exacts from you Less than your iniquity deserves."

Psalms 103:13

"As a father pities his children, So the Lord pities those who fear Him."

Psalms 103:17

"But the mercy of the Lord is from everlasting to everlasting On those who fear Him, And His righteousness to children's children"

Exodus 33:19

"Then He said, 'I will make all My goodness pass before you, and I will proclaim the name of the Lord before you. I will be gracious to whom I will be gracious, and I will have compassion on whom I will have compassion.' "

Hosea 2:23

"Then I will sow her for Myself in the earth, And I will have mercy on her who had not obtained mercy; Then I will say to those who were not My people, 'You are My people!' And they shall say, 'You are my God!' "

Isaiah 60:10

"The sons of foreigners shall build up your walls, And their kings shall minister to you; For in My wrath I struck you, But in My favor I have had mercy on you."

Isaiah 48:9

"For My name's sake I will defer My anger, And for My praise I will restrain it from you, So that I do not cut you off.

Scriptures on Money

Deuteronomy 8:18

"And you shall remember the Lord your God, for it is He who gives you power to get wealth, that He may establish His covenant which He swore to your fathers, as it is this day."

Proverbs 23:4,5

"Do not overwork to be rich; Because of your own understanding, cease! Will you set your eyes on that which is not? For riches certainly make themselves wings; They fly away like an eagle toward heaven."

Psalms 37:16

"A little that a righteous man has Is better than the riches of many wicked."

James 2:5

"Listen, my beloved brethren: Has God not chosen the poor of this world to be rich in faith and heirs of the kingdom which He promised to those who love Him?"

Ecclesiastes 4:6

"Better a handful with quietness Than both hands full, together with toil and grasping for the wind."

Psalms 12:5

" 'For the oppression of the poor, for the sighing of the needy, Now I will arise,' says the Lord; 'I will set him in the safety for which he yearns.' "

Proverbs 17:5

"He who mocks the poor reproaches his Maker; He who is glad at calamity will not go unpunished."

Proverbs 22:22

"Do not rob the poor because he is poor, Nor oppress the afflicted at the gate;"

1 Timothy 6:17-19

"Command those who are rich in this present age not to be haughty, nor to trust in uncertain riches but in the living God, who gives us richly all things to enjoy. Let them do good, that they be rich in good works, ready to give, willing to share, storing up for themselves a good foundation for the time to come, that they may lay hold on eternal life."

Ecclesiates 5:12-14

"The sleep of a laboring man is sweet, Whether he eats little or much; But the abundance of the rich will not permit him to sleep. There is a severe evil which I have seen under the sun: Riches kept for their owner to his hurt. But those riches perish through misfortune; When he begets a son, there is nothing in his hand."

Job 5:15,16

"But He saves the needy from the sword, From the mouth of the mighty, And from their hand. So the poor have hope, And injustice shuts her mouth."

Psalms 9:18

"For the needy shall not always be forgotten; The expectation of the poor shall not perish forever."

Proverbs 11:28

"He who trusts in his riches will fall, But the righteous will flourish like foliage."

Proverbs 28:20

"A faithful man will abound with blessings, But he who hastens to be rich will not go unpunished. "

Proverbs 11:4

"Riches do not profit in the day of wrath, But righteousness delivers from death. "

Ezekiel 7:19

"They will throw their silver into the streets, And their gold will be like refuse; Their silver and their gold will not be able to deliver them In the day of the wrath of the Lord; They will not satisfy their souls, Nor fill their stomachs, Because it became their stumbling block of iniquity."

Proverbs 13:7

"There is one who makes himself rich, yet has nothing; And one who makes himself poor, yet has great riches."

Ecclesiates 5:10

"He who loves silver will not be satisfied with silver; Nor he who loves abundance, with increase. This also is vanity."

Proverbs 22:16

"He who oppresses the poor to increase his riches, And he who gives to the rich, will surely come to poverty."

Proverbs 28:22

"A man with an evil eye hastens after riches, And does not consider that poverty will come upon him."

Proverbs 22:2

"The rich and the poor have this in common, The Lord is the maker of them all."

Job 36:15

"He delivers the poor in their affliction, And opens their ears in oppression."

Proverbs 15:16

"Better is a little with the fear of the Lord, Than great treasure with trouble."

Proverbs 28:6

"Better is the poor who walks in his integrity Than one perverse in his ways, though he be rich."

Psalms 41:1

"Blessed is he who considers the poor; The Lord will deliver him in time of trouble."

Scriptures on Obedience

Deuteronomy 30:15,16

"See, I have set before you today life and good, death and evil, in that I command you today to love the Lord your God, to walk in His ways, and to keep His commandments, His statutes, and His judgments, that you may live and multiply; and the Lord your God will bless you in the land which you go to possess."

Deuteronomy 6:18

"And you shall do what is right and good in the sight of the Lord, that it may be well with you, and that you may go in and possess the good land of which the Lord swore to your fathers"

Deuteronomy 6:3

"Therefore hear, O Israel, and be careful to observe it, that it may be well with you, and that you may multiply greatly as the Lord God of your fathers has promised you – 'a land flowing with milk and honey.' "

Deuteronomy 7:12

"Then it shall come to pass, because you listen to these judgments, and keep and do them, that the Lord your God will keep with you the covenant and the mercy which He swore to your fathers."

Deuteronomy 29:9

"Therefore keep the words of this covenant, and do them, that you may prosper in all that you do."

Deuteronomy 5:29

"Oh, that they had such a heart in them that they would fear Me and always keep all My commandments, that it might be well with them and with their children forever!"

Philippians 4:9

"The things which you learned and received and heard and saw in me, these do, and the God of peace will be with you."

Matthew 5:19

"Whoever therefore breaks one of the least of these commandments, and teaches men so, shall be called least in the kingdom of heaven; but whoever does and teaches them, he shall be called great in the kingdom of heaven."

Matthew 7:24,25

"Therefore whoever hears these sayings of Mine, and does them, I will liken him to a wise man who built his house on the rock: and the rain descended, the floods came, and the winds blew and beat on that house; and it did not fall, for it was founded on the rock."

Job 36:11

"If they obey and serve Him, They shall spend their days in prosperity, And their years in pleasures."

Romans 8:28

"And we know that all things work together for good to those who love God, to those who are the called according to His purpose."

John 15:10

"If you keep My commandments, you will abide in My love, just as I have kept My Father's commandments and abide in His love."

John 13:17

"If you know these things, blessed are you if you do them."

James 1:25

"But he who looks into the perfect law of liberty and continues in it, and is not a forgetful hearer but a doer of the work, this one will be blessed in what he does."

1 John 3:22

"And whatever we ask we receive from Him, because we keep His commandments and do those things that are pleasing in His sight."

Romans 2:13

"for not the hearers of the law are just in the sight of God, but the doers of the law will be justified"

John 5:24

"Most assuredly, I say to you, he who hears My word and believes in Him who sent Me has everlasting life, and shall not come into judgment, but has passed from death into life."

Matthew 12:50

"For whoever does the will of My Father in heaven is My brother and sister and mother."

1 John 2:17

"And the world is passing away, and the lust of it; but he who does the will of God abides forever."

Matthew 7:21

"Not everyone who says to Me, 'Lord, Lord,' shall enter the kingdom of heaven, but he who does the will of My Father in heaven."

Psalms 106:3

"Blessed are those who keep justice, And he who does righteousness at all times!"

Hebrews 5:9

"And having been perfected, He became the author of eternal salvation to all who obey Him,"

John 8:51

"Most assuredly, I say to you, if anyone keeps My word he shall never see death."

Scriptures on Patience

James 5:7,8

"Therefore be patient, brethren, until the coming of the Lord. See how the farmer waits for the precious fruit of the earth, waiting patiently for it until it receives the early and latter rain. You also be patient. Establish your hearts, for the coming of the Lord is at hand."

1 Peter 2:20

"For what credit is it if, when you are beaten for your faults, you take it patiently? But when you do good and suffer, if you take it patiently, this is commendable before God."

Galatians 6:9

"And let us not grow weary while doing good, for in due season we shall reap if we do not lose heart."

Hebrews 10:23

"Let us hold fast the confession of our hope without wavering, for He who promised is faithful."

Matthew 24:13

"But he who endures to the end shall be saved."

Hebrews 6:12

"that you do not become sluggish, but imitate those who through faith and patience inherit the promises."

Hebrews 10:36

"For you have need of endurance, so that after you have done the will of God, you may receive the promise"

James 1:2-4

"My brethren, count it all joy when you fall into various trials, knowing that the testing of your faith produces patience. But let patience have its perfect work, that you may be perfect and complete, lacking nothing."

Romans 5:3,4

"And not only that, but we also glory in tribulations, knowing that tribulation produces perseverance; and perseverance, character; and character, hope."

Scriptures on Peace

Isaiah 57:19

" 'I create the fruit of the lips: Peace, peace to him who is far off and to him who is near,' Says the Lord, 'And I will heal him.' "

Colossians 3:15

"And let the peace of God rule in your hearts, to which also you were called in one body; and be thankful."

Psalms 85:8

"I will hear what God the Lord will speak, For He will speak peace To His people and to His saints; But let them not turn back to folly."

Philippians 4:7

"and the peace of God, which surpasses all understanding, will guard your hearts and minds through Christ Jesus."

Isaiah 32:17

"The work of righteousness will be peace, And the effect of righteousness, quietness and assurance forever."

Luke 7:50

"Then He said to the woman, 'Your faith has saved you. Go in peace.' "

Psalms 37:37

"Mark the blameless man, and observe the upright; For the future of that man is peace."

2 Thessalonians 3:16

"Now may the Lord of peace Himself give you peace always in every way. The Lord be with you all."

John 14:27

"Peace I leave with you, My peace I give to you; not as the world gives do I give to you. Let not your heart be troubled, neither let it be afraid."

Scriptures on Poverty

Psalms 72:12,13

"For He will deliver the needy when he cries, The poor also, and him who has no helper. He will spare the poor and needy, And will save the souls of the needy."

Psalms 107:41

"Yet He sets the poor on high, far from affliction, And makes their families like a flock."

Psalms 69:33

"For the Lord hears the poor, And does not despise His prisoners."

Jeremiah 20:13

"Sing to the Lord! Praise the Lord! For He has delivered the life of the poor From the hand of evildoers."

Psalms 102:17

"He shall regard the prayer of the destitute, And shall not despise their prayer."

Psalms 113:7

"He raises the poor out of the dust, And lifts the needy out of the ash heap"

Psalms 132:15

"I will abundantly bless her provision; I will satisfy her poor with bread."

Psalms 68:10

"Your congregation dwelt in it; You, O God, provided from Your goodness for the poor."

Scriptures on Prayer

Matthew 7:7,8

"Ask, and it will be given to you; seek, and you will find; knock, and it will be opened to you. For everyone who asks receives, and he who seeks finds, and to him who knocks it will be opened."

Matthew 21:22

"And whatever things you ask in prayer, believing, you will receive."

Isaiah 30:19

"For the people shall dwell in Zion at Jerusalem; You shall weep no more. He will be very gracious to you at the sound of your cry; When He hears it, He will answer you."

1 John 5:14,15

"Now this is the confidence that we have in Him, that if we ask anything according to His will, He hears us. And if we know that He hears us, whatever we ask, we know that we have the petitions that we have asked of Him."

Jeremiah 29:12

"Then you will call upon Me and go and pray to Me, and I will listen to you."

Isaiah 65:24

"It shall come to pass That before they call, I will answer; And while they are still speaking, I will hear."

John 16:23,24

"And in that day you will ask Me nothing. Most assuredly, I say to you, whatever you ask the Father in My name He will give you. Until now you have asked nothing in My name. Ask, and you will receive, that your joy may be full."

James 5:16

"Confess your trespasses to one another, and pray for one another, that you may be healed. The effective, fervent prayer of a righteous man avails much."

Job 22:27

"You will make your prayer to Him, He will hear you, And you will pay your vows."

John 14:13,14

"And whatever you ask in My name, that I will do, that the Father may be glorified in the Son. If you ask anything in My name, I will do it."

John 15:7

"If you abide in Me, and My words abide in you, you will ask what you desire, and it shall be done for you."

Matthew 6:6

"But you, when you pray, go into your room, and when you have shut your door, pray to your Father who is in the secret place; and your Father who sees in secret will reward you openly."

Psalms 50:15

"Call upon Me in the day of trouble; I will deliver you, and you shall glorify Me."

Isaiah 58:9

"Then you shall call, and the Lord will answer; You shall cry, and He will say, 'Here I am.' 'If you take away the yoke from your midst, The pointing of the finger, and speaking wickedness ' "

Proverbs 15:29

"The Lord is far from the wicked, But He hears the prayer of the righteous."

Psalms 91:15

"He shall call upon Me, and I will answer him; I will be with him in trouble; I will deliver him and honor him."

Matthew 7:11

"If you then, being evil, know how to give good gifts to your children, how much more will your Father who is in heaven give good things to those who ask Him!"

Psalms 34:17

"The righteous cry out, and the Lord hears, And delivers them out of all their troubles."

Psalms 55:17

"Evening and morning and at noon I will pray, and cry aloud, And He shall hear my voice."

Psalms 145:18 – 21

"The Lord is near to all who call upon Him, To all who call upon Him in truth. He will fulfill the desire of those who fear Him; He also will hear their cry and save them. The Lord preserves all who love Him, But all the wicked He will destroy. My mouth shall speak the praise of the Lord, And all flesh shall bless His holy name Forever and ever."

Zechariah 13:9

"I will bring the one-third through the fire, Will refine them as silver is refined, And test them as gold is tested. They will call on My name, And I will answer them. I will say, 'This is My people'; And each one will say, 'The Lord is my God."

Matthew 6:8

"Therefore do not be like them. For your Father knows the things you have need of before you ask Him."

1 John 3:22

"And whatever we ask we receive from Him, because we keep His commandments and do those things that are pleasing in His sight."

Jeremiah 33:3

"Call to Me, and I will answer you, and show you great and mighty things, which you do not know."

Mark 11:24

"Therefore I say to you, whatever things you ask when you pray, believe that you receive them, and you will have them."

Scriptures on Prisoners

Psalms 72:12,13

"For He will deliver the needy when he cries, The poor also, and him who has no helper. He will spare the poor and needy, And will save the souls of the needy."

Psalms 107:41

"Yet He sets the poor on high, far from affliction, And makes their families like a flock."

Psalms 69:33

"For the Lord hears the poor, And does not despise His prisoners."

Jeremiah 20:13

"Sing to the Lord! Praise the Lord! For He has delivered the life of the poor From the hand of evildoers."

Psalms 102:17

"He shall regard the prayer of the destitute, And shall not despise their prayer."

Psalms 113:7

"He raises the poor out of the dust, And lifts the needy out of the ash heap"

Psalms 132:15

"I will abundantly bless her provision; I will satisfy her poor with bread."

Psalms 68:10

"Your congregation dwelt in it; You, O God, provided from Your goodness for the poor.

Scriptures on Prosperity

Proverbs 15:6

"In the house of the righteous there is much treasure, But in the revenue of the wicked is trouble."

Proverbs 22:4

"By humility and the fear of the Lord Are riches and honor and life."

Deuteronomy 30:9

"The Lord your God will make you abound in all the work of your hand, in the fruit of your body, in the increase of your livestock, and in the produce of your land for good. For the Lord will again rejoice over you for good as He rejoiced over your fathers"

Isaiah 30:23

"Then He will give the rain for your seed With which you sow the ground, And bread of the increase of the earth; It will be fat and plentiful. In that day your cattle will feed In large pastures."

Deuteronomy 28:11- 13

"And the Lord will grant you plenty of goods, in the fruit of your body, in the increase of your livestock, and in the produce of your ground, in the land of which the Lord swore to your fathers to give you. The Lord will open to you His good treasure, the heavens, to give the rain to your land in its season, and to bless all the work of your hand. You shall lend to many nations, but you shall not borrow. And the Lord will make you the head and not the tail; you shall be above only, and not be beneath, if you heed the commandments of the Lord your God, which I command you today, and are careful to observe them."

Ecclesiates 3:13

"and also that every man should eat and drink and enjoy the good of all his labor – it is the gift of God."

Job 22:28

"You will also declare a thing, And it will be established for you; So light will shine on your ways."

Proverbs 8:18,19

"Riches and honor are with me, Enduring riches and righteousness. My fruit is better than gold, yes, than fine gold, And my revenue than choice silver."

Psalms 112:3

"Wealth and riches will be in his house, And his righteousness endures forever."

Deuteronomy 11:15

"And I will send grass in your fields for your livestock, that you may eat and be filled."

Job 22:24,25

"Then you will lay your gold in the dust, And the gold of Ophir among the stones of the brooks. Yes, the Almighty will be your gold And your precious silver."

Psalms 128:2

"When you eat the labor of your hands, you shall be happy, and it shall be well with you."

Isaiah 65:21- 23

"They shall build houses and inhabit them; They shall plant vineyards and eat their fruit. They shall not build and another inhabit; They shall not plant and another eat; For as the days of a tree, so shall be the days of My people, And My elect shall long enjoy the work of their hands. They shall not labor in vain, Nor bring forth children for trouble; For they shall be the descendants of the blessed of the Lord, And their offspring with them."

Psalms 1:3

"He shall be like a tree Planted by the rivers of water, That brings forth its fruit in its season, Whose leaf also shall not wither; And whatever he does shall prosper."

Deuteronomy 28:2- 6

"And all these blessings shall come upon you and overtake you, because you obey the voice of the Lord your God: Blessed shall you be in the city, and blessed shall you be in the country. Blessed shall be the fruit of your body, the produce of your ground and the increase of your herds, the increase of your cattle and the offspring of your flocks. Blessed shall be your basket and your kneading bowl. Blessed shall you be when you come in, and blessed shall you be when you go out."

Scriptures on Remorse

Proverbs 15:6

"In the house of the righteous there is much treasure, But in the revenue of the wicked is trouble."

Proverbs 22:4

"By humility and the fear of the Lord Are riches and honor and life."

Deuteronomy 30:9

"The Lord your God will make you abound in all the work of your hand, in the fruit of your body, in the increase of your livestock, and in the produce of your land for good. For the Lord will again rejoice over you for good as He rejoiced over your fathers"

Isaiah 30:23

"Then He will give the rain for your seed With which you sow the ground, And bread of the increase of the earth; It will be fat and plentiful. In that day your cattle will feed In large pastures."

Deuteronomy 28:11- 13

"And the Lord will grant you plenty of goods, in the fruit of your body, in the increase of your livestock, and in the produce of your ground, in the land of which the Lord swore to your fathers to give you. The Lord will open to you His good treasure, the heavens, to give the rain to your land in its season, and to bless all the work of your hand. You shall lend to many nations, but you shall not borrow. And the Lord will make you the head and not the tail; you shall be above only, and not be beneath, if you heed the commandments of the Lord your God, which I command you today, and are careful to observe them."

Ecclesiates 3:13

"and also that every man should eat and drink and enjoy the good of all his labor – it is the gift of God."

Job 22:28

"You will also declare a thing, And it will be established for you; So light will shine on your ways."

Proverbs 8:18,19

"Riches and honor are with me, Enduring riches and righteousness. My fruit is better than gold, yes, than fine gold, And my revenue than choice silver."

Psalms 112:3

"Wealth and riches will be in his house, And his righteousness endures forever."

Deuteronomy 11:15

"And I will send grass in your fields for your livestock, that you may eat and be filled."

Job 22:24,25

"Then you will lay your gold in the dust, And the gold of Ophir among the stones of the brooks. Yes, the Almighty will be your gold And your precious silver."

Psalms 128:2

"When you eat the labor of your hands, you shall be happy, and it shall be well with you."

Isaiah 65:21- 23

"They shall build houses and inhabit them; They shall plant vineyards and eat their fruit. They shall not build and another inhabit; They shall not plant and another eat; For as the days of a tree, so shall be the days of My people, And My elect shall long enjoy the work of their hands. They shall not labor in vain, Nor bring forth children for trouble; For they shall be the descendants of the blessed of the Lord, And their offspring with them."

Psalms 1:3

"He shall be like a tree Planted by the rivers of water, That brings forth its fruit in its season, Whose leaf also shall not wither; And whatever he does shall prosper."

Deuteronomy 28:2- 6

"And all these blessings shall come upon you and overtake you, because you obey the voice of the Lord your God: Blessed shall you be in the city, and blessed shall you be in the country. Blessed shall be the fruit of your body, the produce of your ground and the increase of your herds, the increase of your cattle and the offspring of your flocks. Blessed shall be your basket and your kneading bowl. Blessed shall you be when you come in, and blessed shall you be when you go out."

Scriptures on Repentance

Mark 1:15

"and saying, 'The time is fulfilled, and the kingdom of God is at hand. Repent, and believe in the gospel.' "

Mark 6:12

"So they went out and preached that people should repent."

Psalms 34:18

"The Lord is near to those who have a broken heart, And saves such as have a contrite spirit."

Psalms 147:3

"He heals the brokenhearted And binds up their wounds."

Job 11:14,15

"If iniquity were in your hand, and you put it far away, And would not let wickedness dwell in your tents; Then surely you could lift up your face without spot; Yes, you could be steadfast, and not fear;"

Ezekiel 18:21,22

"But if a wicked man turns from all his sins which he has committed, keeps all My statutes, and does what is lawful and right, he shall surely live; he shall not die. None of the transgressions which he has committed shall be remembered against him; because of the righteousness which he has done, he shall live."

Matthew 9:13

"But go and learn what this means: 'I desire mercy and not sacrifice.' For I did not come to call the righteous, but sinners, to repentance.' "

Scriptures on Righteousness

Psalms 84:11

"For the Lord God is a sun and shield; The Lord will give grace and glory; No good thing will He withhold From those who walk uprightly."

Psalms 34:10

"The young lions lack and suffer hunger; But those who seek the Lord shall not lack any good thing."

Proverbs 10:24

"The fear of the wicked will come upon him, And the desire of the righteous will be granted."

Proverbs 13:21

"Evil pursues sinners, But to the righteous, good shall be repaid."

Proverbs 12:2

"A good man obtains favor from the Lord, But a man of wicked intentions He will condemn."

Matthew 6:33

"But seek first the kingdom of God and His righteousness, and all these things shall be added to you."

Proverbs 11:28

"He who trusts in his riches will fall, But the righteous will flourish like foliage."

Psalms 58:11

"So that men will say, 'Surely there is a reward for the righteous; Surely He is God who judges in the earth.' "

Psalms 5:12

"For You, O Lord, will bless the righteous; With favor You will surround him as with a shield."

Psalms 3:8

"Salvation belongs to the Lord. Your blessing is upon Your people. Selah"

Romans 8:32

"He who did not spare His own Son, but delivered Him up for us all, how shall He not with Him also freely give us all things?"

Isaiah 3:10

"Say to the righteous that it shall be well with them, For they shall eat the fruit of their doings."

Psalms 23:6

"Surely goodness and mercy shall follow me All the days of my life; And I will dwell in the house of the Lord Forever."

Scriptures on Salvation

Acts 2:21

"And it shall come to pass That whoever calls on the name of the Lord Shall be saved."

Romans 10:9

"that if you confess with your mouth the Lord Jesus and believe in your heart that God has raised Him from the dead, you will be saved."

Ephesians 2:8

"For by grace you have been saved through faith, and that not of yourselves; it is the gift of God"

John 3:16

"For God so loved the world that He gave His only begotten Son, that whoever believes in Him should not perish but have everlasting life."

John 14:6

"Jesus said to him, "I am the way, the truth, and the life. No one comes to the Father except through Me."

John 3:3-7

"Jesus answered and said to him, 'Most assuredly, I say to you, unless one is born again, he cannot see the kingdom of God.' Nicodemus said to Him, 'How can a man be born when he is old? Can he enter a second time into his mother's womb and be born?' Jesus answered, 'Most assuredly, I say to you, unless one is born of water and the Spirit, he cannot enter the kingdom of God. That which is born of the flesh is flesh, and that which is born of the Spirit is spirit. Do not marvel that I said to you, You must be born again.' "

2 Corinthians 5:17

"Therefore, if anyone is in Christ, he is a new creation; old things have passed away; behold, all things have become new."

2 Corinthians 5:21

"For He made Him who knew no sin to be sin for us, that we might become the righteousness of God in Him."

Ephesians 2:1

"And you He made alive, who were dead in trespasses and sins"

1 Timothy 2:3,4

"For this is good and acceptable in the sight of God our Savior, who desires all men to be saved and to come to the knowledge of the truth."

1 John 2:1,2

"My little children, these things I write to you, so that you may not sin. And if anyone sins, we have an Advocate with the Father, Jesus Christ the righteous. And He Himself is the propitiation for our sins, and not for ours only but also for the whole world."

Colossians 2:13

"And you, being dead in your trespasses and the uncircumcision of your flesh, He has made alive together with Him, having forgiven you all trespasses"

1 Timothy 4:9,10

"This is a faithful saying and worthy of all acceptance. For to this end we both labor and suffer reproach, because we trust in the living God, who is the Savior of all men, especially of those who believe."

Romans 5:15

"But the free gift is not like the offense. For if by the one man's offense many died, much more the grace of God and the gift by the grace of the one Man, Jesus Christ, abounded to many."

Titus 3:4 – 6

"But when the kindness and the love of God our Savior toward man appeared, not by works of righteousness which we have done, but according to His mercy He saved us, through the washing of regeneration and renewing of the Holy Spirit, whom He poured out on us abundantly through Jesus Christ our Savior"

John 1:12,13

"But as many as received Him, to them He gave the right to become children of God, to those who believe in His name: who were born, not of blood, nor of the will of the flesh, nor of the will of man, but of God."

Scriptures on Seeking God

Matthew 6:33

"But seek first the kingdom of God and His righteousness, and all these things shall be added to you."

2 Chronicles 15:3

"For a long time Israel has been without the true God, without a teaching priest, and without law"

Hosea 10:12

"Sow for yourselves righteousness; Reap in mercy; Break up your fallow ground, For it is time to seek the Lord, Till He comes and rains righteousness on you."

Hebrews 11:6

"But without faith it is impossible to please Him, for he who comes to God must believe that He is, and that He is a rewarder of those who diligently seek Him."

Acts 17:27

"so that they should seek the Lord, in the hope that they might grope for Him and find Him, though He is not far from each one of us"

Lamentations 3:25

"The Lord is good to those who wait for Him, To the soul who seeks Him. "

Amos 5:4

"For thus says the Lord to the house of Israel: 'Seek Me and live' "

Deuteronomy 4:29,30

"But from there you will seek the Lord your God, and you will find Him if you seek Him with all your heart and with all your soul. When you are in distress, and all these things come upon you in the latter days, when you turn to the Lord your God and obey His voice"

Ezra 8:22

"For I was ashamed to request of the king an escort of soldiers and horsemen to help us against the enemy on the road, because we had spoken to the king, saying, "The hand of our God is upon all those for good who seek Him, but His power and His wrath are against all those who forsake Him."

1 Chronicles 28:9

"As for you, my son Solomon, know the God of your father, and serve Him with a loyal heart and with a willing mind; for the Lord searches all hearts and understands all the intent of the thoughts. If you seek Him, He will be found by you; but if you forsake Him, He will cast you off forever."

Job 8:5,6

"If you would earnestly seek God And make your supplication to the Almighty, If you were pure and upright, Surely now He would awake for you, And prosper your rightful dwelling place."

Psalms 9:10

"And those who know Your name will put their trust in You; For You, Lord, have not forsaken those who seek You."

Jeremiah 29:13

"And you will seek Me and find Me, when you search for Me with all your heart."

Scriptures on Self Denial

Matthew 16:24 – 26

"Then Jesus said to His disciples, 'If anyone desires to come after Me, let him deny himself, and take up his cross, and follow Me. For whoever desires to save his life will lose it, but whoever loses his life for My sake will find it. For what profit is it to a man if he gains the whole world, and loses his own soul? Or what will a man give in exchange for his soul?' "

Romans 8:12,13

"Therefore, brethren, we are debtors – not to the flesh, to live according to the flesh. For if you live according to the flesh you will die; but if by the Spirit you put to death the deeds of the body, you will live."

Galatians 5:24

"And those who are Christ's have crucified the flesh with its passions and desires."

Titus 2:11,12

"For the grace of God that brings salvation has appeared to all men, teaching us that, denying ungodliness and worldly lusts, we should live soberly, righteously, and godly in the present age"

Matthew 5:39 – 41

"But I tell you not to resist an evil person. But whoever slaps you on your right cheek, turn the other to him also. If anyone wants to sue you and take away your tunic, let him have your cloak also. And whoever compels you to go one mile, go with him two."

Luke 18:29,30

"So He said to them, 'Assuredly, I say to you, there is no one who has left house or parents or brothers or wife or children, for the sake of the kingdom of God, who shall not receive many times more in this present time, and in the age to come eternal life."

Scriptures on Selfishness

Leviticus 19:18

"You shall not take vengeance, nor bear any grudge against the children of your people, but you shall love your neighbor as yourself: I am the LORD. "

James 2:8

"If ye fulfil the royal law according to the scripture, Thou shalt love thy XXXeighbor as thyself, ye do well: "

Romans 15:3

"For even Christ pleased not himself; but, as it is written, The reproaches of them that reproached thee fell on me."

2 Timothy 3:2

"For men shall be lovers of their own selves, covetous, boasters, proud, blasphemers, disobedient to parents, unthankful, unholy"

Romans 15:1

"We then that are strong ought to bear the infirmities of the weak, and not to please ourselves."

1 Corinthians 10:33

"Even as I please all men in all things, not seeking mine own profit, but the profit of many, that they may be saved."

Philippians 2:21

"For all seek their own, not the things which are Jesus Christ's."

Isaiah 56:11

"Yea, they are greedy dogs which can never have enough, and they are shepherds that cannot understand: they all look to their own way, every one for his gain, from his quarter. "

1 John 3:17

"But whoso hath this world's good, and seeth his brother have need, and shutteth up his bowels of compassion from him, how dwelleth the love of God in him?"

Scriptures on Self Righteousness

Job 33:8,9

"Surely you have spoken in my hearing, And I have heard the sound of your words, saying, 'I am pure, without transgression; I am innocent, and there is no iniquity in me."

Job 35:2

"Do you think this is right? Do you say, 'My righteousness is more than God's?' "

Isaiah 5:21

"Woe to those who are wise in their own eyes, And prudent in their own sight! "

Job 35:13

"Surely God will not listen to empty talk, Nor will the Almighty regard it."

Proverbs 26:12

"Do you see a man wise in his own eyes? There is more hope for a fool than for him."

Galatians 6:3

"For if anyone thinks himself to be something, when he is nothing, he deceives himself."

2 Corinthians 10:17,18

" ' But he who glories, let him glory in the Lord.' For not he who commends himself is approved, but whom the Lord commends."

John 9:41

"Jesus said to them, 'If you were blind, you would have no sin; but now you say, 'We see.' Therefore your sin remains.' "

Isaiah 64:4

"For since the beginning of the world Men have not heard nor perceived by the ear, Nor has the eye seen any God besides You, Who acts for the one who waits for Him."

Proverbs 28:25,26

"He who is of a proud heart stirs up strife, But he who trusts in the Lord will be prospered. He who trusts in his own heart is a fool, But whoever walks wisely will be delivered."

Luke 16:15

"And He said to them, 'You are those who justify yourselves before men, but God knows your hearts. For what is highly esteemed among men is an abomination in the sight of God.' "

Proverbs 27:2

"Let another man praise you, and not your own mouth; A stranger, and not your own lips."

Scriptures on Sexual Sins

1 Corinthians 6:18-20

"Flee sexual immorality. Every sin that a man does is outside the body, but he who commits sexual immorality sins against his own body. Or do you not know that your body is the temple of the Holy Spirit who is in you, whom you have from God, and you are not your own? For you were bought at a price; therefore glorify God in your body and in your spirit, which are God's."

1 Corinthians 6:13

"Foods for the stomach and the stomach for foods, but God will destroy both it and them. Now the body is not for sexual immorality but for the Lord, and the Lord for the body."

1 Corinthians 7:1

"Now concerning the things of which you wrote to me: It is good for a man not to touch a woman."

1 Corinthians 7:37

"Nevertheless he who stands steadfast in his heart, having no necessity, but has power over his own will, and has so determined in his heart that he will keep his virgin does well."

1 Corinthians 10:13

"No temptation has overtaken you except such as is common to man; but God is faithful, who will not allow you to be tempted beyond what you are able, but with the temptation will also make the way of escape, that you may be able to bear it."

Revelation 14:4

"These are the ones who were not defiled with women, for they are virgins. These are the ones who follow the Lamb wherever He goes. These were redeemed from among men, being firstfruits to God and to the Lamb."

1 Thessalonians 4:3

"For this is the will of God, your sanctification: that you should abstain from sexual immorality"

Hebrews 13:4

"Marriage is honorable among all, and the bed undefiled; but fornicators and adulterers God will judge."

1 Corinthians 6:15

"Do you not know that your bodies are members of Christ? Shall I then take the members of Christ and make them members of a harlot? Certainly not!"

2 Peter 2:9

"then the Lord knows how to deliver the godly out of temptations and to reserve the unjust under punishment for the day of judgment"

James 1:12

"Blessed is the man who endures temptation; for when he has been approved, he will receive the crown of life which the Lord has promised to those who love Him."

Hebrews 2:18

"For in that He Himself has suffered, being tempted, He is able to aid those who are tempted."

Hebrews 4:15,16

"For we do not have a High Priest who cannot sympathize with our weaknesses, but was in all points tempted as we are, yet without sin. Let us therefore come boldly to the throne of grace, that we may obtain mercy and find grace to help in time of need."

Scriptures on Shame

Romans 10:11

"For the Scripture says, 'Whoever believes on Him will not be put to shame.' "

Psalms 119:6

"Then I would not be ashamed, When I look into all Your commandments."

Romans 5:5

"Now hope does not disappoint, because the love of God has been poured out in our hearts by the Holy Spirit who was given to us."

2 Timothy 2:15

"Be diligent to present yourself approved to God, a worker who does not need to be ashamed, rightly dividing the word of truth."

Romans 9:33

"As it is written: 'Behold, I lay in Zion a stumbling stone and rock of offense, And whoever believes on Him will not be put to shame.' "

2 Timothy 2:15

"Be diligent to present yourself approved to God, a worker who does not need to be ashamed, rightly dividing the word of truth."

Psalms 119:80

"Let my heart be blameless regarding Your statutes, That I may not be ashamed."

1 Peter 4:16

"Yet if anyone suffers as a Christian, let him not be ashamed, but let him glorify God in this matter."

Scriptures on Sickness and disease

James 5:14 – 16

"Is anyone among you sick? Let him call for the elders of the church, and let them pray over him, anointing him with oil in the name of the Lord. And the prayer of faith will save the sick, and the Lord will raise him up. And if he has committed sins, he will be forgiven. Confess your trespasses to one another, and pray for one another, that you may be healed. The effective, fervent prayer of a righteous man avails much."

Matthew 9:28 – 30

"And when He had come into the house, the blind men came to Him. And Jesus said to them, 'Do you believe that I am able to do this?' They said to Him, 'Yes, Lord.' Then He touched their eyes, saying, 'According to your faith let it be to you.' And their eyes were opened. And Jesus sternly warned them, saying, 'See that no one knows it.' "

Jeremiah 17:14

"Heal me, O Lord, and I shall be healed; Save me, and I shall be saved, For You are my praise."

Matthew 9:35

"Then Jesus went about all the cities and villages, teaching in their synagogues, preaching the gospel of the kingdom, and healing every sickness and every disease among the people."

Matthew 9:6,7

"But that you may know that the Son of Man has power on earth to forgive sins – then He said to the paralytic, 'Arise, take up your bed, and go to your house.' And he arose and departed to his house."

Jeremiah 30:17

"For I will restore health to you And heal you of your wounds, says the Lord, 'Because they called you an outcast saying: This is Zion; No one seeks her.' "

Exodus 23:25

"So you shall serve the Lord your God, and He will bless your bread and your water. And I will take sickness away from the midst of you."

1 Peter 2:24

"who Himself bore our sins in His own body on the tree, that we, having died to sins, might live for righteousness – by whose stripes you were healed."

Isaiah 53:5

"But He was wounded for our transgressions, He was bruised for our iniquities; The chastisement for our peace was upon Him, And by His stripes we are healed."

Scriptures on Slander

Matthew 5:11,12

"Blessed are you when they revile and persecute you, and say all kinds of evil against you falsely for My sake. Rejoice and be exceedingly glad, for great is your reward in heaven, for so they persecuted the prophets who were before you."

1 Peter 4:14

"If you are reproached for the name of Christ, blessed are you, for the Spirit of glory and of God rests upon you. On their part He is blasphemed, but on your part He is glorified."

Psalms 57:3

"He shall send from heaven and save me; He reproaches the one who would swallow me up. Selah God shall send forth His mercy and His truth."

Isaiah 51:7

"Listen to Me, you who know righteousness, You people in whose heart is My law: Do not fear the reproach of men, Nor be afraid of their insults."

Psalms 31:20

"You shall hide them in the secret place of Your presence From the plots of man; You shall keep them secretly in a pavilion From the strife of tongues."

Job 5:21

"You shall be hidden from the scourge of the tongue, And you shall not be afraid of destruction when it comes."

Psalms 37:6

"He shall bring forth your righteousness as the light, And your justice as the noonday."

Scriptures on Submission

James 4:7

"Therefore submit to God. Resist the devil and he will flee from you."

1 Peter 5:5,6

"Likewise you younger people, submit yourselves to your elders. Yes, all of you be submissive to one another, and be clothed with humility, for 'God resists the proud, But gives grace to the humble.' "

Ephesians 5:33

"Nevertheless let each one of you in particular so love his own wife as himself, and let the wife see that she respects her husband."

Ephesians 5:21-25,28

"Wives, submit to your own husbands, as to the Lord. For the husband is head of the wife, as also Christ is head of the church; and He is the Savior of the body. Therefore, just as the church is subject to Christ, so let the wives be to their own husbands in everything. Husbands, love your wives, just as Christ also loved the church and gave Himself for her"

1 Peter 3:1-4

"Wives, likewise, be submissive to your own husbands, that even if some do not obey the word, they, without a word, may be won by the conduct of their wives, when they observe your chaste conduct accompanied by fear. Do not let your adornment be merely outward—arranging the hair, wearing gold, or putting on fine apparel—rather let it be the hidden person of the heart, with the incorruptible beauty of a gentle and quiet spirit, which is very precious in the sight of God."

Ephesians 6:5-9

"Bondservants, be obedient to those who are your masters according to the flesh, with fear and trembling, in sincerity of heart, as to Christ; not with eyeservice, as men-pleasers, but as bondservants of Christ, doing the will of God from the heart, with goodwill doing service, as to the Lord, and not to men, knowing that whatever good anyone does, he will receive the same from the Lord, whether he is a slave or free. And you, masters, do the same things to them, giving up threatening, knowing that your own Master also[a] is in heaven, and there is no partiality with Him."

Ephesians 6:1-4

"Children, obey your parents in the Lord, for this is right. 'Honor your father and mother,' which is the first commandment with promise: 'that it may be well with you and you may live long on the earth.' And you, fathers, do not provoke your children to wrath, but bring them up in the training and admonition of the Lord."

Scriptures on the Love of God

John 3:16

"For God so loved the world that He gave His only begotten Son, that whoever believes in Him should not perish but have everlasting life."

Deuteronomy 7:13

"And He will love you and bless you and multiply you; He will also bless the fruit of your womb and the fruit of your land, your grain and your new wine and your oil, the increase of your cattle and the offspring of your flock, in the land of which He swore to your fathers to give you."

Psalms 146:8

"The Lord opens the eyes of the blind; The Lord raises those who are bowed down; The Lord loves the righteous."

Proverbs 15:9

"The way of the wicked is an abomination to the Lord, But He loves him who follows righteousness."

Isaiah 62:5

"For as a young man marries a virgin, So shall your sons marry you; And as the bridegroom rejoices over the bride, So shall your God rejoice over you."

Zephaniah 3:17

"The Lord your God in your midst, The Mighty One, will save; He will rejoice over you with gladness, He will quiet you with His love, He will rejoice over you with singing."

Jeremiah 31:3

"The Lord has appeared of old to me, saying: 'Yes, I have loved you with an everlasting love; Therefore with lovingkindness I have drawn you.' "

Hosea 14:4

"I will heal their backsliding, I will love them freely, For My anger has turned away from him."

Jeremiah 32:41

"Yes, I will rejoice over them to do them good, and I will assuredly plant them in this land, with all My heart and with all My soul."

Ephesians 2:4 – 7

"But God, who is rich in mercy, because of His great love with which He loved us, even when we were dead in trespasses, made us alive together with Christ (by grace you have been saved), and raised us up together, and made us sit together in the heavenly places in Christ Jesus, that in the ages to come He might show the exceeding riches of His grace in His kindness toward us in Christ Jesus."

1 John 4:10

"In this is love, not that we loved God, but that He loved us and sent His Son to be the propitiation for our sins."

1 John 4:16

"And we have known and believed the love that God has for us. God is love, and he who abides in love abides in God, and God in him."

1 John 4:19

"We love Him because He first loved us."

John 17:26

"And I have declared to them Your name, and will declare it, that the love with which You loved Me may be in them, and I in them."

John 17:23

"I in them, and You in Me; that they may be made perfect in one, and that the world may know that You have sent Me, and have loved them as You have loved Me."

John 16:27

"for the Father Himself loves you, because you have loved Me, and have believed that I came forth from God."

2 Thessalonians 2:16,17

"Now may our Lord Jesus Christ Himself, and our God and Father, who has loved us and given us everlasting consolation and good hope by grace, comfort your hearts and establish you in every good word and work."

Scriptures on the Word of God

Romans 1:16

"For I am not ashamed of the gospel of Christ, for it is the power of God to salvation for everyone who believes, for the Jew first and also for the Greek."

Revelation 1:3

"Blessed is he who reads and those who hear the words of this prophecy, and keep those things which are written in it; for the time is near."

2 Peter 1:19

"And so we have the prophetic word confirmed, which you do well to heed as a light that shines in a dark place, until the day dawns and the morning star rises in your hearts"

Hebrews 4:12

"For the word of God is living and powerful, and sharper than any two-edged sword, piercing even to the division of soul and spirit, and of joints and marrow, and is a discerner of the thoughts and intents of the heart."

Psalms 119:130

"The entrance of Your words gives light; It gives understanding to the simple."

Proverbs 6:23

"For the commandment is a lamp, And the law a light; Reproofs of instruction are the way of life"

Psalms 119:105

"Your word is a lamp to my feet And a light to my path."

John 5:39

"You search the Scriptures, for in them you think you have eternal life; and these are they which testify of Me."

2 Timothy 3:15,16

"and that from childhood you have known the Holy Scriptures, which are able to make you wise for salvation through faith which is in Christ Jesus. All Scripture is given by inspiration of God, and is profitable for doctrine, for reproof, for correction, for instruction in righteousness"

Romans 10:17

"So then faith comes by hearing, and hearing by the word of God."

1 Peter 2:2

"as newborn babes, desire the pure milk of the word, that you may grow thereby"

James 1:21-25

"Therefore lay aside all filthiness and overflow of wickedness, and receive with meekness the implanted word, which is able to save your souls. But be doers of the word, and not hearers only, deceiving yourselves. For if anyone is a hearer of the word and not a doer, he is like a man observing his natural face in a mirror; for he observes himself, goes away, and immediately forgets what kind of man he was. But he who looks into the perfect law of liberty and continues in it, and is not a forgetful hearer but a doer of the work, this one will be blessed in what he does."

Deuteronomy 11:18

"Therefore you shall lay up these words of mine in your heart and in your soul, and bind them as a sign on your hand, and they shall be as frontlets between your eyes."

Joshua 1:8

"This Book of the Law shall not depart from your mouth, but you shall meditate in it day and night, that you may observe to do according to all that is written in it. For then you will make your way prosperous, and then you will have good success."

1 Peter 1:23

"having been born again, not of corruptible seed but incorruptible, through the word of God which lives and abides forever"

Acts 20:32

"So now, brethren, I commend you to God and to the word of His grace, which is able to build you up and give you an inheritance among all those who are sanctified."

Scriptures on Trust

Psalms 46:1,2

"God is our refuge and strength, A very present help in trouble. Therefore we will not fear, Even though the earth be removed, And though the mountains be carried into the midst of the sea"

Psalms 84:11,12

"For the Lord God is a sun and shield; The Lord will give grace and glory; No good thing will He withhold From those who walk uprightly. O Lord of hosts, Blessed is the man who trusts in You!"

Psalms 37:3-5

"Trust in the Lord, and do good; Dwell in the land, and feed on His faithfulness. Delight yourself also in the Lord, And He shall give you the desires of your heart. Commit your way to the Lord, Trust also in Him, And He shall bring it to pass."

Proverbs 3:5,6

"Trust in the Lord with all your heart, And lean not on your own understanding; In all your ways acknowledge Him, And He shall direct your paths."

Luke 12:32

"Do not fear, little flock, for it is your Father's good pleasure to give you the kingdom."

Matthew 6:31,32

"Therefore do not worry, saying, 'What shall we eat?' or 'What shall we drink?' or 'What shall we wear?' For after all these things the Gentiles seek. For your heavenly Father knows that you need all these things."

1 Peter 5:7

"casting all your care upon Him, for He cares for you."

Psalms 40:4

"Blessed is that man who makes the Lord his trust, And does not respect the proud, nor such as turn aside to lies."

Psalms 125:1

"Those who trust in the Lord Are like Mount Zion, Which cannot be moved, but abides forever."

Scriptures on Wisdom

James 1:5

"If any of you lacks wisdom, let him ask of God, who gives to all liberally and without reproach, and it will be given to him."

Isaiah 2:3

"Many people shall come and say, 'Come, and let us go up to the mountain of the Lord, To the house of the God of Jacob; He will teach us His ways, And we shall walk in His paths.' For out of Zion shall go forth the law, And the word of the Lord from Jerusalem. "

Psalms 32:8

"I will instruct you and teach you in the way you should go; I will guide you with My eye."

Ecclesiastes 2:26

"For God gives wisdom and knowledge and joy to a man who is good in His sight; but to the sinner He gives the work of gathering and collecting, that he may give to him who is good before God. This also is vanity and grasping for the wind."

Psalms 16:7

"I will bless the Lord who has given me counsel; My heart also instructs me in the night seasons."

Proverbs 2:5-7

"Then you will understand the fear of the Lord, And find the knowledge of God. For the Lord gives wisdom; From His mouth come knowledge and understanding; He stores up sound wisdom for the upright; He is a shield to those who walk uprightly;"

1 John 5:20

"And we know that the Son of God has come and has given us an understanding, that we may know Him who is true; and we are in Him who is true, in His Son Jesus Christ. This is the true God and eternal life."

2 Corinthians 4:6

"For it is the God who commanded light to shine out of darkness, who has shone in our hearts to give the light of the knowledge of the glory of God in the face of Jesus Christ."

Proverbs 28:5

"Evil men do not understand justice, But those who seek the Lord understand all."

Psalms 51:6

"Behold, You desire truth in the inward parts, And in the hidden part You will make me to know wisdom."

***

Made in the USA
Lexington, KY
08 September 2015